His Excel. G. WASHINGTON Esq. LLD. Late Commander in Chief of the ARMIES of THE U.S. of AMERICA & PRESIDENT of THE CONVENTION OF 1787

MAXIMS
—of—
George Washington

Political, Military, Social, Moral, and Religious

Collected and Arranged by

JOHN FREDERICK SCHROEDER, D.D.

A citizen of the United States

With an Introduction by

GERALD R. FORD

Chapter Introductions by John P. Riley
Illustrations from the Stanley D. Scott Collection

THE MOUNT VERNON LADIES' ASSOCIATION
MOUNT VERNON, VIRGINIA
1989

Cover illustration: George Washington by Rembrandt Peale, 1823. Known as the Porthole Portrait, this is one of 79 copies of the portrait that Peale painted throughout his life, some depicting Washington in military uniform as shown, others in civilian dress. The portrait is based on Peale's study of Washington done from life in 1795, when the artist was 17 years old. *Mount Vernon Ladies' Association.*

Frontispiece: *His Excel. G. Washington Esq: L.L.D. Late Commander in Chief of the Armies of the U.S. of America & President of the Convention of 1787,* engraved by John Sartain, after Charles Willson Peale, [1865]. *The Stanley D. Scott Collection, Mount Vernon Ladies' Association.*

Back cover: George Washington's tambour secretary at Mount Vernon, where he penned numerous letters during the last years of his life. Washington purchased the desk in Philadelphia in 1797 at the end of his second term as President, and used it during his final retirement. *Photograph by G. E. Garrison.*

Library of Congress Cataloging-in-Publication Data

Washington, George, 1732-1799.
  Maxims of George Washington.

  Previous eds. published under title: Maxims of
Washington.
  Bibliography: p.
  Includes index.
  1. Washington, George, 1732-1799—Quotations.
2. Quotations, American.   I. Schroeder, John Frederick,
1800-1857.   II. Title.
E312.79.W3127   1989   973.4'1'0924   89-2964
ISBN 0-931917-16-6

First Printing, April 1942
Second Printing, April 1947
Third Printing, April 1953
Fourth Printing, April 1963
Fifth Printing, June 1974
Revised Edition, February 1989

TO ALL MEN
WHO REVERE THE SACRED MEMORY
OF

WASHINGTON

ADMIRE HIS EXALTED VIRTUES,
AND APPLAUD HIS GREAT AND
GLORIOUS ACHIEVEMENTS,

THIS VOLUME

A REPOSITORY OF HIS
ENNOBLING SENTIMENTS,
IS RESPECTFULLY DEDICATED
BY
THE AUTHOR.

Geo. Washington by Grainger after Archibald Robertson, published by H. D. Symonds, July 1, 1794. Washington's portrait stands above symbols of liberty and justice.

INTRODUCTION

When as a young boy I first began to learn about George Washington, the greatest of all American heroes, he seemed to be a larger-than-life figure. Like the eagle and the flag, George Washington served as an American icon, more a symbol than a flesh-and-blood man.

I expected to learn a great deal more about Washington as I grew older. But in fact, the "Father of our Country" remained an enigma, a soldier and statesman with a spotless reputation, a man so perfect that he seemed to lack color, depth or imagination.

This is the special curse of becoming the ultimate hero, for as Ralph Waldo Emerson warned us, "Every hero becomes a bore at last."

Now more than ever, we can ill afford to allow the image of Washington to become so perfect that it fails to fascinate, so one-dimensional that it discourages analysis. Perhaps Washington's most significant contribution to our nation was the example he set for others to follow, and we cannot allow the true essence and worthiness of Washington's character to be taken for granted.

To best understand the true impact of his fame and influence, we must put aside the tired myths of our childhood and travel back to Washington's own milieu. To his contemporaries he came to symbolize the strength and unity of the new American nation, yet it is in their accounts that we also find his human dimensions. To Alexander Hamilton, he was a "kind and unchanging friend." To Thomas Jefferson, he was "a wise, a good, and a great man." But perhaps no one was more deeply affected by him than the Marquis de Lafayette who wrote to Washington in 1781: "Every mark of friendship I receive from you adds to my happiness, as I love you with all the sincerity and warmth of my heart."

More than 200 years later, it is difficult—perhaps impossible—to imagine what it would have been like to serve as a loyal friend of George Washington. If his weaknesses existed, we know little about them today. One of our first lessons in grade school is the familiar tribute to Washington, "First in war, first in peace, and first in the hearts of his countrymen." Even in his own time, amidst a host of courageous heroes, Washington stood apart from the crowd.

One could argue that the pedestal upon which this heroic figure stands is much too lofty for the 20th-century American to scale. We could not climb high enough to look this man straight in the eye, to know his personality, to share his experiences, to understand what it might have been like to have been part of his intimate circle.

Despite the ever-present crowds of people that tend to surround any president, the role of commander in chief can prove to be a lonely one. As the first of his kind, a presidential trailblazer, Washington found himself alone at the apex, a symbol of democracy in an elitist world ruled by monarchs and dictators. Scholars have stated that it was Washington's character that inspired the delegates at the Constitutional Convention as they created the Executive Office. He was the obvious, and only, choice to be first President of the United States. There were those among his countrymen who would have made him king, but Washington's personal commitment to a democratic form of government saved our new nation from the fate of the French, who just a few years later discovered that their liberator, Napoleon, would quickly crown himself an all-powerful emperor.

By refusing a crown, Washington selected a much more difficult challenge—to make effective a government based on a complex system of checks and balances. In following the eloquent directions of the Constitution to the letter, Washington resisted a remarkable number of political temptations, and his commitment to the public good was nothing short of miraculous. In the words of poet Robert Frost, "George Washington was one of the few in the whole history of the world who was not carried away by power."

As unbelievable as it may seem to the countless candidates who seek the presidency today, Washington accepted the office with great reluctance, even though he was the unanimous choice of both his political colleagues and the American people. Washington would have much preferred to retire to Mount Vernon, his tranquil and beautiful estate on the banks of the Potomac River, to spend his final years in his favorite occupation, farming. Without a doubt, it was duty to country, rather than personal ambition, that drove this man. Yet ironically, this devotion to the cause, this hesitation to promote himself, simply enhanced Washington's reputation and made it that much more difficult for him to ignore the pleas of his countrymen.

We owe our heartfelt appreciation to the founding fathers who so adeptly twisted General Washington's arm, and who successfully convinced this "indispensable man" to serve two full terms. The 39 men who have tried to follow in his footsteps are most certainly indebted to Washington for creating an office that reflects the dignity, the democracy and the determination of the American people.

How can we possibly show our appreciation to this singular expression of patriotism, to this man who sacrificed so much for the good of the American people? During the nearly 200 years since his death, we have named thousands of city streets in honor of Washington, and at least 100 towns and villages proudly bear his name. No fewer than nine colleges and ten lakes are named after Mount Vernon's owner, and his image is everywhere, from the halls of our statehouses to the face of our dollar bill.

Yet these memorials to Washington, in spite of their good intentions, fail to add dimension to his character. We can use these tributes to celebrate the enormous contributions of the man, but we learn little about his personality in the process.

Rather than studying the thousands of references to Washington made by countless scholars, poets and politicians, perhaps we should direct our attentions to the words of the master himself. Although he did not have the opportunity to attend college, Washington was an avid reader and a remarkably prolific writer. His papers are currently being edited by a team of scholars in Charlottesville, Virginia, who predict that their research will eventually result in no less than 90 volumes of Washington's writings, ranging from personal letters to his farewell address.

The *Maxims of George Washington* is a condensation of Washington's most memorable statements. By reading Washington's own words, we begin to understand the many facets of his character. Slowly but surely, the myth begins to sound like a man. We stand in awe of his intellect and wisdom as a soldier and statesman, and at the same time, are touched by his sensitivity and practicality as a husband and father, a farmer and businessman, a man who appreciates fine wine and somehow has time to worry about the weather.

I have always appreciated and respected George Washington. By reading this superb book of quotations, I have come to better understand both the man and his unique place in history. The wisdom that fills these pages is his most enduring legacy to each rising generation of Americans. This is the genius of George Washington.

Gerald R. Ford

Gen. Washington by William Angus after Charles Willson Peale, published by J. Fielding, September 23, 1785.

PREFACE TO THE NEW EDITION

Although no single hero in American history is more respected or more revered than George Washington, this great man's words are seldom remembered or recited. In fact, modern Americans tend to picture Washington as a larger-than-life general on horseback providing inspiration to our tattered troops, or as the severe-looking President memorialized in Gilbert Stuart's famous portrait. American children are taught that Washington was indeed a man of action, whether it be as a child chopping down a cherry tree, or as an Olympic-style tosser of silver dollars across a mile-wide river.

No doubt Washington would be proud of his seemingly indestructible reputation as a dynamic leader, a man who did not hesitate when the time for decision was at hand. "First in war, first in peace, and first in the hearts of his countrymen"—indeed, Washington's pedestal seems just a bit higher than the rest.

But this modest "gentleman farmer" might be surprised—and perhaps just a bit disappointed—to know that the thoughts and beliefs he so carefully recorded on paper over a period of more than five decades are seldom read, either in grade school classrooms or by modern scholars and speechwriters. Thomas Jefferson, James Madison and Benjamin Franklin have somehow survived the generations as creative, clever and almost poetic authors. In fact, this trio of intellectuals did indeed possess an elegant way with words which may have escaped George Washington, and this is perhaps why we recall their words as well as their actions.

Nevertheless, it is an oversight, if not an age-old injustice, to underestimate the writings of George Washington. In thousands of letters this "indispensable man" displayed his remarkable leadership, his strong character, his love of family, God and country.

Those of us who serve in the Mount Vernon Ladies' Association are fortunate—we are exposed to the words and thoughts of George Washington on an almost continuous basis. In a very practical way, the writings of Washington have established the course for Mount Vernon's restoration, which began in 1853 and continues today. His remarkably detailed household account books, cash memoranda and ledgers have been invaluable to us in furnishing the Mansion, and his diaries and letters offer countless clues about Washington's daily life at Mount Vernon.

For nearly two decades the *Maxims of George Washington* has been a familiar sight on my cluttered desktop. I refer to the *Maxims* when I need just the right Washington quotation for a speech, or perhaps a letter to a history-minded friend. I often find myself just flipping through its pages for no particular reason, perhaps in an effort to learn more about Washington's personality and character.

What sets the *Maxims* apart from most other works about Washington is its purity—Washington is communicating directly to the reader. When the Reverend John Frederick Schroeder first brought together these "best and brightest" quotations in 1854, he wisely decided to present them in an unadorned format, void of interpretation or analysis. In preparing this revised version, the Association has remained true to Schroeder's mission, and the vast majority of quotations are identical to those in his original version. In some cases, however, our scholarly staff members have shortened the lengthier quotations. Several entries have been removed from our new edition. We determined that they are perhaps less meaningful and relevant as we approach the 21st century, and quite frankly, their omission has released the space which was required for additional quotations. Our new entries touch upon subjects—such as slavery—which were often avoided in the mid-19th century, when Dr. Schroeder first assembled this important volume.

We have also attempted to reorganize Washington's *Maxims* in a more concise manner, and are hopeful that readers will be able to turn to their favorite quotations in a faster and more efficient manner. The brief introductions to each section are an attempt to set the stage for the ennobling words which follow.

Those who revere George Washington will most certainly appreciate the illustrations which are spaced throughout this new edition. As we read George Washington's words, we can watch him mature in the 31 portraits created by a variety of accomplished artists and engravers. We are deeply indebted to Mr. Stanley DeForest Scott of New York City, who contributed his superb collection of prints to the Association in 1985, from which each of our illustrations is taken. Mr. Scott is a lifelong collector, a true connoisseur of Washingtoniana.

We also owe our appreciation to Ellen McCallister Clark, Mount Vernon's devoted Librarian from 1975-1988; John P. Riley, Archivist; and James C. Rees, Associate Director of Mount Vernon, who together served as our editors for this revised edition. Ann M. Rauscher successfully guided the *Maxims* through its long publication process, and Anne M. Johnson served dutifully as our computer processor through countless drafts of the manuscript.

We also received the expert advice of Dr. W. W. Abbot, editor of *The Papers of George Washington* at the University of Virginia in Charlottesville. Dr. Abbot and his staff are immersed in the words of George Washington, day in and day out, as they pursue the challenging task of assembling all of Washington's writings in a single, definitive work. To date, 17 volumes have been published, and Dr. Abbot expects that the entire project will result in no less than 90 volumes! There is indeed a great deal of exhausting work that remains to be accomplished. Yet the vision of *The Papers of George Washington* is much greater than the cumulative effects of several dozen volumes—the editors are in search of the character and personality of George Washington, as reflected in his own words.

It would be an exaggeration to declare that the *Maxims of George Washington* includes all of the very best quotations from these volumes, some published, and still others years away from the printed page. The Association believes, however, that the maxims selected by Dr. Schroeder more than a century ago remain among the most meaningful and memorable in existence. We hope that these excerpts will lead the reader back to the source which, in every instance, is among the published writings, letters or speeches of George Washington.

Finally, I feel moved to recognize the extraordinary efforts of a single member of the Association who is responsible for breathing new life into the *Maxims of George Washington* project. When the Association announced three years ago that budgetary restrictions would postpone indefinitely the reprinting of the *Maxims of George Washington,* the Vice Regent for Michigan, Mrs. Alexander L. Wiener, accepted the responsibility of raising the necessary funds from private sources. With the help of her husband, Mrs. Wiener appealed to two generous couples in Michigan, Mr. and Mrs. Rogers I. Marquis and Mr. and Mrs. Stanley P. Sax. Together, these three couples have underwritten the entire cost of this project. With the addition of former President Ford's fine introduction, the *Maxims* is a reflection of the strength, the determination and the patriotism of Michiganders.

We can only hope that this book does indeed touch the hearts and minds of tens of thousands, so that future generations can declare with true conviction that George Washington is still "First in the hearts of his countrymen."

Mrs. Robert Channing Seamans, Jr.
Regent
Mount Vernon Ladies' Association

Mount Vernon, *February 22, 1989*

About the Editor

———————————— ϶∈ ————————————

The Reverend John Frederick Schroeder was born in Baltimore in 1800, graduated from Princeton in 1819, was assistant minister at Trinity Church and its associated Chapel in New York for 14 years. He established Saint Ann's Hall, Flushing, Long Island and also had pastoral duties in the Church of the Crucifixion, New York, and Saint Tomas' Church in Brooklyn. His literary work included horticultural and biblical subjects and translations from the German on the use of the Syriac language. Besides compiling the *Maxims,* he wrote the *Life and Times of George Washington* in two volumes published posthumously.

Through the painstaking research of Mrs. Katherine Clagett, who for many years worked as secretary to Dr. John C. Fitzpatrick, the well known authority on Washingtoniana, it has been possible to add to the original publication the source and date of the quotations.

Preface

Lord Broughman, in speaking of the Father of our Country, calls him "the Greatest *man of our own or any age;* the Only One upon whom an epithet, so thoughtlessly lavished by men to foster the crimes of their worst enemies, may be innocently and justly bestowed." He adds, "It will be the duty of the historian and the sage in all ages, to let no occasion pass, of commemorating this illustrious man; and, until time shall be no more, will a test of the progress which our race has made in wisdom and in virtue, be derived from the veneration paid to the immortal name of Washington."

The powerful influence of his character, his achievements, and his opinions, is acknowledged by all men. It has long been extending and increasing. And it cannot fail to produce, eventually, the most important and happy results, in the fulfillment of the final destinies of nations, and the attainment of the chief end of human existence.

By common consent, Washington is regarded as not merely the Hero of the American Revolution, but the World's Apostle of Liberty. The war of the Revolution was a war of principle, that involved the interests of all mankind. England's violation of our sacred rights, was the stirring of the eagle's nest. It naturally awakened emotions of resistance. British prerogative was opposed by American freedom. . . . Prerogative became oppressive and cruel, and Freedom took up arms and declared her independence. The Spirit of America's cause was impersonated in her great chief. He was a manifestation of the nation's heart and mind. And under his judicious guidance, by the providence of God, America not only stood erect, before the world, clothed in the panoply of justice, but moved steadily onward in her course; her shield, and breastplate, and whole armor flashing, at every step, with the light that shone on her from heaven.

Our victory being won, Washington sheathed his sword, and sat, for a brief space, under the shadow of his own vine and fig-tree. Soon, at the nation's call, he guided her in establishing the foundation, and rearing the superstructure, of her vast and imposing political fabric. He saw its topstone laid. And he was exulting, with holy joy, at the completion of his work, when the Supreme Disposer of events, by suddenly removing him from earth, in the fullness of his glory and renown, consecrated his character, and imparted to his opinions the commanding authority which they now possess.

The first name of America, not only is, but always will be, that of Washington. We pronounce it with filial reverence, as well as gratitude; for we admire and love him, not merely in consideration of what he did, but what he was. There is a sacred charm in his actions and his sentiments, as well as a divine philosophy in his remarkable career.

But his example and his precepts are a legacy, not only to America, but to all mankind. And as they are contemplating and admiring his virtues, they are invited to read, in his own words, his golden maxims. These are adapted to the use of Statesmen, Soldiers, Citizens, heads of families, teachers of youth, and, in a word, all who should aim at what is great and good, in public and in private life, and who would avail themselves of such sagacious, profound, and ennobling sentiments.

With a view to furnish, for popular use, a small volume of the words of Washington, the labor of culling and arranging his memorable precepts in this collection, was originally undertaken. Public documents and private letters, manuscripts and printed volumes, have accordingly been examined, with a view to the completeness and interest of the collection; and none but undoubtedly authentic materials have been used in forming it.

The late Earl of Buchan, whose uniform regard for the American States was manifested long before the epoch of their Federal Union, said of our Washington, "I recommend the constant remembrance of the moral and political Maxims conveyed to its citizens by the Father and Founder of the United States. It seems to me, that *such Maxims and such advice ought to be engraved on every Forum or Place of common Assembly among the people, and read by parents, teachers, and guardians, to their children and pupils, so that true Religion, and virtue, its inseparable attendant,* may be imbibed by the rising generations, to remote ages."

That generation after generation may enjoy the blessedness of the benign influence which these Maxims are so eminently calculated to exert, should surely be the prayer of patriots, philanthropists, and Christians, until all men shall be animated by the spirit of Washington, and exemplify his precepts.

J. F. Schroeder

New York, *September 12, 1854*

GEORGE WASHINGTON

Né en Virginie le 11 Février 1732.

Gravé d'après le Camée peint par Madame de Brehan à Newyork en 1789.

Dirigé par P.F. Tardieu.   *Gravé par Roger.*

George Washington Ne en Virginie le 11 Fevrier 1732 by Roger after Madame de Brehan. The Marchioness de Brehan, a sis-ter-in-law of the French minister in America, Comte de Mous-tier, visited Washington at Mount Vernon and again in New York after he had assumed the presidency. On October 3, 1789, the President noted in his diary: "sat about two o'clock for Madame de Brienne, to complete a miniature profile of me which she had begun from memory and which she had made exceedingly like the original." This print, based on her work, was published in Paris in 1801.

TABLE OF CONTENTS

———————————— ❦ ————————————

I. POLITICAL MAXIMS

A. POLITICS AND GOVERNMENT

B. LIBERTY AND PATRIOTISM

C. INDEPENDENCE

D. THE CONSTITUTION

E. NATIONAL PROSPERITY

F. NATIONAL POLICY

G.   FOREIGN RELATIONS

H.   FINANCE

I.   AGRICULTURE AND COMMERCE

J. COMMUNICATION AND TRANSPORTATION

K. NATIONAL EDUCATION

II. MILITARY MAXIMS

A. WAR

B. THE ARMY

III. SOCIAL MAXIMS

A. FRIENDSHIP

B. BENEVOLENCE

C. DOMESTIC LIFE

IV. MORAL MAXIMS

A. VIRTUE AND VICE

B. APPROBATION AND CENSURE

C.   INTEMPERANCE AND GAMING

D.   PUNISHMENTS

E.   SLAVERY

V. RELIGIOUS MAXIMS

A. GOD

B. RELIGION AND THE STATE

C. RELIGIOUS ACTS AND EMOTIONS

D. CHRISTIANITY

E.   DEATH

DRAWN BY B.TROTT.   ENGRAVED BY C.GOBRECHT

GEORGE WASHINGTON.

George Washington by C. Gobrecht after B. Trott and Gilbert Stuart. This familiar image was published in *The Cyclopedia or Universal Dictionary of Arts, Sciences, and Literature* by Abraham Rees (Philadelphia, 1821).

LIST OF ILLUSTRATIONS

———————— ✖ ————————

I.
POLITICAL MAXIMS

POLITICAL MAXIMS

George Washington first tested the turbulent waters of politics in 1755 at the age of 23. The results were hardly auspicious. While campaigning for his friend George William Fairfax, who eyed a vacant seat in the Virginia House of Burgesses, Washington scuffled with a supporter of a rival candidate and was knocked to the ground. Washington later apologized, admitting he was at fault. Insult was added to injury when the young Virginian lost his bid to represent Frederick County in Williamsburg. Washington's next attempt in 1758 was successful and, indeed, he never experienced another political defeat.

As a Burgess, Washington was more comfortable in the role of studied observer, allowing fiery orators such as Patrick Henry to take center stage. Yet when tensions elevated between Britain and her American colonies, Washington was not shy in defending the natural rights he felt the mother country was violating. In 1769, he teamed with neighbor George Mason to establish a Virginia non-importation plan. Conservatives and radicals alike approved this economic rebuttal to British taxes, which called for a boycott of certain imported items bearing unfair taxes.

Elected to the First and Second Continental Congresses, Washington was described by a fellow delegate as "a modest man, but sensible and speaks little — in action, cool, like a Bishop at his prayers." This characterization would be apt, too, while Washington presided over the Constitutional Convention in Philadelphia in 1787.

Washington again answered the call of his country in 1789, accepting the office of first President of the United States. Realizing that unity and stability were America's greatest friends, Washington established a neutral stance in foreign affairs, although most Americans were experiencing great sympathy for the French, remaining ever-grateful for her ally's aid at Yorktown. This bond was further enhanced in 1792, when France followed in America's footsteps, substituting a monarchy with a democratic republic. Washington found it more and more difficult to garner support for his proclamation of neutrality. It did not help that two members of the President's cabinet, Alexander Hamilton, an Anglophile and Secretary of the Treasury, and Thomas Jefferson, supporter of the French Republic and Secretary of State, were constantly at odds.

During Washington's eight-year tenure, he established a number of important precedents that continue to shape the presidency today. Regular meetings of the cabinet evolved, wherein the President received, as he did during earlier War Councils, the advice and comments of his underlings. He endured the shaky beginnings of what would become a unique party system of government, although Washington himself believed that parties would fracture rather than cement the Union. In 1783, several months before he resigned his commission as commander in chief, Washington had addressed a circular letter to the governors of the states urging "an indissoluble Union of the States under one Federal Head." In his Farewell Address, the departing President reiterated this theme, offering unity as the fountain from which all other blessings of liberty flow.

In 1797, Washington may have finally found the peace he had yearned for since 1775, the year he took command of the Continental forces. After a second term, Washington retired to his beloved home, Mount Vernon. His political career ended, the Virginia farmer returned to his plantation where he spent the final two-and-a-half years of his life.

A. POLITICS AND GOVERNMENT

POLITICAL INFALLIBILITY

... If any power on earth could, or the great power above would, erect the standard of infallibility in political opinions, there is no being that inhabits this terrestrial globe that would resort to it with more eagerness than myself, so long as I remain a servant of the public. But as I have found no better guide hitherto than upright intentions, and close investigation, I shall adhere to these maxims while I keep the watch; leaving it to those who will come after me to explore new ways, if they like; or think them better.

To Henry Knox, September 20, 1795   *Writings* Vol. 34 p. 310*

THE END OF GOVERNMENT

... The aggregate happiness of the society, which is best promoted by the practice of a virtuous policy, is, or ought to be, the end of all government ....

To Comte de Moustier, November 1, 1790   *Writings Vol. 31 p. 142*

... Influence is no Government.

To Henry Lee, October 31, 1786   *Writings Vol. 29 p. 34*

... Let us have one by which our lives, liberties and properties will be secured ....

To Henry Lee, October 31, 1786   *Writings Vol. 29 p. 34*

---

*John C. Fitzpatrick, ed. *The Writings of George Washington*, 1745-1799 (39 vols.), Washington, D.C.: United States George Washington Bicentennial Commission.

THE RIGHT OF A NATION TO ESTABLISH ITS OWN GOVERNMENT

... My politics are plain and simple. I think every nation has a Right to establish that form of Government under which It conceives It shall live most happy; provided it infracts no Right or is not dangerous to others. And that no Governments ought to interfere with the internal concerns of Another, except for the security of what is due to themselves.

To Marquis de Lafayette, December 25, 1798   *Writings Vol. 37 p. 70*

NATIONAL REVOLUTIONS

... The rapidity of national revolutions appear no less astonishing, than their magnitude. In what they will terminate, is known only to the great ruler of events; and confiding in his wisdom and goodness, we may safely trust the issue to him, without perplexing ourselves to seek for that, which is beyond human ken; only taking care to perform the parts assigned us, in a way that reason and our own consciences approve of.

To David Humphreys, March 23, 1793   *Writings Vol. 32 p. 398*

POLITICAL IMPROVEMENTS IN EUROPE

... A spirit for political improvements seems to be rapidly and exten-sively spreading through the European Countries. I shall rejoice in seeing the condition of the Human Race happier than ever it has hitherto been. But I should be sorry to see, that those who are for prematurely accelerat-ing those improvements, were making *more haste than good speed,* in their innovations. So much prudence, so much perseverance, so much disinter-estedness and so much patriotism are necessary among the Leaders of a Nation, in order to promote the national felicity, that sometimes my fears nearly preponderate over my expectations.

To Marquis de LaLuzerne, April 29, 1790   *Writings Vol. 31 p. 40*

... Born, Sir, in a land of liberty; having early learned its value; having engaged in a perilous conflict to defend it; having, in a word, devoted the best years of my life to secure its permanent establishment in my own country; my anxious recollections, my sympathetic feelings, and my best wishes are irresistibly excited, whensoever, in any country, I see an op-pressed nation unfurl the banners of Freedom.

To the French Minister, January 1, 1796   *Writings Vol. 34 p. 413*

THE FRENCH REVOLUTION

... My greatest fear has been, that the nation would not be sufficiently cool and moderate in making arrangements for the security of that lib-erty, of which it seems to be fully possessed.

To Mrs. C. M. Graham, January 9, 1790   *Writings Vol. 30 p. 498*

ANARCHY AND TYRANNY

... there is a natural and necessary progression, from the extreme of anarchy to the extreme of Tyranny; and that arbitrary power is most easily established on the ruins of Liberty abused to licentiousness.

Circular to the States, June 8, 1783   *Writings Vol. 26 p. 489*

REPUBLICANISM

... republicanism is not the phantom of a deluded imagination: on the contrary, that under no form of government, will laws be better supported, liberty and property better secured, or happiness be more effectually dispensed to mankind.

To Edmund Pendleton, January 22, 1795   *Writings Vol. 34 p. 99*

THE GOVERNMENT OF THE UNITED STATES

... That the Government, though not absolutely perfect, is one of the best in the world, I have little doubt.

To Mrs. C. M. Graham, January 9, 1790   *Writings Vol. 30 p. 496*

MONARCHY

... I am told that even respectable characters speak of a monarchial form of Government without horror. From thinking proceeds speaking, thence to acting is often but a single step. But how irrevocable and tremendous! what a triumph for our enemies to verify their predictions! what a triumph for the advocates of despotism to find that we are incapable of governing ourselves, and that systems founded on the basis of equal liberty are merely ideal and fallacious!

To the Secretary for Foreign Affairs, August 1, 1786   *Writings Vol. 28 p. 503*

NOBILITY AND KNIGHTHOOD

... it appears to be incompatible with the principles of our national constitution to admit the introduction of any kind of Nobility, Knighthood, or distinctions of a similar nature, amongst the Citizens of our republic.

To Jean de Heintz, January 21, 1784   *Writings Vol. 27 p. 310*

B. LIBERTY AND PATRIOTISM

CIVIL LIBERTY

... Liberty, when it begins to take root, is a plant of rapid growth.

To James Madison, March 2, 1788   *Writings Vol. 29 p. 431*

... the American Revolution, or the peculiar light of the age seems to have opened the eyes of almost every nation in Europe.

To Hector St. John de Crevecoeur, April 10, 1789   *Writings Vol. 30 p. 281*

... a spirit of equal liberty appears fast to be gaining ground everywhere, which must afford satisfaction to every friend of mankind.

To Hector St. John de Crevecoeur, April 10, 1789   *Writings Vol. 30 p. 281*

... if we mean to support the Liberty and Independence which it has cost us so much blood and treasure to establish, we must drive far away the demon of party spirit and local reproach.

To Governor Arthur Fenner, June 4, 1790   *Writings Vol. 31 p. 48*

... Should the conduct of the Americans, whilst promoting their own happiness, influence the feelings of other nations, and thereby render a service to mankind, they will receive a double pleasure.

To Comte de Segur, July 1, 1790   *Writings Vol. 31 p. 67*

... Interwoven as is the love of liberty with every ligament of your hearts, no recommendation of mine is necessary to fortify or confirm the attachment.

Farewell Address, September 19, 1796   *Writings Vol. 35 p. 218*

... none of them will ever submit to the loss of those valuable rights and privileges, which are essential to the happiness of every free state, and without which, life, liberty, and property are rendered totally insecure.

To Robert MacKenzie, October 9, 1774   *Writings Vol. 3 p. 246*

... In a government as free as ours where the people are at liberty, and will express their sentiments, oftentimes imprudently, and for want of information sometimes unjustly, allowances must be made for occasional effervescences; but after the declaration which I have here made of my political creed, you can run no hazard in asserting, that the Executive branch of this government never has, nor will suffer, while I preside, any improper conduct of its officers to escape with impunity; or will give its sanctions to any disorderly proceedings of its citizens.

To Gouverneur Morris, December 22, 1795   *Writings Vol. 34 p. 402*

THE CAUSE OF THE AMERICAN COLONIES

... If Historiographers should be hardy enough to fill the page of History with the advantages that have been gained with unequal numbers (on the part of America) in the course of this contest, and attempt to relate the distressing circumstances under which they have been obtained, it is more than probable that Posterity will bestow on their labors the epithet and marks of fiction; for it will not be believed that such a force as Great

Britain has employed for eight years in this Country could be baffled in their plan of Subjugating it by numbers infinitely less, composed of Men oftentimes half starved; always in Rags, without pay, and experiencing, at times, every species of distress which human nature is capable of under-going.

To Nathanael Greene, February 6, 1785   *Writings Vol. 26 p. 104*

... Great Britain; who thought it was only to hold up the rod, and all would be hush!

To Joseph Jones, February 11, 1783   *Writings Vol. 26 p. 123*

... When we consider the magnitude of the prize we contended for, the doubtful nature of the contest, and the favorable manner in which it has terminated, we shall find the greatest possible reason for gratitude and rejoicing ....

Circular to the States, June 8, 1783   *Writings Vol. 26 p. 484*

... this is a theme that will afford infinite delight to every benevolent and liberal mind, whether the event in contemplation, be considered as the source of present enjoyment or the parent of future happiness; and we shall have equal occasion to felicitate ourselves on the lot which Provi-dence has assigned us, whether we view it in a natural, a political or moral point of light.

Circular to the States, June 8, 1783   *Writings Vol. 26 p. 484*

... the rights of Mankind, the privileges of the people, and the true princi-ples of liberty, seem to have been more generally discussed and better understood throughout Europe since the American revolution than they were at any former period.

To Thomas Jefferson, January 1, 1788   *Writings Vol. 29 p. 350*

THE SPIRIT OF THE REVOLUTION

... The value of liberty was thus enhanced in our estimation by the diffi-culty of its attainment, and the worth of characters appreciated by the trial of adversity. The tempest of war having at length been succeeded by the sunshine of peace; our citizen-soldiers impressed an useful lesson of patriotism on mankind, by nobly returning with impaired constitutions and unsatisfied claims, after such long sufferings and severe disappoint-ments, to their former occupations. Posterity as well as the present age will doubtless regard with admiration and gratitude the patience, perser-verance, and valour, which achieved our revolution they will cherish the remembrance of virtues which had but few parallels in former times, and which will add new lustre to the most splendid page of history.

To the People of the State of South Carolina, May 1790   Writings Vol. 31 p. 67

... I concur with the Legislature in repeating, with pride and joy, what will be an everlasting honor to our country, that our revolution was so distinguished for moderation virtue and humanity, as to merit the eulogium they have pronounced of being unsullied with a crime.

To Governor John Hawkins Stone, December 23, 1796   *Writings Vol. 35 p. 343*

FALSE AND CRUEL POLICY OF GREAT BRITAIN

... great Britain understood herself perfectly well in this dispute but did not comprehend America....they meant to drive us into what they termed rebellion, that they might be furnished with a pretext to disarm and then strip us of the rights and privileges of Englishmen and Citizens. If they were actuated by principles of justice, why did they refuse indignantly to accede to the terms which were humbly supplicated before hostilities commenced and this Country deluged in Blood; and now make their principal Officers and even the Comrs. themselves say, that these terms are just and reasonable; Nay that more will be granted than we have yet asked, if we will relinquish our Claim to Independency. What Name does such conduct as this deserve? and what punishment is there in store for the Men who have distressed Millions, involved thousands in ruin, and plunged numberless families in inextricable woe? Could that wch. is just and reasonable now, have been unjust four Years ago?

To Bryan Fairfax, March 1, 1778   *Writings Vol. 11 p. 3*

... they must either be wantonly wicked and cruel, or (which is only anr. mode of describing the same thing) under false colours are now endeavouring to deceive the great body of the people, by industriously propagating a belief that G. B. is willing to offer any, and that we will accept of no terms; thereby hoping to poison and disaffect the Minds of those who wish for peace, and create feuds and dissentions among ourselves. In a word, having less dependance now, in their Arms than their Arts, they are practising such low and dirty tricks, that Men of Sentiment and honr. must blush at their Villainy, among other manoeuvres, in this way they are counterfeiting Letters, and publishing them, as intercepted ones of mine to prove that I am an enemy to the present measures, and have been led into them step by step still hoping that Congress would recede from their present claims.

To Bryan Fairfax, March 1, 1778   *Writings Vol. 11 p. 4*

THE STAMP ACT: ITS PASSAGE CONDEMNED

... The Stamp Act Imposed on the Colonies by the Parliament of Great Britain engrosses the conversation of the Speculative part of the Colonists, who look upon this unconstitutional method of Taxation as a direful attack upon their Liberties, and loudly exclaim against the Violation;

... the advantage accrueing to the Mother Country will fall greatly short of the expectations of the Ministry; for certain it is, our whole Substance does already in a manner flow to Great Britain and that whatsoever contributes to lessen our Importation's must be hurtful to their Manufactures. And the Eyes of our People, already beginning to open, will perceive, that many Luxuries which we lavish our substance to Great Britain for, can well be dispensd with whilst the necessaries of Life are (mostly) to be had within ourselves. This consequently will introduce frugality, and be a necessary stimulation to Industry. If Great Britain therefore Loads her Manufactures with heavy Taxes, will it not facilitate these Measures? they will not compel us I think to give our Money for their exports, whether we will or no, and certain I am none of their Traders will part from them without a valuable consideration. Where then is the Utility of these Restrictions?

To Francis Dandridge, September 20, 1765   *Writings Vol. 2 p. 425*

... As to the Stamp Act, taken in a single view, one, and the first bad consequences attending it I take to be this. Our Courts of Judicature must inevitably be shut up; for it is impossible (or next of kin to it) under our present Circumstances that the Act of Parliam't can be complyd with were we ever so willing to enforce the execution; for not to say, which alone would be sufficient, that we have not Money to pay the Stamps, there are many other Cogent Reasons to prevent it; and if a stop be put to our judicial proceedings I fancy the Merchants of G. Britain trading to the Colonies will not be among the last to wish for a Repeal of it.

To Francis Dandridge, September 20, 1765   *Writings Vol. 2 p. 426*

THE STAMP ACT: ITS REPEAL

... those therefore who wisely foresaw this, and were Instrumental in procuring the repeal of it, are, in my opinion, deservidly entitled to the thanks of the well wishers to Britain and her Colonies; and must reflect with pleasure that through their means, many Scenes of confusion and distress have been avoided: Mine they accordingly have, and always shall have, for their opposition to any Act of Oppression, for that Act could be looked upon in no other light by every person who would view it in its proper colours.

To Capel and Osgood Hanbury, July 25, 1767   *Writings Vol. 2 p. 466*

... The Repeal of the Stamp Act, to whatsoever causes owing, ought much to be rejoiced at, for had the Parliament of Great Britain resolved upon enforcing it the consequences I conceive would have been more direful than is generally apprehended both to the Mother Country and her Colonies. All therefore who were Instrumental in procuring the Repeal are entitled to the Thanks of every British Subject and have mine cordially.

To Robert Cary & Company, July 21, 1766   *Writings Vol. 2 p. 440*

TAXATION

... I would heartily join you in them, so far as relates to a humble and dutiful petition to the throne, provided there was the most distant hope of success. But have we not tried this already? Have we not addressed the Lords, and remonstrated to the Commons? And to what end? Did they deign to look at our petitions?

To Bryan Fairfax, July 4, 1774   *Writings Vol. 3 p. 228*

TAXATION, A QUESTION OF RIGHT AND HONOR

... what is it we are contending against? Is it against paying the duty of three pence per pound on tea because burthensome? No, it is the right only, we have all along disputed.

To Bryan Fairfax, July 20, 1774   *Writings Vol. 3 p. 232*

... If, then, as the fact really is, it is against the right of taxation that we now do, and, (as I before said,) all along have contended, why should they suppose an exertion of this power would be less obnoxious now than formerly? And what reasons have we to believe, that they would make a second attempt, while the same sentiments filled the breast of every American, if they did not intend to enforce it if possible?

To Bryan Fairfax, July 20, 1774   *Writings Vol. 3 p. 232*

... I think the Parliament of Great Britain hath no more right to put their hands into my pocket, without my consent, than I have to put my hands into yours for money; and this being already urged to them in a firm, but decent manner, by all the colonies, what reason is there to expect any thing from their justice?

To Bryan Fairfax, July 20, 1774   *Writings Vol. 3 p. 233*

... should much distrust my own judgment upon the occasion, if my nature did not recoil at the thought of submitting to measures, which I think subversive of every thing that I ought to hold dear and valuable, and did I not find, at the same time, that the voice of mankind is with me.

To Bryan Fairfax, July 20, 1774   *Writings Vol. 3 p. 234*

... an intimate spirit of freedom first told me, that the measures, which administration hath for some time been, and now are most violently pursuing, are repugnant to every principle of natural justice; whilst much abler heads than my own hath fully convinced me, that it is not only repugnant to natural right, but subversive of the laws and constitution of Great Britain itself, in the establishment of which some of the best blood in the kingdom hath been spilt.

To Bryan Fairfax, August 24, 1774   *Writings Vol. 3 p. 240*

THE PATRIOT CHIEF

... as the Congress desires I will enter upon the momentous duty, and exert every power I Possess In their Service for the Support of the glorious Cause.

Acceptance of Appointment as General and Commander in Chief,
June 16, 1775   *Writings Vol. 3 p. 292*

THE COUNTRY'S CALL

... I was summoned by my Country, whose voice I can never hear but with veneration and love.

The First Inaugural Address, April 30, 1789   *Writings Vol. 30 p. 292*

... I have obeyed a summons, to which I can never be insensible. ... when my country demands the sacrifice, personal ease must always be a secondary consideration.

To the Connecticut Legislature, October 17, 1789   *Writings Vol. 30 p. 453*

THE PATRIOT'S VOW

... the love of my country will be the ruling influence of my conduct.

Answer to the New Hampshire Executive, November 3, 1789
                                            Writings Vol. 30 p. 453

THE RULER'S GLORY AND THE PEOPLE'S HAPPINESS

... It is a wonder to me, there should be found a single monarch, who does not realize that his own glory and felicity must depend on the prosperity and happiness of his People. How easy is it for a sovereign to do that which shall not only immortalize his name, but attract the blessings of millions.

To Marquis de Lafayette, June 19, 1788   *Writings Vol. 29 p. 524*

THE AMERICAN PATRIOT

... When the councils of the British nation had formed a plan for enslaving America, and depriving her sons of their most sacred and invaluable privileges, against the clearest remonstrances of the constitution, of justice, and of truth, and, to execute their schemes, had appealed to the sword, I esteemed it my duty to take a part in the contest, and more especially on account of my being called thereto by the unsolicited suffrages of the representatives of a free people; wishing for no other reward, than that arising from a conscientious discharge of the important trust, and that my services might contribute to the establishment of freedom and peace, upon a permanent foundation, and merit the applause of my countrymen, and every virtuous citizen.

Answer to an Address from the Massachusetts Legislature, March 1776
Writings Vol. 4 p. 440

SPIRIT OF FREEDOM

... With respect to myself, I have never entertained an idea of an accommodation, since I heard of the measures, which were adopted in consequence of the Bunker's Hill fight. The king's speech has confirmed the sentiments I entertained upon the news of that affair; and if every man was of my mind, the ministers of Great Britain should know, in a few words, upon what issue the cause should be put. I would not be deceived by artful declarations, nor specious pretences; nor would I be amused by unmeaning propositions; but in open, undisguised, and manly terms proclaim our wrongs, and our resolution to be redressed. I would tell them, that we had borne much, that we had long and ardently sought for reconciliation upon honorable terms, that it had been denied us, that all our attempts after peace had proved abortive, and had been grossly misrepresented, that we had done every thing which could be expected from the best of subjects, that the spirit of freedom beat too high in us to submit to slavery, and that, if nothing else could satisfy a tyrant and his diabolical ministry, we are determined to shake off all connexions with a state so unjust and unnatural. This I would tell them, not under covert, but in words as clear as the sun in its meridian brightness.

To Joseph Reed, February 10, 1776   *Writings Vol. 4 p. 321*

... If we do our duty we may even hope to make the campaign decisive on this Continent. But we must do our duty in earnest, or disgrace and ruin will attend us.

To Joseph Reed, May 28, 1780   *Writings Vol. 18 p. 438*

TRUST IN GOD

... as it has been a kind of destiny, that has thrown me upon this service, I shall hope that my undertaking it is designed to answer some good purpose. ... I shall rely, therefore, confidently on that Providence, which has heretofore preserved and been bountiful to me.

To Martha Washington, June 18, 1775   *Writings Vol. 3 p. 294*

PUBLIC SPIRIT

... In exchanging the enjoyments of domestic life for the duties of my present honorable but arduous station, I only emulate the virtue and public spirit of the whole province of the Massachusetts Bay, which, with a firmness and patriotism without example in modern history, have sacrificed all the comforts of social and political life, in support of the rights of mankind, and the welfare of our common country. My highest ambition is to be the happy instrument of vindicating those rights, and to see this devoted province again restored to peace, liberty, and safety.

Answer to an Address of the Massachusetts Legislature, July 4, 1775

Writings Vol. 3 p. 307

OBEDIENCE TO CONGRESS

... while I have the honor to remain in the service of the United States, obey to the utmost of my power and to the best of my Abilities, all orders of Congress with a scrupulous exactness.

To the Board of War and Ordnance, July 29, 1776   *Writings Vol. 5 p. 347*

... Connecticut wants no Massachusetts man in their corps; Massachusetts thinks there is no necessity (for a Rhode-Islander) to be introduced amongst them; and New Hampshire says, it's very hard, that her valuable and experienced officers (who are willing to serve) should be discarded, because her own regiments, under the new establishment, cannot provide for them.

To Joseph Reed, November 8, 1775   *Writings Vol. 4 p. 77*

... it is maxim with me, that in times of imminent danger to a Country, every true Patriot should occupy the Post in which he can render them the most effectually.

To the Secretary of War, February 25, 1799   *Writings Vol. 37 p. 136*

BRAVERY

... I have a Constitution hardy enough to encounter and undergo the most severe tryals, and, I flatter myself, resolution to Face what any Man durst, as shall be prov'd when it comes to the Test.

To Robert Dinwiddie, May 29, 1754   *Writings Vol. 1 p. 60*

HONOR

... The Rank of Officers, which to me, Sir, is much dearer than the Pay.

To Robert Dinwiddie, June 12, 1754   *Writings Vol. 1 p. 83*

... You make mention in your letter of my continuing in the Service, and retaining my Colo's Commission. This idea has filled me with surprise; for if you think me capable of holding a commission that has neither rank nor emolument annexed to it, you must entertain a very contemptible opinion of my weakness, and believe me to be more empty than the Commission itself.

To William Fitzhugh, November 15, 1754   *Writings Vol. 1 p. 105*

THE PATRIOT'S OFFERING

... it is my full intention to devote my Life and Fortune in the cause we are engaged in, if need be.

To John Augustine Washington, March 25, 1775   *Writings Vol. 3 p. 277*

... the principle by which my conduct has been actuated through life, would not suffer me, in any great emergency, to withhold any services I could render, required by my Country, especially in a case where its dearest rights are assailed by lawless ambition, and intoxicated power, contrary to every principle of justice, and in violation of solemn compact, and Laws which govern all Civilized Nations. And this too with obvious intent to sow thick the Seeds of disunion for the purpose of subjugating the Government and destroying our Independence and happiness.

To the Secretary of War, July 4, 1798   *Writings Vol. 36 p. 305*

RECTITUDE

... The consciousness of having attempted faithfully to discharge my duty, and the approbation of my Country will be a sufficient recompense for my Services.

To the President of Congress, March 18, 1783   *Writings Vol. 26 p. 232*

... Conscious that it is the aim of my actions to promote the public good, and that no part of my conduct is influenced by personal enmity to individuals, I cannot be insensible to the artifices employed by some men to prejudice me in the public esteem.

To John Jay, April 14, 1779   *Writings Vol. 14 p. 378*

SACRIFICES TO PRINCIPLE

... I think, at least I hope, that there is public virtue enough left among us to deny ourselves every thing but the bare necessaries of life to accomplish this end.

To Bryan Fairfax, July 20, 1774   *Writings Vol. 3 p. 234*

... To share a common lot, and participate the inconveniencies wch. the Army (from the peculiarity of our circumstances are obliged to undergo) has, with me, been a fundamental principle.

To Nathanael Greene, January 22, 1780   *Writings Vol. 17 p. 423*

A Display of the United States by Amos Doolittle after Joseph Wright, New Haven, 1794. Published during Washington's presidency, this engraving features the seals of the United States and the 13 original states in interlocking circles, each ring containing statistics on the state's population and congressional representation. The unbroken chain surrounds a portrait of Washington, symbolically linking the first President with the strength of the new government.

ENDURANCE

... We should never despair, our Situation before has been unpromising and has changed for the better, so I trust, it will again. If new difficulties arise, we must only put forth New Exertions and proportion our Efforts to the exigency of the times.

To Philip Schuyler, July 15, 1777   *Writings Vol. 8 p. 408*

... The value of liberty was thus enhanced in our estimation by the difficulty of its attainment, and the worth of characters appreciated by the trial of adversity.

To the People of the State of South Carolina
                    Addresses and Answers, Vol. 29 p. 142, Washington Papers

THE SACRIFICES AND REWARDS OF PATRIOTISM

... it is but justice to assign great merit to the temper of those citizens, whose estates were more immediately the scene of warfare. Their personal services were rendered without constraint, and the derangement of their affairs submitted to without dissatisfaction. It was the triumph of patriotism over personal considerations. And our present enjoyments of peace and freedom reward the sacrifice.

Answer to the New Jersey Legislature, December 1, 1789 Writings Vol. 30 p. 476

THE PATRIOT'S TWO-FOLD DEPENDENCE

... I have every thought, and am still of Opinion that no terms of accommodation will be offered by the British Ministry, but such as cannot be accepted by America. We have nothing my Dear Sir, to depend upon but the protection of a kind Providence and unanimity among ourselves.

To John Adams, April 15, 1776   *Writings Vol. 4 p. 483*

SELF-CONTROL

... It is our duty to make the best of our misfortunes, and not to suffer passion to interfere with our interest and the public good.

To William Heath, August 28, 1778   *Writings Vol. 12 p. 365*

THE PATRIOT'S GREAT OBJECT

... The welfare of our Country is the great object to which our Cares and efforts ought to be directed. And I shall derive great satisfaction from a co-operation with you, in the pleasing though arduous task of ensuring to our fellow-citizens the blessings which they have a right to expect from a free, efficient and equal Government.

To the Senate and the House of Representatives, January 8, 1790
                    Writings Vol. 30 p. 494

TALENTS, RECTITUDE, PATRIOTISM

. . . In these honorable qualifications, I behold the surest pledges, that as on one side, no local prejudices, or attachments; no seperate views, nor party animosities, will misdirect the comprehensive and equal eye which ought to watch over this great assemblage of communities and interests: so, on another, that the foundations of our National policy will be laid in the pure and immutable principles of private morality; and the pre-eminence of a free Government, be exemplified by all the attributes which can win the affections of its Citizens, and command the respect of the world.

The First Inaugural Address, April 30, 1789   *Writings Vol. 30 p. 294*

PATRIOTISM, FIRMNESS, WISDOM

. . . to secure the blessings which a Gracious Providence has placed within our reach, will in the course of the present important Session, call for the cool and deliberate exertion of your patriotism, firmness and wisdom.

First Annual Address, January 8, 1790   *Writings Vol. 30 p. 491*

. . . Our conflict is not likely to cease so soon as every good Man would wish. The measure of iniquity is not yet filled; and unless we can return more to first principles, and act a little more upon patriotic ground, I do not know when it will, or, what may be the Issue of the contest.

To James Warren, March 31, 1779   *Writings Vol. 14 p. 312*

. . . General Washington, replied, he was not vested with any powers on this subject by those from whom he derived his authority and power. But from what had appeared or transpired on this head, Lord Howe and General Howe were only to grant pardons; that those who had committed no fault wanted no pardon, that we were only defending what we deemed our indisputable right.

Memorandum, July 20, 1776   *Writings Vol. 5 p. 323*

PRUDENCE, TEMPER, MODERATION

. . . Nothing but disunion can hurt our cause. This will ruin it, if great prudence, temper, and moderation is not mixed in our counsels, and made the governing principles of the contending parties.

To Joseph Reed, April 15, 1776   *Writings Vol. 4 p. 483*

THE PATRIOT'S HAPPINESS

. . . to stand well in the good opinion of my Countrymen constitutes my chiefest happiness; and will be my best support under the perplexities and difficulties of my present Station.

To Benjamin Harrison, December 18–30, 1778   *Writings Vol. 13 p. 463*

... to be in any degree instrumental in procuring to my American Brethren a restitution of their just rights and Priviledges, will constitute my chief happiness.

To the President of Congress, April 18, 1776   *Writings Vol. 4 p. 489*

THE PATRIOT'S REWARD

... Whatever services I have rendered to my country, in its general approbation I have received an ample reward.

To the Massachusetts Senators, February 24, 1797   *Writings Vol. 35 p. 398*

POPULAR SPIRIT

... It is a happy circumstance, that such an animation prevails among the people. I would wish to let it operate and draw as many as possible together, which will be a great discouragement to the Enemy, by Showing that the popular Spirit is at such a height, and at the same time, will inspire the people themselves with confidence in their own Strength, by discovering to every individual the zeal and Spirit of his neighbours. But after they have been collected a few days, I would have the greatest part of them dismissed, as not being immediately wanted, desiring them to hold themselves in readiness for any sudden call, and concerting Signals with them, at the appearance of which they are to fly to Arms.

To Benedict Arnold, June 17, 1777   *Writings Vol. 8 p. 261*

NATIONALITY

... No expressions of personal politeness to me can be acceptable, accompanied by reflections on the Representatives of a free People, under whose Authority I have the Honor to act. The delicacy I have observed in refraining from every thing offensive in this way, entitled me to expect a similar Treatment from you. I have not indulged myself in invective against the present Rulers of Great Britain, in the course of our Correspondence, nor will I even now avail myself of so fruitful a Theme.

To Sir William Howe, January 30, 1778   *Writings Vol. 10 p. 409*

THE PATRIOT, REFUSING A CROWN

... With a mixture of great surprise and astonishment I have read with attention the Sentiments you have submitted to my perusal. Be assured Sir, no occurrence in the course of the War, has given me more painful sensations than your information of there being such ideas existing in the Amry as you have expressed, and I must view with abhorrence, and reprehend with severity. For the present, the communicatn. of them will rest in my own bosom, unless some further agitation of the matter, shall make a disclosure necessary. I am much at a loss to conceive what part of my conduct could have given encouragement to an address which to me seems big with the greatest mischiefs that can befall my Country. If I am not deceived in the knowledge of myself, you could not have found a person to whom your schemes are more disagreeable; at the same time in justice to my own feelings I must add, that no Man possesses a more sincere wish to see ample justice done to the Army than I do, and as far as my powers and influence, in a constitutional way extend, they shall be employed to the utmost of my abilities to effect it, should there be any occasion. Let me conjure you then, if you have any regard for your Country, concern for yourself or posterity, or respect for me, banish these thoughts from your mind, and never communicate, as from yourself, or any one else, a sentiment of the like Nature.

To Lewis Nicola, May 22, 1782   *Writings Vol. 24 p. 272*

FEMALE PATRIOTISM

... I very much admire the patriotic spirit of the Ladies of Philada., and shall with great pleasure give them my advice, as to the application of their benevolent and generous donation to the soldiers of the Army.

To Joseph Reed, June 25, 1780   *Writings Vol. 19 p. 71*

... I ... cannot forbear taking the earliest moment to express the high sense I entertain of the patriotic exertions of the Ladies of Maryland in favor of the Army.

To Mary Lee, October 11, 1780   *Writings Vol. 20 p. 168*

... Amidst all the distresses and sufferings of the Army, from whatever sources they have arisen, it must be consolation to our *Virtuous Country Women* that they have never been accused of with holding their most zealous efforts to support the cause we are engaged in, and encourage those who are defending them in the Field. The Army do not want gratitude, nor do they Misplace it in this instance.

To Sarah Bache, January 15, 1781   *Writings Vol. 21 p. 102*

... It embellishes the American character with a new trait; by proving that the love of country is blended with those softer domestic virtues, which have always been allowed to be more peculiarly *your own.*

You have not acquired admiration in your own country only; it is paid you abroad; and you will learn with pleasure by a part of your own sex, where female accomplishments have attained their highest perfection, and who from the commencement have been the patronesses of American liberty.

To Anne Francis, Henrietta Hillegas, Mary Clarkson, Sarah Bache, and Susan Blair, February 13, 1781   *Writings Vol. 21 p. 221*

ON HIS ACCEPTING THE PRESIDENCY

... Among the vicissitudes incident to life, no event could have filled me with greater anxieties than that of which the notification was transmitted by your order, and received on the fourteenth day of the present month. On the one hand, I was summoned by my Country, whose voice I can never hear but with veneration and love, from a retreat which I had chosen with the fondest predilection, and, in my flattering hopes, with an immutable decision, as the asylum of my declining years: a retreat which was rendered every day more necessary as well as more dear to me, by the addition of habit to inclination, and of frequent interruptions in my health to the gradual waste committed on it by time. On the other hand, the magnitude and difficulty of the trust to which the voice of my Country called me, being sufficient to awaken in the wisest and most experienced of her citizens, could not but overwhelm with dispondence, one, who, inheriting inferior endowments from nature and unpractised in the duties of civil administration, ought to be peculiarly conscious of his own deficencies. In this conflict of emotions, all I dare aver is, that it has been my faithful study to collect my duty from a just appreciation of every circumstance, by which it might be affected. All I dare hope, is, that, if in executing this task I have been too much swayed by a grateful remembrance of former instances, or by an affectionate sensibility to this transcendent proof, of the confidence of my fellow-citizens; and have thence too little consulted my incapacity as well as disinclination for the weighty and untried cares before me; my *error* will be palliated by the motives which misled me, and its consequences be judged by my Country, with some share of the partiality in which they originated.

The First Inaugural Address, April 30, 1789   *Writings Vol. 30 p. 291*

... I feel for those Members of the new Congress, who, hitherto, have given an unavailing attendance at the theatre of business. For myself, the delay may be compared to a reprieve; for in confidence I assure *you,* with the *world* it would obtain *little credit,* that my movements to the chair of Government will be accompanied by feelings not unlike those of a culprit who is going to the place of his execution: so unwilling am I, in the evening of a life nearly consumed in public cares, to quit a peaceful abode for an Ocean of difficulties, without that competency of political skill, abilities and inclination which is necessary to manage the helm.

... I am sensible, that I am embarking the voice of my Countrymen and a good name of my own, on this voyage, but what returns will be made for them, Heaven alone can foretell. Integrity and firmness is all I can promise; these, be the voyage long or short, never shall forsake me although I may be deserted by all men. For of the consolations which are to be derived from these (under any circumstances) the world cannot deprive me.

To the Acting Secretary at War, April 1, 1789   *Writings Vol. 30 p. 268*

HIS PROGRESS TO THE SEAT OF GOVERNMENT

... When I was first honoured with a call into the Service of my Country, then on the eve of an arduous struggle for its liberties, the light in which I contemplated my duty required that I should renounce every pecuniary compensation. From this resolution I have in no instance departed. And being still under the impressions which produced it, I must decline as inapplicable to myself, any share in the personal emoluments, which may be indispensably included in a permanent provision for the Executive Department; and must accordingly pray that the pecuniary estimates for the Station in which I am placed, may, during my continuance in it, be limited to such actual expenditures as the public good may be thought to require.

The First Inaugural Address, April 30, 1789   *Writings Vol. 30 p. 295*

... When I was first called to the station with which I was honored during the late conflict for our liberties, to the diffidence which I had so many reasons to feel in accepting it, I thought it my duty to join a firm resolution to shut my hand against every pecuniary recompense. To this resolution I have invariably adhered, and from it (if I had the inclination) I do not consider myself at liberty now to depart.

To Patrick Henry, October 29, 1785   *Writings Vol. 28 p. 304*

ON RETIRING FROM OFFICE

... Though in reviewing the incidents of my Administration, I am unconscious of intentional error, I am nevertheless too sensible of my defects not to think it probable that I may have committed many errors. Whatever they may be I fervently beseech the Almighty to avert or mitigate the evils to which they may tend. I shall also carry with me the hope that my Country will never cease to view them with indulgence; and that after forty five years of my life dedicated to its Service, with an upright zeal, the faults of incompetent abilities will be consigned to oblivion, as myself must soon be to the Mansions of rest.

... Relying on its kindness in this as in other things, and actuated by that fervent love towards it, which is so natural to a Man, who views in it the native soil of himself and his progenitors for several Generations; I anticipate with pleasing expectation that retreat, in which I promise myself to realize, without alloy, the sweet enjoyment of partaking, in the midst of my fellow Citizens, the benign influence of good Laws under a free Government, the ever favourite object of my heart, and the happy reward, as I trust, of our mutual cares, labours and dangers.

Farewell Address, September 19, 1796   *Writings Vol. 35 p. 237*

... when, in the decline of Life, I gratify the fond wish of my heart in retiring from public labours, and find the language of approbation and fervent prayers for future happiness following that event, my heart expands with gratitude and my feelings become unutterable.

To the General Assembly of the State of Rhode Island, April 3, 1797
                                              Writings Vol. 35 p. 431

GRATITUDE TO THE COUNTRY

... In looking forward to the moment, which is intended to terminate the career of my public life, my feelings do not permit me to suspend the deep acknowledgment of that debt of gratitude wch. I owe to my beloved country, for the many honors it has conferred upon me; still more for the stedfast confidence with which it has supported me; and for the opportunities I have thence enjoyed of manifesting my inviolable attachment, by services faithful and persevering, though in usefulness unequal to my zeal. If benefits have resulted to our country from these services, let it always be remembered to your praise, and as an instructive example in our annals, that, under circumstances in which the Passions agitated in every direction were liable to mislead, amidst appearances sometimes du-. bious, viscissitudes of fortune often discouraging, in situations in which not unfrequently want of Success has countenanced the spirit of criticism, the constancy of your support was the essential prop of the efforts, and a guarantee of the plans by which they were effected. Profoundly penetrated with this idea, I shall carry it with me to my grave, as a strong incitement to unceasing vows that Heaven may continue to you the choicest tokens of its beneficence; that your Union and brotherly affection may be perpetual; that the free constitution, which is the work of your hands, may be sacredly maintained; that its administration in every department may be stamped with wisdom and Virtue; that, in fine, the happiness of the people of these States, under the auspices of liberty, may be made complete, by so careful a preservation and so prudent a use of this blessing as will acquire to them the glory of recommending it to the applause, the affection, and adoption of every nation which is yet a stranger to it.

Farewell Address, September 19, 1796   *Writings Vol. 35 p. 217*

HIS FAREWELL TO THE ARMY

... being now to conclude these his last public Orders, and to bid a final adieu to the Armies he has so long had the honor to Command, he can only again offer in their behalf his recommendations to their grateful country, and his prayers to the God of Armies. May ample justice be done them here, and may the choicest of heaven's favours, both here and here-after, attend those who, under the devine auspices, have secured innumerable blessings for others; with these wishes, and this benediction, the Commander in Chief is about to retire from Service. The Curtain of seperation will soon be drawn, and the military scene to him will be closed for ever.

Farewell Orders to the Armies of the United States, November 2, 1783
Writings Vol. 27 p. 227

FAREWELL TO CONGRESS, AT THE CLOSE OF THE WAR

... Happy in the confirmation of our Independence and Sovereignty, and pleased with the oppertunity afforded the United States of becoming a respectable Nation, I resign with satisfaction the Appointment I accepted with diffidence. A diffidence in my abilities to accomplish so arduous a task, which however was superseded by a confidence in the rectitude of our Cause, the support of the Supreme Power of the Union, and the patronage of Heaven . . . .

... I consider it an indispensable duty to close this last solemn act of my Official life, by commending the Interest of our dearest Country to the protection of Almighty God, and those who have the superintendence of them, to his holy keeping.

Address to Congress on Resigning His Commission, December 23, 1783
Writings Vol. 27 p. 284

ON HIS RETURN TO MOUNT VERNON, AFTER THE WAR

... The Scene is at last closed.

To George Clinton, December 28, 1783   *Writings Vol. 27 p. 288*

... on the Eve of Christmas entered these doors an older man by near nine years, than when I left them.

To Marquis de Lafayette, February 1, 1784   *Writings Vol. 27 p. 318*

... I am just beginning to experience that ease, and freedom from public cares which, however desirable, takes some time to realize; for strange as it may tell, it is nevertheless true, that it was not 'till lately I could get the better of my usual custom of ruminating as soon as I waked in the Morning, on the business of the ensuing day; and of my surprize, after having revolved many things in my mind, to find that I was no longer a public

Man, or had any thing to do with public transactions.

To Henry Knox, February 20, 1784   *Writings Vol. 27 p. 340*

CONSECRATION OF THE PATRIOT'S WEAPONS

... To each of my Nephews, William Augustine Washington, George Lewis, George Steptoe Washington, Bushrod Washington, and Samuel Washington, I give one of the Swords or Cutteaux of which I may die possessed; and they are to chuse in the order they are named. —These Swords are accompanied with an injunction not to unsheath them for the purpose of shedding blood, except it be for defense, or in defense of their Country and its rights; and in the latter case, to keep them unsheathed, and prefer falling with them in their hands, to the relinquishment thereof.

Will, July 9, 1799   *Writings Vol. 37 p. 288*

C. INDEPENDENCE

THE CAUSE OF AMERICAN INDEPENDENCE

... Our cause is noble, it is the cause of Mankind! and the danger to it, is to be apprehended from ourselves. Shall we slumber and sleep then while we should be punishing those miscreants who have brot. these troubles upon us and who are aimg. to continue us in them, while we should be striving to fill our Battalions, and devising ways and means to appreciate the currency; on the credit of wch. every thing depends? I hope not.

To James Warren, March 31, 1779   *Writings Vol. 14 p. 313*

... I trust the goodness of the cause and the exertions of the people under divine protection will give us that honourable peace for which we are contending.

To the Minister, Elders, and Deacons of the Dutch Reformed Church at Raritan, June 2, 1779   *Writings Vol. 15 p. 210*

... The favourable disposition of Spain; the promised succour from France; the combined force in the West Indies; The declaration of Russia (acceded to by other powers of Europe, humiliating to the Naval pride and power of Great Britain); the Superiority of France and Spain by Sea in Europe; The Irish claims and English disturbances, formed in the aggregate, an opinion in my breast (which is not very susceptable of peaceful dreams) that the hour of deliverance was not far distant; for that however unwilling Great B: might be to yield the point, it would not be in her power to continue the contest. but alas! these prospects, flattering as they were, have prov'd delusory, and I see nothing before us but accumulating distress.

To John Cadwalader, October 5, 1780　　　　　*Writings Vol. 20 p. 121*

... we must not despair; the game is yet in our own hands; to play it well is all we have to do, and I trust the experience of error will enable us to act better in future. A cloud may yet pass over us, individuals may be ruined; and the Country at large, or particular States, undergo temporary distress; but certain I am, that it is in our power to bring the War to a happy conclusion.

To John Mathews, June 7, 1781　　　　　*Writings Vol. 22 p. 176*

... I am happy to be informed by Accounts from all Parts of the Continent, of the agreeable Prospect of a very plentifull Supply of almost all the Productions of the Earth. Blessed as we are with the Bounties of Providence, necessary for our support and Defence, the Fault must surely be our own (and great indeed will it be), if we do not, by a proper Use of them, attain the noble Prize for wch. we have so long been contending, the Establishment of Peace, Liberty and Independence.

To Thomas McKean, President of Congress, July 21, 1781

　　　　　Writings Vol. 22 p. 405

THE COMMON WEAL

... it appears as clear to me as ever the Sun did in its meredian brightness, that America never stood in more eminent need of the wise, patriotic, and Spirited exertions of her Sons than at this period and if it is not a sufficient cause for genl. lamentation, my misconception of the matter impresses it too strongly upon me; that the States seperately are too much engaged in their local concerns, and have too many of their ablest men withdrawn from the general Council for the good of the common weal.

To Benjamin Harrison, December 18–30, 1778　　*Writings Vol. 13 p. 464*

... I think our political system may, be compared to the mechanism of a Clock; and that our conduct should derive a lesson from it for it answers no good purpose to keep smaller Wheels in order if the greater one which is the support and prime mover of the whole is neglected.

To Benjamin Harrison, December 18–30, 1778　　*Writings Vol. 13 p. 464*

... as there can be no harm in a pious wish for the good of ones Country I shall offer it as mine that each State wd. not only choose, but absolutely compel their ablest Men to attend Congress; that they would instruct them to go into a thorough investigation of the causes that have produced so many disagreeable effects in the Army and Country; in a word that public abuses should be corrected.

To Benjamin Harrison, December 18–30, 1778   *Writings Vol. 13 p. 464*

INDEPENDENCE, WON

... A contemplation of the compleat attainment (at a period earlier than could have been expected) of the object for which we contended against so formidable a power cannot but inspire us with astonishment and gratitude.

Farewell Orders to the Armies of the United States, November 2, 1783
                                          Writings Vol. 27 p. 223

... The disadvantageous circumstances on our part, under which the war was undertaken, can never be forgotten. The singular interpositions of Providence in our feeble condition were such, as could scarcely escape the attention of the most unobserving; while the unparalleled perseverence of the Armies of the U States, through almost every possible suffering and discouragement for the space of eight long years, was little short of a standing miracle.

Farewell Orders to the Armies of the United States, November 2, 1783
                                          Writings Vol. 27 p. 223

... It is universally acknowledged, that the enlarged prospects of happiness, opened by the confirmation of our independence and sovereignty, almost exceed the power of description.

Farewell Orders to the Armies of the United States, November 2, 1783
                                          Writings Vol. 27 p. 224

... the foundation of a great Empire is laid, and I please myself with a persuasion, that Providence will not leave its work imperfect.

To Chevalier de LaLuzerne, August 1, 1786   *Writings Vol. 28 p. 501*

... The establishment of our new Government seemed to be the last great experiment for promoting human happiness by reasonable compact in civil Society. It was to be, in the first instance, in a considerable degree a government of accommodation as well as a government of Laws.

To Mrs. C. M. Graham, January 9, 1790   *Writings Vol. 30 p. 496*

MOMENTOUS INFLUENCE OF THE REVOLUTION

... the preservation of the sacred fire of liberty, and the destiny of the Republican model of Government, are justly considered as *deeply,* perhaps as *finally* staked, on the experiment entrusted to the hands of the American people.

First Inaugural Address, April 30, 1789   *Writings Vol. 30 p. 294*

His Excellency George Washington Lieut. Genl. of the Armies of the United States of America by D. Edwin after Gilbert Stuart. This print was published in 1798 following Washington's reappointment as commander in chief by President John Adams.

SITUATION AND PROSPECTS OF THE COUNTRY

... The Citizens of America, placed in the most enviable condition, as the sole Lords and Proprietors of a vast Tract of Continent, comprehending all the various soils and climates of the World, and abounding with all the necessaries and convencies of life, are now by the late satisfactory pacification, acknowledged to be possessed of absolute freedom and Independency; They are, from this period, to be considered as the Actors on a most conspicuous Theatre, which seems to be peculiarly designated by Providence for the display of human greatness and felicity; Here, they are not only surrounded with every thing which can contribute to the completion of private and domestic enjoyment, but Heaven has crowned all its other blessings, by giving a fairer opportunity for political happiness, than any other Nation has ever been favored with.

Circular to the States, June 8, 1783   *Writings Vol. 26 p. 484*

... The foundation of our Empire was not laid in the gloomy age of Ignorance and Superstition, but at an Epocha when the rights of mankind were better understood and more clearly defined, than at any former period, the researches of the human mind, after social happiness, have been carried to a great extent, the Treasures of knowledge, acquired by the labours of Philosophers, Sages and Legislatures, through a long succession of years, are laid open for our use, and their collected wisdom may be happily applied in the Establishment of our forms of Government; the free cultivation of Letters, the unbounded extension of Commerce, the progressive refinement of Manners, the growing liberality of sentiment, and above all, the pure and benign light of Revelation, have had a meliorating influence on mankind and increased the blessings of Society. At this auspicious period, the United States came into existence as a Nation, and if their Citizens should not be completely free and happy, the fault will be intirely their own.

Circular to the States, June 8, 1783   *Writings Vol. 26 p. 485*

D. THE CONSTITUTION

CHOICE OF THE FORM OF GOVERNMENT

We exhibit at present the Novel and astonishing Spectacle of a whole People deliberating calmly on what form of government will be most conducive to their happiness; and deciding with an unexpected degree of unanimity in favour of a System which they conceive calculated to answer the purpose.

To Sir Edward Newenham, August 29, 1788   *Writings Vol. 30 p. 73*

... I do not believe, that Providence has done so much for nothing. It has always been my creed that we should not be left as an awful monument to prove, "that Mankind, ... are unequal to the task of Governing themselves, ..."

To Marquis de Lafayette, June 19, 1788   *Writings Vol. 29 p. 526*

THE FOUR PILLARS OF INDEPENDENCE

... There are four things, which I humbly conceive, are essential to the well being, I may even venture to say, to the existence of the United States as an Independent Power:

1st. An indissoluble Union of the States under one Federal Head.

2dly. A Sacred regard to Public Justice.

3dly. The adoption of a proper Peace Establishment, and

4thly. The prevalence of that pacific and friendly Disposition, among the People of the United States, which will induce them to forget their local prejudices and policies, to make those mutual concessions which are requisite to the general prosperity, and in some instances, to sacrifice their individual advantages to the interest of the Community.

... These are the Pillars on which the glorious Fabrick of our Independency and National Character must be supported; Liberty is the Basis, and whoever would dare to sap the foundation, or overturn the Structure, under whatever specious pretexts may he attempt it, will merit the bitterest execration, and the severest punishment which can be inflicted by his injured Country.

Circular to the States, June 8, 1783   *Writings Vol. 26 p. 487*

IMPORTANCE OF THE FEDERAL UNION

... Thirteen Sovereignties pulling against each other, and all tugging at the federal head will soon bring ruin on the whole; whereas a liberal, and energetic Constitution, well guarded and closely watched ... might restore us to that degree of respectability and consequence, to which we had a fair claim, and the brightest prospect of attaining.

To James Madison, November 5, 1786   *Writings Vol. 29 p. 52*

... unless the States will suffer Congress to exercise those prerogatives, they are undoubtedly invested with by the Constitution, every thing must very rapidly tend to Anarchy and confusion ....

Circular to the States, June 8, 1783   *Writings Vol. 26 p. 488*

... it is indispensable to the happiness of the individual States, that there should be lodged somewhere, a Supreme Power to regulate and govern the general concerns of the Confederated Republic, without which the Union cannot be of long duration.

Circular to the States, June 8, 1783   *Writings Vol. 26 p. 488*

... whatever measures have a tendency to dissolve the Union, or contribute to violate or lessen the Sovereign Authority, ought to be considered as hostile to the Liberty and Independency of America, and the Authors of them treated accordingly ....

Circular to the States, June 8, 1783   *Writings Vol. 26 p. 488*

... unless we can be enabled, by the concurrence of the States, to participate of the fruits of the Revolution, and enjoy the essential benefits of Civil Society, under a form of Government so free and uncorrupted, ... it will be a subject of regret, that so much blood and treasure have been lavished for no purpose, that so many sufferings have been encountered without a compensation, and that so many sacrifices have been made in vain.

Circular to the States, June 8, 1783   *Writings Vol. 26 p. 488*

... It is only in our united Character as an Empire, that our Independence is acknowledged, that our power can be regarded, or our Credit supported among Foreign Nations. The Treaties of the European Powers with the United States of America, will have no validity on a dissolution of the Union. We shall be left nearly in a state of Nature, or we may find by our own unhappy experience, that there is a natural and necessary progression, from the extreme of anarchy to the extreme of Tyranny; and that arbitrary power is most easily established on the ruins of Liberty abused to licentiousness.

Circular to the States, June 8, 1783   *Writings Vol. 26 p. 488*

... The Unity of Government which constitutes you one people is also now dear to you. It is justly so; for it is a main Pillar in the Edifice of your real independence, the support of your tranquility at home; your peace abroad; of your safety; of your prosperity; of that very Liberty which you so highly prize.

Farewell Address, September 19, 1796   *Writings Vol. 35 p. 218*

AMERICANS, UNITED IN SYMPATHY AND INTEREST

... Citizens by birth or choice, of a common country, that country has a right to concentrate your affections. The name of AMERICAN, which belongs to you, in your national capacity, must always exalt the just pride of Patriotism, more than any appellation derived from local discriminations. With slight shades of difference, you have the same Religion, Manners, Habits and political Principles. You have in a common cause fought

and triumphed together. The independence and liberty you possess are
the work of joint councils, and joint efforts; of common dangers, sufferings and successes.

Farewell Address, September 19, 1796   *Writings Vol. 35 p. 219*

THE PRESERVATION OF THE UNION, OUR INTEREST

... Here every portion of our country finds the most commanding motives for carefully guarding and preserving the Union of the whole.

Farewell Address, September 19, 1796   *Writings Vol. 35 p. 220*

THE POWER OF THE UNION

... While then every part of our country thus feels an immediate and particular Interest in Union, all the parts combined cannot fail to find in the
united mass of means and efforts greater strength, greater resource, pro-
portionably greater security from external danger, a less frequent interruption of their Peace by foreign Nations; ... your Union ought to be
considered as a main prop of your liberty, and that the love of the one
ought to endear to you the preservation of the other.

Farewell Address, September 19, 1796   *Writings Vol. 35 p. 221*

THE EXTENT OF THE UNION

... Is there a doubt, whether a common government can embrace so large
a sphere? Let experience solve it. To listen to mere speculation in such a
case were criminal. We are authorized to hope that a proper organization
of the whole, with the auxiliary agency of governments for the respective
Sub divisions, will afford a happy issue to the experiment. 'Tis well worth
a fair and full experiment.

Farewell Address, September 19, 1796   *Writings Vol. 35 p. 222*

CAUSES OF DISTURBANCE OF THE UNION

... In contemplating the causes wch. may disturb our Union, it occurs as a
matter of serious concern, that any ground should have been furnished
for characterizing parties by *Geographical* discriminations: *Northern and
Southern: Atlantic* and *Western;* whence designing men may endeavour to
excite a belief that there is a real difference of local interest and views.
One of the expedients of Party to acquire influence, within particular districts, is to misrepresent the opinions and aims of other Districts. You
cannot shield yourselves too much against the jealousies and heart burn-
ings which spring from these misrepresentations. They tend to render

Alien to each other those who ought to be bound together by fraternal affection.

Farewell Address, September 19, 1796   *Writings Vol. 35 p. 223*

UNION, NOT MERE ALLIANCE

... To the efficacy and permanency of Your Union, a Government for the whole is indispensable. No Alliances, however strict between the parts can be an adequate substitute. They must inevitably experience the infractions and interruptions which all Alliances in all times have experienced.

Farewell Address, September 19, 1796   *Writings Vol. 35 p. 224*

... Sensible of this momentous truth, you have improved upon your first essay, by the adoption of a Constitution of Government, better calculated than your former for an intimate Union, and for the efficacious management of your common concerns.

Farewell Address, September 19, 1796   *Writings Vol. 35 p. 224*

... This government, the offspring of our own choice uninfluenced and unawed, adopted upon full investigation and mature deliberation, completely free in its principles, in the distribution of its powers, uniting security with energy, and containing within itself a provision for its own amendment, has a just claim to your confidence and your support. Respect for its authority, compliance with its Laws, acquiescence in its measures, are duties enjoined by the fundamental maxims of true Liberty.

Farewell Address, September 19, 1796   *Writings Vol. 35 p. 224*

... The basis of our political systems is the right of the people to make and to alter their Constitutions of Government. But the Constitution which at any time exists, 'till changed by an explicit and authentic act of the whole People, is sacredly obligatory upon all.

Farewell Address, September 19, 1796   *Writings Vol. 35 p. 224*

... The very idea of the power and the right of the People to establish Government presupposes the duty of every Individual to obey the established Government.

Farewell Address, September 19, 1796   *Writings Vol. 35 p. 224*

FACTION

... All obstructions to the execution of the Laws, all combinations and Associations, under whatever plausible character, with the real design, controul, counteract, or awe the regular deliberation and action of the Constituted authorities are destructive of this fundamental principle and of fatal tendency. They serve to organize faction, to give it an artificial and extraordinary force; to put in the place of the delegated will of the Nation, the will of a party; often a small but artful and enterprizing minority of the Community; and, according to the alternate triumphs of different parties, to make the public administration the Mirror of the ill concerted and incongruous projects of faction, rather than the Organ of consistent and wholesome plans digested by common councils, and modefied by mutual interests. However combinations or Associations of the above description may now and then answer popular ends, they are likely, in the course of time and things, to become potent engines, by which cunning, ambitious and unprincipled men will be enabled to subvert the Power of the People, and to usurp for themselves the reins of Government; destroying afterwards the very engines which have lifted them to unjust dominion.

Farewell Address, September 19, 1796   *Writings Vol. 35 p. 224*

... In all the changes to which you may be invited, remember that time and habit are at least as necessary to fix the true character of Governments, as of other human institutions; that experience is the surest standard, by which to test the real tendency of the existing Constitution of a country; ... Liberty itself will find in such a Government, with powers properly distributed and adjusted, its surest Guardian.

Farewell Address, September 19, 1796   *Writings Vol. 35 p. 225*

... It is indeed little else than a name, where the Government is too feeble to withstand the enterprises of faction, to confine each member of the Society within the limits prescribed by the laws and to maintain all in the secure and tranquil enjoyment of the rights of person and property.

Farewell Address, September 19, 1796   *Writings Vol. 35 p. 226*

ALLEGED BENEFIT OF PARTIES

... It is also most devoutly to be wished that faction was at an end and that those to whom everything dear and valuable is entrusted would lay aside party views and return to first principles. happy, happy, thrice happy Country if such was the government of it, but alas! we are not to expect that the path is to be strewed wt. flowers. That great and good Being who rules the Universe has disposed matters otherwise and for wise purposes I am perswaded.

To Joseph Reed, November 27, 1778   *Writings Vol. 13 p. 347*

... I am under more apprehensions on account of our own dissentions than of the efforts of the Enemy.

To Benedict Arnold, December 13, 1778   *Writings Vol. 13 p. 393*

... Unanimity in our Councils, disinterestedness in our pursuits, and steady perseverence in our national duty, are the only means to avoid misfortunes; if they come upon us after these we shall have the consolation of knowing that we have done our best, the rest is with the Gods.

To Thomas Nelson, March 15, 1779   *Writings Vol. 14 p. 246*

... The hour therefore is certainly come when party differences and disputes should subside; when every Man (especially those in Office) should with one hand and one heart pull the same way and with their whole strength.

To John Armstrong, May 18, 1779   *Writings Vol. 15 p. 99*

... Providence has done, and I am perswaded is disposed to do, a great deal for us, but we are not to forget the fable of Jupiter and the Countryman.

To John Armstrong, May 18, 1779   *Writings Vol. 15 p. 99*

USURPATION

... It is important, likewise, that the habits of thinking in a free Country should inspire caution in those entrusted with its administration, to confine themselves within their respective Constitutional spheres; ... If in the opinion of the People, the distribution or modification of the Constitutional powers be in any particular wrong, let it be corrected by an amendment in the way which the Constitution designates. But let there be no change by usurpation; for though this, in one instance, may be the instrument of good, it is the customary weapon by which free governments are destroyed.

Farewell Address, September 19, 1796   *Writings Vol. 35 p. 228*

SUPREME IMPORTANCE OF THE FEDERAL UNION

... notwithstanding the cup of blessing is thus reached out to us, notwithstanding happiness is ours, if we have a disposition to seize the occasion and make it our own; yet, it appears to me there is an option still left to the United States of America, that it is in their choice, and depends upon their conduct, whether they will be respectable and prosperous, or contemptable and miserable as a Nation; This is the time of their political probation, this is the moment when the eyes of the whole World are turned upon them, this is the moment to establish or ruin their national Character forever ....

Circular to the States, June 8, 1783   *Writings Vol. 26 p. 485*

... it is yet to be decided, whether the Revolution must ultimately be considered as a blessing or a curse: a blessing or a curse, not to the present

age alone, for with our fate will the destiny of unborn Millions be involved.

Circular to the States, June 8, 1783   *Writings Vol. 26 p. 486*

RECIPROCITY

... There must be reciprocity or no Union, which is preferable will not
become a question in the Mind of any true patriot.

To David Stuart, October 17, 1787   *Writings Vol. 29 p. 290*

POWERS OF CONGRESS

... the fear of giving sufficient powers to Congress for the purposes I have
mentioned is futile, without it, our Independence fails, and each Assembly under its present Constitution will be annihilated, and we must once
more return to the Government of G: Britain, and be made to kiss the rod
preparing for our correction.

To John Parke Custis, February 28, 1781   *Writings Vol. 21 p. 320*

... unless the principles of the federal government were properly supported and the powers of the union increased, the honour, dignity, and
justice of the nation would be lost forever.

Farewell Orders to the Armies of the United States, November 2, 1783
                                                     Writings Vol. 27 p. 226

... To *me*, it is a solecism in politics: indeed it is one of the most extraordinary things in nature, that we should confederate as a Nation, and yet be
afraid to give the rulers of that nation, who are the creatures of our making, appointed for a limited and short duration, and who are amenable
for every action, and recallable at any moment, and are subject to all the
evils which they may be instrumental in producing, sufficient powers to
order and direct the affairs of the same. By such policy as this the wheels
of Government are clogged, and our brightest prospects, and that high
expectation which was entertained of us by the wondering world, are
turned into astonishment; and from the high ground on which we stood,
we are descending into the vale of confusion and darkness.

To James Warren, October 7, 1785   *Writings Vol. 28 p. 290*

... we have probably had too good an opinion of human nature in forming our confederation. Experience has taught us, that men will not adopt
and carry into execution measures the best calculated for their own good,
without the intervention of a coercive power.

To the Secretary for Foreign Affairs, August 1, 1786   *Writings Vol. 28 p. 502*

G. Washington, President of the United States by William Rollinson, published by I. Reid, New York, 1796. This portrait, based on a miniature by Walter Robertson, was published in William Winterbotham's *An Historical, Geographical, Commercial and Philosophical View . . . of the United States of America* (New York, 1796).

THE UNION, OUR SAFETY

... Common danger brought the States into confederacy, and on their union our safety and importance depend.

To David Stuart, March 28, 1790   *Writings Vol. 31 p. 29*

SPIRIT OF ACCOMMODATION

... A spirit of accommodation was the basis of the present constitution.

To David Stuart, March 28, 1790   *Writings Vol. 31 p. 29*

NATIONAL INFLUENCE

... It should be the highest ambition of every American to extend his views beyond himself, and to bear in mind that his conduct will not only affect himself, his country, and his immediate posterity; but that its influence may be co-extensive with the world, and stamp political happiness or misery on ages yet unborn. To establish this desirable end, and to establish the government of *laws*, the *union* of these States is absolutely necessary; therefore in every proceeding, this great, this important object should ever be kept in view; and so long as our measures tend to this; and are marked with the wisdom of a well informed and enlightened people, we may reasonably hope, under the smiles of Heaven, to convince the world that the happiness of nations can be accomplished by pacific revolutions in their political systems, without the destructive intervention of the sword.

To Legislature of Pennsylvania, September 5, 1789   *Writings Vol. 30 p. 395*

CONSTITUTIONAL CONVENTION

... That a thorough reform of the present system is indispensable, none who have capacities to judge will deny; and with hands (and heart) I hope the business will be essayed in a full Convention.

To James Madison, March 31, 1787   *Writings Vol. 29 p. 190*

... The business of this Convention is as yet too much in embryo to form any opinion of the result. Much is expected from it by some; but little by others; and nothing by a few. That something is necessary, all will agree; for the situation of the General Governmt. (it can be called a governmt.) is shaken to its foundation, and liable to be overset by every blast.

To Thomas Jefferson, May 30, 1787   *Writings Vol. 29 p. 224*

... General Government is now suspended by a thread. I might go farther and say it is really at an end, and what will be the consequence of a fruitless attempt to amend the [Constitution] which is offered, before it is tried, ... does not in my Judgement need the gift of prophecy to predict.

To Charles Carter, December 14, 1787   *Writings Vol. 29 p. 340*

... It [the Constitution] is now a Child of fortune, to be fostered by some and buffeted by others. What will be the General opinion on, or the reception of it, is not for me to decide, nor shall I say any thing for or against it: if it be good I suppose it will work its way good; if bad, it will recoil on the Framers.

To Marquis de Lafayette, September 18, 1787   *Writings Vol. 29 p. 277*

... Weak at home and disregarded abroad is our present Condition, and contemptible enough it is.

To David Stuart, July 1, 1787   *Writings Vol. 29 p. 238*

... my wish is, that the Convention may adopt no temporizing espedient, but probe the defects of the Constitution to the bottom, and provide radical cures ....

To James Madison, March 31, 1787   *Writings Vol. 29 pp. 191–192*

... Let us look to our National character, and to things beyond the present period. No morn ever dawned more favourably than ours did; and no day was ever more clouded than the present! Wisdom and good examples are necessary at this time to rescue the political machine from the impending storm.

To James Madison, November 5, 1786   *Writings Vol. 29 p. 51*

... I wish the Constitution which is offered had been made more perfect, but I sincerely believe it is the best that could be obtained at this time. ...

To Patrick Henry, September 24, 1787   *Writings Vol. 29 p. 278*

THE CONSTITUTION, UNANIMITY OF ITS ADOPTION

... The various and opposite interests which were to be conciliated; the local prejudices which were to be subdued, the diversity of opinions and sentiments which were to be reconciled; and in fine, the sacrifices which were necessary to be made on all sides for the General welfare, combined to make it a work of so intricate and difficult a nature, that I think it is much to be wondered at, that any thing could have been produced with such unanimity as the Constitution proposed.

To Catharine Macaulay Graham, November 16, 1787   *Writings Vol. 29 p. 316*

... When the situation of this Country calls loudly for unanimity and vigor, it is to be lamented that Gentlemen of talents and character should disagree in their sentiments for promoting the public weal; but unfortunately, this ever has been, and most probably ever will be the case, in the affairs of man.

To Alexander Hamilton, October 18, 1787   *Writings Vol. 29 p. 291*

... I am better pleased that the proceedings of the Convention are submitted from Congress by a unanimous vote (feeble as it is) than if they had appeared under strong marks of approbation without it. This apparent unanimity will have its effect. Not every one has opportunities to peep behind the curtain; and as the multitude are often deceived by externals, the appearance of unanimity in that body on this occasion will be of great importance.

To James Madison, October 10, 1787   *Writings Vol. 29 p. 285*

THE CONSTITUTION OR DISUNION

... I then did conceive, and do now most firmly believe, that, in the aggregate, it is the best Constitution that can be obtained at this Epocha, and that this, or a dissolution of the Union awaits our choice, and are the only alternatives before us.

To Governor Edmund Randolph, January 8, 1788   *Writings Vol. 29 p. 358*

THE CONSTITUTION, AN IMPERFECT DOCUMENT

... The warmest friends and the best supporters the Constitution has, do not contend that it is free from imperfections ... and ... I think the People ... can ... decide with as much propriety on the alterations and amendments which are necessary [as] ourselves. I do not think we [the Framers] are more inspired, have more wisdom, or possess more virtue than those who will come after us.

To Bushrod Washington, November 10, 1787   *Writings Vol. 29 p. 311*

THE CONSTITUTION, TO BE VINDICATED

... let the reins of government then be braced and held with a steady hand, and every violation of the Constitution be reprehended: if defective, let it be amended, but not suffered to be trampled upon whilst it has an existence.

To Henry Lee, October 31, 1786   *Writings Vol. 29 p. 34*

THE GENERAL GOVERNMENT, AND LOCAL POLITICS

... We now stand an Independent People, and have yet to learn political Tactics. We are placed among the Nations of the Earth, and have a character to establish; but how we shall acquit ourselves time must discover ....

To Marquis de Lafayette, April 5, 1783   *Writings Vol. 26 p. 298*

... I see one head gradually changing into thirteen. I see one Army branching into thirteen; and instead of looking up to Congress as the supreme controuling power of the United States, are considering themselves as dependent on their respective States. In a word, I see the powers of Congress declining too fast for the consequence and respect which is due to them as the grand representative body of America, and am fearful of the consequences of it.

To Joseph Jones, May 31, 1780   *Writings Vol. 18 p. 453*

STATE RIGHTS

... The disinclination of the individual States to yield competent powers to Congress for the Federal Government, their unreasonable jealousy of that body and of one another, and the disposition which seems to pervade each, of being all-wise and all-powerful within itself, will, if there is not a change in the system be our downfall as a nation. This is as clear to me as the A, B, C; and I think we have opposed Great Britain, and have arrived at the present state of peace and independency, to very little purpose, if we cannot conquer our own prejudices. . . .They know that individual opposition to their measures is futile, and *boast* that we are not sufficiently united as a Nation to give a general one! Is not the indignity alone, of this declaration, while we are in the very act of peacemaking and conciliation, sufficient to stimulate us to vest more extensive and adequate powers in the sovereign of these United States?

To Governor Benjamin Harrison, January 18, 1784   *Writings Vol. 27 p. 305*

AMITY AND CONCESSION

... It is a fact declared by the General Convention, and universally understood, that the Constitution of the United States was the result of a spirit of amity and mutual concession. And it is well known that under this influence the smaller States were admitted to an equal representation in the Senate with the larger States; and that this branch of the government was invested with great powers: for on the equal participation of those powers, the sovereignty and political safety of the smaller States were deemed essentially to depend.

To the House of Representatives, March 30, 1796   *Writings Vol. 35 p. 4*

CONGRESS: CHOICE OF DELEGATES

... Men, chosen as the Delegates in Congress are, cannot officially be dangerous; they depend upon the breath, nay, they are so much the creatures of the people, under the present constitution, that they can have no views (which could possibly be carried into execution,) nor any interests, distinct from those of their constituents.

To Governor Benjamin Harrison, January 18, 1784   *Writings Vol. 27 p. 306*

... My political creed therefore is, to be wise in the choice of Delegates, support them like Gentlemen while they are our representatives, give them competent powers for all federal purposes, support them in the due exercise thereof, and lastly, to compel them to close attendance in Congress during their delegation.

To Governor Benjamin Harrison, January 18, 1784   *Writings Vol. 27 p. 306*

FREE AND EQUAL REPRESENTATIONS

... I always believed that an unequivocally free and equal Representation of the People in the Legislature, together with an efficient and responsable Executive, were the great Pillars on which the preservation of American Freedom must depend.

To Catharine Macaulay Graham, January 9, 1790   *Writings Vol. 30 p. 496*

THE AFFECTIONS OF THE PEOPLE

... It is desirable on all occasions, to unite with a steady and firm adherence to constitutional and necessary Acts of Government, the fullest evidence of a disposition, as far as may be practicable, to consult the wishes of every part of the Community, and to lay the foundations of the public administration in the affection of the people.

Third Annual Address to Congress, October 25, 1791   *Writings Vol. 31 p. 400*

PUBLIC CONFIDENCE

... In general I esteem it a good maxim, that the best way to preserve the confidence of the people durably is to promote their true interest; there are particular exigencies when this maxim has peculiar force. When any great object is in view, the popular mind is roused into expectation and prepared to make sacrifices both of ease and property; if those to whom they confide the management of their affairs do not call them to make these sacrifices, and the object is not attained, or they are involved in the reproach of not having contributed as much as they ought to have done towards it; they will be mortified at the disappointment they will feel the censure, and their resentment will rise against those who with sufficient authority have omitted to do what their interest and their honor required.

To Joseph Reed, July 4, 1780   *Writings Vol. 19 p. 114*

THE CONSTITUTION, THE PEOPLE'S CHOICE

... To complete the American character, it remains for the citizens of the United States to shew to the world, that the reproach heretofore cast on republican Governments for their want of stability, is without founda-tion, when that government is the deliberate choice of an enlightened people: and I am fully persuaded, that every well-wisher to the happiness and prosperity of this Country will evince by his conduct, that we live under a government of laws; and that, while we preserve inviolate our national faith, we are desirous to live in amity with all mankind.

To the Inhabitants of Alexandria, July 4, 1793   *Writings Vol. 33 p. 3*

PUBLIC OPINION, TO BE ENLIGHTENED

... Promote then as an object of primary importance, Institutions for the general diffusion of knowledge. In proportion as the structure of a gov-ernment gives force to public opinion, it is essential that public opinion should be enlightened.

Farewell Address, September 19, 1796   *Writings Vol. 35 p. 230*

THE VOICE OF THE MULTITUDE

... in a free, and republican Government, you cannot restrain the voice of the multitude; every Man will speak as he thinks, or more properly with-out thinking, consequently will judge of Effects without attending to the Causes.

To Marquis de Lafayette, September 1, 1778   *Writings Vol. 12 p. 383*

THE GOVERNMENT; ITS BRANCHES

... the general Government is not invested with more Powers than are indispensably necessary to perform the functions of a good Government ... these Powers (as the appointment of all Rulers will for ever arise from, and, at short stated intervals, recur to the free suffrage of the People) are so distributed among the Legislative, Executive, and Judicial Branches, into which the general Government is arranged, that it can never be in danger of degenerating into a monarchy, an Oligarchy, an Aristocracy, or any other despotic or oppressive form, so long as there shall remain any virtue in the body of the People.

To Marquis de Lafayette, February 7, 1788   *Writings Vol. 29 p. 410*

THE CONSTITUTION, OUR GUIDE

... the constitution is the guide, which I never will abandon.

To the Boston Selectmen, July 28, 1795   *Writings Vol. 34 p. 253*

COMPREHENSIVE NATIONAL VIEWS

... In every act of my administration, I have sought the happiness of my fellow-citizens. My system for the attainment of this object has uniformly been to overlook all personal, local and partial considerations: to contemplate the United States, as one great whole: to confide, that sudden impressions, when erroneous, would yield to candid reflection: and to consult only the substantial and permanent interests of our country.

To the Boston Selectmen, July 28, 1795   *Writings Vol. 34 p. 252*

THE SOURCE OF POWER

... The Power under the Constitution will always be in the People. It is entrusted for certain defined purposes, and for a certain limited period, to representatives of their own chusing; and whenever it is executed contrary to their Interest, or not agreeable to their wishes, their Servants can, and undoubtedly will be, recalled.

To Bushrod Washington, November 10, 1787   *Writings Vol. 29 p. 311*

THE DUTIES OF THE PEOPLE

... It remains with the people themselves to preserve and promote the great advantages of their political and natural situation; nor ought a doubt to be entertained that men, who so well understand the value of social happiness, will ever cease to appreciate the blessings of a free, equal, and efficient government.

To the Rhode Island Legislature, August 18, 1790   *Writings Vol. 31 p. 94*

POPULAR COMMOTION

... The tumultous populace of large cities are ever to be dreaded. Their indiscrimate violence prostrates for the time all public authority, and its consequences are sometimes extensive and terrible.

To Marquis de Lafayette, July 28, 1791   *Writings Vol. 31 p. 324*

PARTY DISPUTES

... such (for wise purposes it is presumed) is the turbulence of human passions in party disputes; when victory, more than truth, is the palm contended for, "that the Post of honor is a private Station."

To the Secretary of War, July 27, 1795   *Writings Vol. 34 p. 251*

POWER OF TRUTH

... I am *Sure* the Mass of Citizens in these United States *mean well, and I firmly believe they will always act well*, whenever they can obtain a right un-

derstanding of matters ... serious misfortunes originating in misrepresentation frequently flow and spread before they can be dissipated by
truth.

To John Jay, May 8, 1796   *Writings Vol. 35 p. 37*

INFLUENCE OF THE PEOPLE

... From the gallantry and fortitude of her citizens, under the auspices of
heaven, America has derived her independence. To their industry and
the natural advantages of the country she is indebted for her prosperous
situation. From their virtue she may expect long to share the protection
of a free and equal government, which their wisdom has established, and
which experience justifies, as admirably adapted to our social wants and
individual felicity.

To the Congregational Church and Society at Midway, Georgia, May 13, 1791
Writings, Vol. 31 p. 288

THE PEOPLE; NOT THE PRESIDENT

... As, under the smiles of Heaven, America is indebted for freedom and
independence rather to the joint exertions of the citizens of the several
States, in which it may be your boast to have borne no inconsiderable
share, than to the conduct of the Commander in chief, so is she indebted
for their support rather to a continuation of those exertions, than to the
prudence and ability manifested in the exercise of the powers delegated
to the President of the United States.

To the Inhabitants of Providence, August 18, 1790   *Writings Vol. 31 p. 94*

LIBERTY AND POWER

... A change in the national constitution, conformed to experience and
the circumstances of our country, has been most happily effected by the
influence of reason alone; in this change the liberty of the citizen continues unimpaired, while the energy of government is so encreased as to
promise full protection to all the pursuits of science and industry; together with the firm establishment of public credit, and the vindication of
our national character.

To the Rhode Island Legislature, August 18, 1790   *Writings Vol. 31 p. 94*

APPOINTMENTS TO OFFICE

... of two men equally well affected to the true interests of their country,
of equal abilities and equally disposed to lend their support, it is the part
of prudence to give a preference to him, against whom the *least* clamour
can be excited.

To the Acting Secretary of State, September 27, 1795   *Writings Vol. 34 p. 315*

FITNESS OF CHARACTER

... In every nomination to office I have endeavored, as far as my own knowledge extended, or information could be obtained, to make fitness of character my primary object.

To Joseph Jones, November 30, 1789   *Writings Vol. 30 p. 469*

FREEDOM OF CHOICE

... it is really my wish to have my mind, and my actions which are the result of contemplation, as free and independent as the air.

To Benjamin Harrison, January 22, 1785   *Writings Vol. 28 p. 35*

POLITICAL SUICIDE

... I shall not, whilst I have the honor to Administer the government, bring a man into my office, of consequence knowingly whose political tenets are adverse to the measures which the *general* government are pursuing; for this, in my opinion, would be a sort of political Suicide.

To the Acting Secretary of State, September 27, 1795   *Writings Vol. 34 p. 315*

ALLUREMENTS OF OFFICE

... All see, and most admire, the glare which hovers round the external trappings of elevated office. To me there is nothing in it, beyond the lustre which may be reflected from its connection with a power of promoting human felicity.

To Catharine Macauley Graham, January 9, 1790   *Writings Vol. 30 p. 496*

FOREIGN MINISTERS

... The interests of the United States requires that our intercourse with other nations should be facilitated, by such provisions as will enable me to fulfill my duty in that respect, in the manner which circumstances may render most conducive to the public good: And to this end that the compensations to be made to the persons who may be employed, should according to the nature of their appointments, be defined by law; and a competent fund designated for defraying the expenses incident to the conduct of our foreign affairs.

First Annual Address, January 8, 1790   *Writings Vol. 30 p. 492*

MAXIMS FOR EXECUTIVE OFFICERS

... let me, in a friendly way, impress the following maxims upon the Executive Officers. In all important matters, to deliberate maturely, but to execute promptly and vigorously. And not to put things off until the Morrow which can be done, and require to be done, today. Without an adherence to these rules, business never will be *well* done, or done in an easy manner; but will always be in arrear, with one thing treading upon the heels of another.

To the Secretary of War, July 13, 1796   *Writings Vol. 35 p. 138*

... men in responsible situations cannot, like those in private life, be governed *solely* by the dictates of their own inclinations, or by such motives as can only affect themselves.

To the Duc De Liancourt, August 8, 1796   *Writings Vol. 35 p. 167*

... Good measures should always be executed as soon as they are conceived and circumstances will permit.

To the Secretary of State, August 1, 1796   *Writings Vol. 35 p. 161*

COMPENSATION OF OFFICERS OF GOVERNMENT

... If private wealth, is to supply the defect of public retribution, it will greatly contract the sphere within which, the selection of Characters for Office, is to be made, and will proportionally diminish the probability of a choice of Men, able as well as upright: Besides that it would be repugnant to the vital principles of our Government, virtually to exclude from public trusts, talents and virtue, unless accompanied by wealth.

Eighth Annual Address to Congress, December 7, 1796   Writings Vol. 35 p. 318

CIVIL MAGISTRATES

... The dispensation of this justice belongs to the civil Magistrate and let it ever be our pride and our glory to leave the sacred deposit there unviolated.

To Governor Henry Lee, October 20, 1794   *Writings Vol. 34 p. 6*

THE JUDICIARY SYSTEM

... I have always been persuaded that the stability and success of the national Government, and consequently the happiness of the People of the United States, would depend in a considerable degree on the Interpretation and Execution of its Laws.

To the Chief Justice and Associate Justices of the Supreme Court of the United States, April 3, 1790   *Writings Vol. 31 p. 31*

... In my opinion, therefore, it is important, that the Judiciary System should not only be independent in its operations, but as perfect as possible in its formation.

To the Chief Justice and Associate Justices of the Supreme Court of the United States, April 3, 1790   *Writings Vol. 31 p. 31*

E. NATIONAL PROSPERITY

PROSPERITY OF THE UNITED STATES

... Contemplating the internal situation, as well as the external relations of the United States, we discover equal cause for contentment and satisfaction. While many of the nations of Europe, with their American Dependencies, have been involved in a contest unusually bloody, exhausting and calamitous; in which the evils of foreign war have been aggravated by domestic convulsion and insurrection; in which many of the arts most useful to society have been exposed to discouragement and decay; in which scarcity of subsistence has embittered other sufferings; while even the anticipations of a return of the blessings of peace and repose, are alloyed by the sense of heavy and accumulating burthens, which press upon all the departments of industry, and threaten to clog the future springs of Government: Our favored country, happy in a striking contrast, has enjoyed general tranquility; a tranquility the more satisfactory, because maintained at the expense of no duty. Faithful to ourselves, we have violated no obligation to others.

Seventh Annual Address, December 8, 1795　　　　*Writings Vol. 34 p. 388*

... Our Agriculture, commerce and Manufactures, prosper beyond former example; the molestations of our trade (to prevent a continuance of which, however, very pointed remonstrances have been made) being over-balanced by the aggregate benefits which it derives from a Neutral position.

Seventh Annual Address, December 8, 1795　　　　*Writings Vol. 34 p. 389*

... Our population advances with a celerity, which exceeding the most sanguine calculations, proportionally augments our strength and resources, and guarantees our future security.

Seventh Annual Address, December 8, 1795　　　　*Writings Vol. 34 p. 389*

... Every part of the union displays indications of rapid and various improvement, and with burthens so light as scarcely to be perceived; with resources fully adequate to our present exigencies; with Governments founded on genuine principles of rational liberty, and with mild and wholesome laws; is it too much to say, that our country exhibits a spectacle of national happiness never surpassed if ever before equalled?

Seventh Annual Address, December 8, 1795　　　　*Writings Vol. 34 p. 389*

... Placed in a situation every way so auspicious, motives of commanding force impel us, with sincere acknowledgment to heaven, and pure love to our country, to unite our efforts to preserve, prolong, and improve, our immense advantages.

Seventh Annual Address, December 8, 1795　　　　*Writings Vol. 34 p. 389*

Washington by J. B. Longacre after Gilbert Stuart. This was published in
The National Portrait Gallery of Distinguished Americans (Philadelphia, 1834).

AMERICA AND EUROPE

... With respect to the Nations of Europe, their situation appears so awful, that nothing short of Omnipotence can predict the issue, although every humane mind must feel for the miseries they endure. Our course is plain; they who run may read it. Theirs is so bewildered and dark, so entangled and embarrassed, and so obviously under the influence of Intriegue, that one would suppose, if any thing could open the eyes of our misled citizens, the deplorable situation of those people could not fail to accomplish it.

To the Secretary of the Treasury, May 29, 1797   *Writings Vol. 35 p. 457*

NATIONAL PROSPECTS

... It should be the policy of United America to administer to their wants, without being engaged in their quarrels. And it is not in the ability of the proudest and most potent people on earth to prevent us from becoming a great, a respectable and a commercial Nation, if we shall continue United and faithful to ourselves.

To Sir Edward Newenham, August 29, 1788   *Writings Vol. 30 p. 72*

AMERICA'S FUTURE

... I begin to look forward, with a kind of political faith, to scenes of National happiness, which have not heretofore been offered for the fruition of the most favoured Nations. The natural political, and moral circumstances of our Nascent empire justify the anticipation.

To Sir Edward Newenham, August 29, 1788   *Writings Vol. 30 p. 72*

... We have an almost unbounded territory whose natural advantages for agriculture and Commerce equal those of any on the globe. In a civil point of view we have unequalled previledge of choosing our own political Institutions and of improving upon the experience of Mankind in the formation of a confoederated government, where due energy will not be incompatible with unalienable rights of freemen. To complete the picture, I may observe, that the information and morals of our Citizens appear to be peculiarly favourable for the introduction of such a plan of government.

To Sir Edward Newenham, August 29, 1788   *Writings Vol. 30 p. 72*

... In such a Country, so happily circumstanced, the pursuits of Commerce and the cultivation of the soil will unfold to industry the certain road to competence.   To those hardy Soldiers, who are actuated by the spirit of adventure the Fisheries will afford ample and profitable employment, and the extensive and fertile regions of the West will yield a most happy asylum to those, who, fond of domestic enjoyments are seeking for personal independence.

Farewell Orders to the Armies of the United States, November 2, 1783

Writings Vol. 27 p. 224

... The prospect of national prosperity now before us is truly animating, and ought to exite the exertions of all good men to establish and secure the happiness of their country, in the permanent duration of its freedom and independence. America, under the smiles of a divine Providence, the protection of a good government, the cultivation of manners, morals, and piety, can hardly fail of attaining an uncommon degree of eminence in literature, commerce, agriculture, improvements at home, and respectability abroad.

Address to Catholics, March 15, 1790   *Writings Vol. 31 p. 22*

... I expect, that many blessings will be attributed to our new government ... I really believe, that there never was so much labour and economy to be found before in the country as at the present moment.

To Marquis de Lafayette, June 19, 1788   *Writings Vol. 29 p. 525*

... When the people shall find themselves secure under an energetic government, when foreign nations shall be disposed to give us equal advantages in commerce from dread of retaliation ... when the seeds of happiness which are sown here shall begin to expand themselves and when every one under his own vine and fig-tree shall begin to taste the fruits of freedom, then all these blessings (for all these blessings will come) will be referred to the fostering influence of the new government.

To Marquis de Lafayette, June 19, 1788   *Writings Vol. 29 pp. 525–526*

... If we may calculate upon rectitude in the views, and prudence in the conduct of the leading characters throughout the States, accompanied by industry and honesty in the Mass of the people, we may assuredly anticipate a new era ....

To John Lanzton, July 20, 1788   *Writings Vol. 30 p. 19*

NATIONAL REPUTATION

... The virtue, moderation, and patriotism which marked the steps of the American People in framing, adopting, and thus far carrying into effect our present system of Government, has excited the admiration of Nations; and it only now remains for us to act up to those principles, which should characterize a free and enlightened People, that we may gain respect abroad and ensure happiness and safety to ourselves and to our posterity.

Address Legislature Pennsylvania, September 5, 1789   *Writings Vol. 30 p. 395*

FOUNDERS OF THE FABRIC OF FREEDOM

... happy, thrice happy shall they be pronounced hereafter, who have contributed any thing, who have performed the meanest office in erecting this steubendous *fabrick of Freedom* and *Empire* on the broad basis of Independency; who have assisted in protecting the rights of humane nature and establishing an Asylum for the poor and oppressed of all nations and religions.

General Orders, April 18, 1783   *Writings Vol. 26 p. 335*

AMERICA, AN ASYLUM FOR THE OPPRESSED

... under an energetic general Government such regulations might be made, and such measures taken, as would render this Country the asylum of pacific and industrious characters from all parts of Europe, would encourage the cultivation of the Earth by the high price which its products would command, and would draw the wealth, and wealthy men of other Nations into our bosom, by giving security to property, and liberty to its holders.

To Thomas Jefferson, January 1, 1788   *Writings Vol. 29 p. 351*

... It is a flattering and consolatory reflection, that our rising Republics have the good wishes of all the Philosophers, Patriots, and virtuous men in all nations; and that they look upon them as a kind of Asylum for mankind. God grant that we may not disappoint their honest expectations, by our folly or perverseness.

To Marquis de Chastellux, April 25–May 1, 1788   *Writings Vol. 29 p. 484*

THE WORLD'S GRANARY

... I hope, some day or another, we shall become a storehouse and granary for the world.

To Marquis de Lafayette, June 19, 1788   *Writings Vol. 29 p. 526*

THE HOME OF INDUSTRY

... it is a point conceded, that America, under an efficient government, will be the most favorable Country of any in the world for persons of industry and frugality, possessed of a moderate capital, to inhabit. It is also believed, that it will not be less advantageous to the happiness of the lowest class of people because of the equal distribution of property the great plenty of unoccupied lands, and the facility of procuring the means of subsistence.

To Richard Henderson, June 19, 1788   *Writings Vol. 29 p. 520*

EMIGRATION TO AMERICA

... My opinion, with respect to emigration, is, that except of useful Mechanics and some particular descriptions of men or professions, there is no need of encouragement: while the policy or advantage of its taking place in a body (I mean the settling of them in a body) may be much questioned; for, by so doing, they retain the Language, habits and principles (good or bad) which they bring with them. Whereas by an intermixture with our people, they, or their descendants, get assimilated to our customs, measures and laws: in a word, soon become one people.

To the Vice President, November 15, 1794   *Writings Vol. 34 p. 23*

F. NATIONAL POLICY

FOREIGN INFLUENCE

... Against the insidious wiles of foreign influence, (I conjure you to believe me fellow citizens) the jealousy of a free people ought to be *constantly* awake; since history and experience prove that foreign influence is one of the most baneful foes of Republican Government. But that jealousy to be useful must be impartial; else it becomes the instrument of the very influence to be avoided, instead of a defence against it.

Farewell Address, September 19, 1796   *Writings Vol. 35 p. 233*

... Excessive partiality for one foreign nation and excessive dislike of another, cause those whom they actuate to see danger only on one side, and serve to veil and even second the arts of influence on the other.

Farewell Address, September 19, 1796   *Writings Vol. 35 p. 233*

THE TRUE POLICY OF AMERICA

... The Great rule of conduct for us, in regard to foreign Nations is in extending our commercial relations to have with them as little *political* connection as possible. So far as we have already formed engagements let them be fulfilled with perfect good faith. Here let us stop.

Farewell Address, September 19, 1796   *Writings Vol. 35 p. 233*

FOREIGN ALLIANCES

... Our detached and distant situation invites and enables us to pursue a different course. If we remain one People, under an efficient government, the period is not far off, when we may defy material injury from external annoyance; when we may take such an attitude as will cause the neutrality we may at any time resolve upon to be scrupulously respected; when belligerent nations, under the impossibility of making acquisitions upon us, will not lightly hazard the giving us provocation; when we may choose peace or War, as our interest guided by our justice shall Counsel. Why forego the advantages of so peculiar a situation? Why quit our own to stand upon foreign ground? Why, by interweaving our destiny with that of any part of Europe, entangle our peace and prosperity in the toils of European Ambition, Rivalship, Interest, Humour or Caprice?

Farewell Address, September 19, 1796   *Writings Vol. 35 p. 234*

... 'Tis our true policy to steer clear of permanent Alliances, with any portion of the foreign world. So far, I mean, as we are now at liberty to do it, for let me not be understood as capable of patronizing infidelity to existing engagements.

Farewell Address, September 19, 1796   *Writings Vol. 35 p. 234*

... (I hold the maxim not less applicable to public than to private affairs that honesty is always the best policy). I repeat it therefore, let those engagements be observed in their genuine sense. But in my opinion, it is unnecessary and would be unwise to extend them.

Farewell Address, September 19, 1796   *Writings Vol. 35 p. 235*

NATIONAL ANTIPATHIES AND ATTACHMENTS

... Observe good faith and justice towds. all Nations ... In the execution of such a plan nothing is more essential than that permanent, inveterate antipathies against particular Nations and passionate attachments for others should be excluded; and that in place of them just and amicable feelings towards all should be cultivated.

Farewell Address, September 19, 1796   *Writings Vol. 35 p. 231*

... The Nation, which indulges towards another an habitual hatred, or an habitual fondness, is in some degree a slave. It is a slave to its animosity or to its affection, either of which is sufficient to lead it astray from its duty and its interest.

Farewell Address, September 19, 1796   *Writings Vol. 35 p. 231*

... a passionate attachment of one Nation for another produces a variety of evils. Sympathy for the favourite nation, facilitating the illusion of an imaginary common interest, in cases where no real common interest exists, and infusing into one the enmities of the other, betrays the former into a participation in the quarrels and Wars of the latter, without adequate inducement or justification: It leads also to concessions to the favourite Nation of priviledges denied to others, which is apt doubly to injure the Nation making the concessions; by unnecessarily parting with what ought to have been retained; and by exciting jealousy, ill will, and a disposition to retaliate, in the parties from whom eql. priviledges are withheld: And it gives to ambitious, corrupted, or deluded citizens (who devote themselves to the favourite Nation) facility to betray, or sacrifice the interest of their own country, without odium, sometimes even with popularity; gilding with the appearances of a virtuous sense of obligation and commendable deference for public opinion, or a laudable zeal for public good, the base or foolish compliances of ambition corruption or infatuation.

Farewell Address, September 19, 1796   *Writings Vol. 35 p. 232*

... As avenues to foreign influence in innumerable ways, such attachments are particularly alarming to the truly enlightened and independent Patriot. How many opportunities do they afford to tamper with domestic factions, to practise the arts of seduction, to mislead public opinion, to influence or awe the public Councils! Such an attachment of a small or weak, towards a great and powerful Nation, dooms the former to be the satellite of the latter.

Farewell Address, September 19, 1796   *Writings Vol. 35 p. 233*

FOREIGN POLICY OF THE NATION

... my aim has been ... to comply strictly with *all* our engagemts. foreign and domestic; but to keep the U States free from *political* connexions with *every* other Country. To see that they *may be* independent of *all,* and under the influence of *none.* In a word, I want an *American* character, that the powers of Europe may be convinced we act for *ourselves* and not for *others;* this in my judgment, is the only way to be respected abroad and happy at home.

To Patrick Henry, October 9, 1795   *Writings Vol. 34 p. 335*

... My policy has been, and will continue to be, while I have the honor to remain in the administration of the government, to be upon friendly terms with, but independent of, all the nations of the earth. To share in the broils of none. To fulfil our own engagements. To supply the wants, and be carriers for them all: being thoroughly convinced that it is our policy and interest to do so.

To Gouverneur Morris, December 22, 1795   *Writings Vol. 34 p. 401*

... nothing short of self respect, and that justice which is essential to a national character, ought to involve us in War; for sure I am, if this country is preserved in tranquillity twenty years longer, it may bid defiance, in a just cause, to any power whatever, such, in that time, will be its population, wealth, and resource.

To Gouverneur Morris, December 22, 1795   *Writings Vol. 34 p. 401*

NON-INTERVENTION

... I have always given it as my decided opinion that no Nation had a right to intermeddle in the internal concerns of another; that every one had a right to form and adopt whatever government they liked best to live under themselves. and that if this country could, consistently with its engagements, maintain a strict neutrality and thereby preserve peace, it was bound to do so by motives of policy, interest, and every other consideration, that ought to actuate a people situated and circumstanced as we are; already deeply in debt, and in a convalescent state, from the struggle we have been engaged in ourselves.

To James Monroe, August 25, 1796   *Writings Vol. 35 p. 189*

PEACE WITH OTHER NATIONS

... Observations on the value of peace with other Nations are unnecessary. It would be wise, however, by timely provisions, to guard against those acts of our own Citizens, which might tend to disturb it, and to put ourselves in a condition to give that satisfaction to foreign Nations which we may sometimes have occasion to require from them.

Fourth Annual Address to Congress, November 6, 1792 Writings Vol. 32 p. 209

... Where individuals shall within the United States, array themselves in hostility against any of the powers, at war; or enter upon Military expeditions, or enterprizes within the jurisdiction of the United States; or usurp and exercise judicial authority within the United States; or where the penalties on violations of the law of Nations may have been indistinctly marked, or are inadequate; these offences cannot receive too early and close an attention, and require prompt and decisive remedies.

Fifth Annual Address to Congress, December 3, 1793   Writings Vol. 33 p. 165

... True to our duties and interest as Americans, firm to our purpose as lovers of peace, let us unite our fervent prayers to the great ruler of the Universe, that the justice and moderation of all concerned may permit us to continue in the uninterrupted enjoyment of a blessing, which we so greatly prize, and of which we ardently wish them a speedy and permanent participation.

To the Inhabitants of Richmond, August 28, 1793   *Writings Vol. 33 p. 72*

PEACE WITH ALL THE WORLD

... my policy in our foreign transactions has been, to cultivate peace with all the world; to observe treaties with pure and absolute faith; to check every deviation from the line of impartiality; to explain what may have been misapprehended, and correct what may have been injurious to any nation; and having thus acquired the right, to lose no time in acquiring the ability, to insist upon justice being done to ourselves.

To the House of Representatives, November 19, 1794   *Writings Vol. 34 p. 37*

PEACE, OUR POLICY

... I rejoice most exceedingly that there is an end to our Warfare, and that such a field is opening to our view as will, with wisdom to direct the cultivation of it, make us a great, a respectable, and happy People.

To Alexander Hamilton, March 31, 1783   *Writings Vol. 26 p. 276*

... Peace, with all the world is my sincere wish. I am sure it is our true policy. and am persuaded it is the Ardent desire of the Government.

To Reverend Jonathan Boucher, August 15, 1798   *Writings Vol. 36 p. 413*

... Standing, as it were in the midst of falling empires, it should be our aim to assume a station and attitude, which will preserve us from being overwhelmed in their ruins.

To the Secretary of War, December 13, 1798   *Writings Vol. 37 p. 36*

... It is not uncommon, however, in prosperous gales, to forget that adverse winds may blow. Such *was* the case with France. Such *may* be the case of the Coalesced Powers, against her. A bye stander sees more of the game, generally, than those who are playing it; so, Neutral Nations may be better enabled to draw a line between the contending Parties, than those who are Actors in the War. My own wish is, to see everything settled upon the best and surest foundation for the Peace and happiness of mankind, without regard to this, that, or the other Nation. A more destructive Sword never was drawn (at least in modern times) than this war has produced. It is time to sheathe it, and give Peace to mankind.

To William Vans Murray, October 26, 1799   *Writings Vol. 37 p. 399*

FALSE SECURITY

... The satisfaction I have in any successes that attend us or even in the alleviation of misfortunes is always allayed by a fear that it will lull us into security. Supineness and a disposition to flatter ourselves seem to make parts of our national character; when we receive a check and are not quite undone, we are apt to fancy we have gained a victory; and when we do gain any little advantage, we imagine it decisive and expect the war is immediately to end. The history of the war is a history of false hopes and temporary expedients. Would to God they were to end here!

To James Duane, October 4, 1780   *Writings Vol. 20 p. 117*

S. E. George Washington by "J. L." after "Le B.," [undated]. This is one of the many images of Washington based on Charles Willson Peale's portraits, which were circulated in Europe.

THE FLATTERY OF SUCCESS

... Particular successes obtained against all the chances of war have had too much influence to the prejudice of general and substantial principles.

To the President of Congress, February 26, 1781   *Writings Vol. 21 p. 301*

UNINTERMITTED EFFORT

... altho' we cannot, by the best concerted plans, absolutely command success, altho', the race is not always to the swift, or the Battle to the strong, yet without presumptuously waiting for Miracles to be wrought in our favour, it is our *indispensible Duty*, with the deepest gratitude to Heaven for the past, and humble confidence in its smiles on our future operations, to make use of all the Means in our power for our defence and security.

Circular to the States, January 31, 1782   *Writings Vol. 23 p. 478*

HONORABLE PEACE

... there is nothing which will so soon produce a speedy and honorable Peace as a State of preparation for War, and we must either do this, or lay our acct. for patched up inglorious Peace, after all the Toil, Blood, and treasure we have spent. This has been my uniform opinion, a doctrine I have endeavoured, amidst the torrent of expectation of an approaching Peace, to inculcate; the event, I am sure, will justify me in it.

To James McHenry, September 12, 1782   *Writings Vol. 25 p. 151*

... There is nothing so likely to produce peace as to be well prepared to meet an Enemy.

To Elbridge Gerry, January 29, 1780   *Writings Vol. 17 p. 463*

PEACE WITHOUT INDEPENDENCE TO BE DEPLORED

... to discerning Men, nothing can be more evident, than that a Peace on the principles of dependance, however limited, after what has happened, would be to the last degree dishonourable and ruinous.

To John Bannister, April 21, 1778   *Writings Vol. 11 p. 287*

... Nothing short of Independence, it appears to me, can possibly do. A Peace, on other terms, would, if I may be allowed the expression, be a Peace of War. The injuries we have received from the British Nation were so unprovoked; have been so great and so many, that they can never be forgotten. Besides the feuds, the jealousies; the animosities that would ever attend a Union with them. Besides the importance, the advantages we should derive from an unrestricted commerce; Our fidelity as a people; Our gratitude; Our Character as Men, are opposed to a coalition with them as subjects, but in case of the last extremity. Were we easily to accede to terms of dependence, no nation, upon future occasions, let the oppressions of Britain be never so flagrant and unjust, would interpose for our relief, or at least they would do it with a cautious reluctance and upon conditions, most probably, that would be hard, if not dishonourable to us. France, by her supplies, has saved us from the Yoke thus far, and a wise and virtuous perseverence, would and I trust will, free us entirely.

To John Bannister, April 21, 1778   *Writings Vol. 11 p. 289*

NEUTRALITY

... The considerations, which respect the right to hold this conduct, it is not necessary on this occasion to detail. I will only observe, that according to my understanding of the matter, that right, so far from being denied by any of the Belligerent Powers has been virtually admitted by all. The duty of holding a Neutral conduct may be inferred, without anything more, from the obligation which justice and humanity impose on every Nation, in cases in which it is free to act, to maintain inviolate the relations of Peace and amity towards other Nations.

Farewell Address, September 19, 1796   *Writings Vol. 35 p. 237*

... With me, a predominant motive has been to endeavour to gain time to our country to settle and mature its yet recent institutions, and to progress without interruption, to that degree of strength and consistency, which is necessary to give it, humanly speaking, the command of its own fortunes.

Farewell Address, September 19, 1796   *Writings Vol. 35 p. 237*

... Separated as we are by a world of water from other Nations, if we are wise we shall surely avoid being drawn into the labyrinth of their politics and involved in their destructive wars.

To Chevalier de La Luzerne, February 7, 1788   *Writings Vol. 29 p. 406*

... America may think herself happy in having the Atlantic for a barrier.

To Comte de Rochambeau, December 1, 1785   *Writings Vol. 28 p. 339*

NATIONAL SYMPATHY

The impressions naturally produced by similarity of political sentiment are justly to be regarded as causes of national sympathy; calculated to confirm the amicable ties which may otherwise subsist between nations. This reflection, independent of its more particular reference, must dispose every benevolent mind to unite in the wish, that a general diffusion of true principles of liberty, assimilating as well as ameliorating the condition of Mankind and fostering the maxims of an ingenuous and virtuous policy, may tend to strengthen the fraternity of the human race, to assuage the jealousies and animosities of its various subdivisions, and to convince them more and more, that their true interest and felicity will best be promoted by mutual good will and universal harmony.

To the President of the National Assembly of France, January 27, 1791

Writings Vol. 31 p. 206

G. FOREIGN RELATIONS

TREATIES

... The nature of foreign negotiations requires caution; and their success must often depend on secrecy: and even when brought to a conclusion, a full disclosure of all the measures, demands, or eventual concessions, which have been proposed or contemplated, would be extremely impolitic: for this might have a pernicious influence on future negotiations; or produce immediate inconveniences, perhaps danger or mischief, in relation to other powers.

To the House of Representatives, March 30, 1796   *Writings Vol. 35 p. 2*

... It doubtless is important that all treaties and compacts formed by the United States with other nations, whether civilized or not, should be made with caution and executed with fidelity.

To the Senate, September 17, 1789   *Writings Vol. 30 p. 406*

TREATY-MAKING POWER

... Having been a member of the General Convention, and knowing the principles on which the Constitution was formed, I have ever entertained but one opinion on this subject ... that the power of making treaties is exclusively vested in the President, by and with the advice and consent of the Senate, provided two thirds of the Senators present concur, and that every treaty so made, and promulgated, thenceforward became the Law of the land.

To the House of Representatives, March 30, 1796   *Writings Vol. 35 p. 3*

THE PRESIDENT, THE TREATY-MAKER

... the constitution is the guide, which I never will abandon. It has assigned to the President the power of making treaties, with the advice and consent of the senate. It was doubtless supposed that these two branches of government would combine, without passion, (and with the best means of information), those facts and principles upon which the success of our foreign relations will always depend: that they ought not to substitute for their own conviction the opinions of others . . . .

To the Boston Selectmen, July 28, 1795   *Writings Vol. 34 p. 253*

OPPRESSIVE TREATIES

. . . I believe it is among nations as with individuals, the party taking advantage of the distresses of another will lose infinitely more in the opinion of mankind and in subsequent events than he will gain by the stroke of the moment.

To Gouverneur Morris, July 28, 1791   *Writings Vol. 31 p. 328*

EQUITABLE TREATIES

. . . Treaties which are not built upon reciprocal benefits, are not likely to be of long duration.

To Comte de Moustier, March 26, 1788   *Writings Vol. 29 p. 448*

. . . unless treaties are mutually beneficial to the Parties, it is in vain to hope for a continuance of them beyond the moment when the one which conceives itself to be over-reached is in a situation to break off the connexion.

To Gouverneur Morris, July 28, 1791   *Writings Vol. 31 p. 328*

NATIONAL FRIENDSHIPS

. . . Nations are not influenced, as individuals may be, by disinterested friendships; but, when it is their interest to live in amity, we have little reason to apprehend any rupture.

To Marquis de Lafayette, August 15, 1786   *Writings Vol. 28 p. 518*

NATIONAL OBLIGATIONS

. . . I do not like to add to the number of our national obligations. I would wish as much as possible to avoid giving a foreign power new claims of merit for services performed, to the United States, and would ask no assistance that is not indispensible.

To Henry Laurens, November 14, 1778   *Writings Vol. 13 p. 257*

THE POLITICS OF PRINCES

. . . The politic's of Princes are fluctuating, more guided often by a particular prejudice, whim, or interest, than by extensive views of policy.

To the President of Congress, August 20, 1780   *Writings Vol. 19 p. 407*

NATIONAL CANDOR

... Candour is not a more conspicuous trait in the character of Government, than it is of Individuals.

To the Secretary of State, August 29, 1797   *Writings Vol. 36 p. 18*

NATIONAL SENTIMENTS

... I had always believed that some apparent cause, powerful in its nature and progressive in its operation, must be employed to produce a change in National sentiments.

To Comte de Moustier, March 26, 1788   *Writings Vol. 29 p. 448*

NATIONAL HONESTY

... Honesty in States, as well as Individuals will ever be found the soundest policy.

To David Stuart, November 5, 1787   *Writings Vol. 29 p. 302*

FRENCH OFFICERS IN AMERICA

... in the midst of a war, the nature and difficulties of which are peculiar and uncommon, I cannot flatter myself in any way to attone for the sacrafices they have made; but by giving them such opportunities in the field of glory as will enable them to display that gallantry and those talents which we shall always be happy to acknowledge with applause.

To Comte de Rochambeau, July 16, 1780   *Writings Vol. 19 p. 186*

FRENCH MILITARY CHARACTER

... To call your nation brave, were to pronounce but common praise. Wonderful people! Ages to come will read with astonishment the history of your brilliant exploits!

Reply to the French Minister, January 1, 1796   *Writings Vol. 34 p. 413*

FRANCE

... A Country to which I shall ever feel a Warm Affection.

To Marquis de Lafayette, April 5, 1783   *Writings Vol. 26 p. 299*

FRENCH REVOLUTION

... Happy am I, my good friend, that amidst all the tremendous benefits which have assailed your political Ship, you have had address and fortitude enough to steer her hitherto safely through the quick-sands and rocks, which threatened instant destruction on every side ....

To Marquis de Lafayette, August 11, 1790   *Writings Vol. 31 p. 86*

... we cannot help looking forward with a lively wish to the period, when order Shall be established by a government respectfully energetic, and founded on the broad basis of liberality, and the rights of man, which will make millions happy, and place your nation in the rank which she ought to hold.

To Marquis de Lafayette, September 10, 1791   *Writings Vol. 31 p. 301*

H. FINANCE

PUBLIC CREDIT

... As a very important source of strength and security, cherish public credit. One method of preserving it is to use it as sparingly as possible: avoiding occasions of expence by cultivating peace, but remembering also that timely disbursements to prepare for danger frequently prevent much greater disbursements to repel it; avoiding likewise the accumulation of debt, not only by shunning occasions of expence, but by vigorous exertions in time of Peace to discharge the Debts which unavoidable wars may have occasioned, not ungenerously throwing upon posterity the burthen which we ourselves ought to bear.

Farewell Address, September 19, 1796   *Writings Vol. 35 p. 230*

... an adequate provision for the support of the public credit is a matter of high importance to the national honor and prosperity.

To the House of Representatives, January 8, 1790   *Writings Vol. 30 p. 494*

NATIONAL RESOURCES

... No nation will have it more in its power to repay what it borrows than this. Our debts are hitherto small. The vast and valuable tracts of unlocated lands, the variety and fertility of climates and soils; the advantages of every kind, which we possess for commerce, insure to this country a rapid advancement in population and prosperity and certainty, its independence being established, of redeeming in a short term of years, the comparitively inconsiderable debts it may have occasion to contract.

To John Laurens, January 15, 1781   *Writings Vol. 21 p. 109*

... The concurrence of virtuous individuals, and the combination of economical societies, to rely, as much as possible, on the resources of our own country, may be productive of great national advantages, by establishing the habits of industry and economy.

To Delaware Society, April 19, 1789   *Writings Vol. 30 p. 289*

NATIONAL DEBT

... let us then as a Nation be just, let us fulfil the public Contracts, which Congress had undoubtedly a right to make for the purpose of carrying on the War, with the same good faith we suppose ourselves bound to perform our private engagements.

Circular to the States, June 8, 1783   *Writings Vol. 26 p. 489*

... I entertain a strong hope that the state of the national finances is now sufficiently matured to enable you to enter upon a Systematic and effectual arrangement for the regular redemption and discharge of the public debt, according to the right which has been reserved to the Government. No measure can be more desireable, whether viewed with an eye to its intrinsic importance, or to the general sentiment and wish of the Nation.

To the House of Representatives, November 6, 1792   *Writings Vol. 32 p. 211*

... No pecuniary consideration is more urgent, than the regular redemption and discharge of the public debt: on none can delay be more injurious, or an economy of time more valuable.

To the House of Representatives, December 3, 1793   *Writings Vol. 33 p. 168*

SPEEDY EXTINGUISHMENT OF THE NATIONAL DEBT

... Posterity may have cause to regret, if, from any motive, intervals of tranquillity are left unimproved for accelerating this valuable end.

To the House of Representatives, December 7, 1796   *Writings Vol. 35 p. 319*

THE CURRENCY

... I am well aware that appearances ought to be upheld, and that we should avoid as much as possible recognizing by any public Act, the depreciation of our currency; but I conceive this end would be answered, as far as might be necessary, by stipulating that all money payments should be made in Gold and Silver, being the common Medium of Commerce among Nations ... and providing for the payment of what we may owe, by sending in provisions and selling it at their market.

To the President of Congress, April 4, 1778   *Writings Vol. 11 p. 217*

... It is therefore our interest and truest policy to give a Currency, to fix a value, as far as it may be practicable, upon all occasions, upon that which is to be the medium of our internal commerce and the support of the War.

To Gouverneur Morris, September 5, 1778   *Writings Vol. 12 p. 404*

... Can *we* carry on the War much longer? certainly NO, unless some measures can be devised, and speedily executed, to restore the credit of our

Currency, restrain extortion, and punish forestallers. Without these can be effected, what funds can stand the present expences of the Army? And what Officer can bear the weight of prices, that every necessary Article is now got to? A Rat, in the shape of a Horse, is not to be bought at this time for less than £200; a Saddle under thirty or Forty; Boots twenty, and Shoes and other articles in like proportion. How is it possible therefore for Officers to stand this, without an increase of pay? And how is it possible to advance their Pay when Flour is selling (at different places) from five to fifteen pounds pr. Ct., Hay from ten to thirty pounds pr. Tunn, and Beef and other essentials, in this proportion.

To Gouverneur Morris, October 4, 1778   *Writings Vol. 13 p. 21*

... it is well worthy the ambition of a patriot Statesman at this juncture, to endeavour to pacify party differences, to give fresh vigor to the springs of government, to inspire the people with confidence, and above all to restore the credit of our currency.

To Gouverneur Morris, May 8, 1779   *Writings Vol. 15 p. 26*

CREDIT OF THE CURRENCY, TO BE RESTORED

... every other effort is in vain unless something can be done to restore its credit.   Congress, the States individually, and individuals of each state, should exert themselves to effect this great end. It is the only hope; the last resource of the enemy; and nothing but our want of public virtue can induce a continuance of the War. Let them once see, that as it is in our power, so it is our inclination and intention to overcome this difficulty, and the idea of conquest, or hope of bringing us back to a state of dependence, will vanish like the morning dew; they can no more encounter this kind of opposition than the hoar frost can withstand the rays of an all chearing Sun. The liberties and safety of this Country depend upon it. the way is plain, the means are in our power, but it is virtue alone that can effect it.

To Edmund Pendleton, November 1, 1779   *Writings Vol. 17 p. 52*

... To make and extort money in every shape that can be devised, and at the same time to decry its value seems to have become a mere business and an epedemical disease, calling for the interposition of every good Man, and body of Men.

To Andrew Lewis, October 15, 1778   *Writings Vol. 13 p. 80*

THE STATE OF THE CURRENCY, THE NATION'S GREAT EVIL

... Nothing I am convinced but the depreciation of our Currency proceeding in a great measure from the foregoing Causes, aided by Stock jobbing, and party dissensions has fed the hopes of the Enemy and kept the B. Arms in America to this day. They do not scruple to declare this themselves, and add, that we shall be our own conquerers. Cannot our common Country Am. possess virtue enough to disappoint them? Is the paltry consideration of a little dirty pelf to individuals to be placed in competition with the essential rights and liberties of the present genera- tion, and of Millions yet unborn? Shall a few designing men for their own aggrandizement, and to gratify their own avarice, overset the goodly fab- ric we have been rearing at the expence of so much time, blood, and trea- sure? and shall we at last become the victims of our own abominable lust of gain? Forbid it heaven! forbid it all and every State in the Union! by enacting and enforcing efficacious laws for checking the growth of these monstrous evils, and restoring matters, in some degree to the pristine state they were in at the commencement of the War.

To James Warren, March 31, 1779   *Writings Vol. 14 p. 312*

... It is much to be lamented that each State long ere this has not hunted them down as the pests of society, and the greatest Enemys we have to the happiness of America. I would to God that one of the most attrocious of each State was hung in Gibbets upon a gallows five times as high as the one prepared by Haman. No punishment in my opinion is too great for the Man who can build his greatness upon his Country's ruin.

To Joseph Reed, December 12, 1778   *Writings Vol. 13 p. 383*

... Let vigorous measures be adopted; not to limit the prices of Articles, for this I believe is inconsistent with the very nature of things, and im- practicable in itself, but to punish Speculators, forestallers, and extor- tioners, and above all to sink the money by heavy taxes. To promote pub- lic and private economy; Encourage Manufacturers &ca. Measures of this sort gone heartily into by the several States would strike at once at the root of all our evils and give the coup de grace to British hope of subjugat- ing this Continent, either by their Arms or their Arts. The first, as I have before observed, they acknowledge is unequal to the task; the latter I am sure will be so if we are not lost to every thing that is good and virtuous.

To James Warren, March 31, 1779   *Writings Vol. 14 p. 313*

THE MINT

... The disorders in the existing currency, and especially the scarcity of small change, a scarcity so peculiarly distressing to the poorer classes, strongly recommend the carrying into immediate effect the resolution al- ready entered into concerning the establishment of a Mint.

To the Senate and the House of Representatives, October 25, 1791

Writings Vol. 31 p. 403

COINAGE

... a coinage of Gold, Silver and Copper; a measure which in my opinion is become indispensably necessary.... Without a Coinage, or without some stop can be put to the cutting and clipping of money; our Dollars, pistareens &c. will be converted (as Teague says) into *five* quarters; and a man must travel with a pair of money scales in his pocket, or run the risk of receiving Gold at one fourth less by weight than it counts.

To William Grayson, August 22, 1785 *Writings Vol. 28 p. 233*

... The mint of the United States has entered upon the coinage of the precious metals; and considerable sums of defective coins and bullion have been lodged with the director by individuals. There is a pleasing prospect that the institution will, at no remote day, realize the expectation which was originally formed of its utility.

To the Gentlemen of the Senate and of the House of Representatives, November 19, 1794 *Writings Vol. 34 p. 37*

I. AGRICULTURE AND COMMERCE

IMPORTANCE OF AGRICULTURE

... It will not be doubted, that with reference either to individual, or National Welfare, Agriculture is of primary importance. In proportion as Nations advance in population, and other circumstances of maturity, this truth becomes more apparent; and renders the cultivation of the Soil more and more, an object of public patronage.

Eighth Annual Address to Congress, December 7, 1796 *Writings Vol. 35 p. 315*

PROPER CULTIVATION OF LANDS

... Nothing in my opinion would contribute more to the welfare of these States, than the proper management of our Lands; and nothing, in this State particularly, seems to be less understood. The present mode of cropping practised among us, is destructive to landed property; and must, if persisted in much longer, ultimately ruin the holders of it.

To William Drayton, March 25, 1786 *Writings Vol. 28 p. 394*

AGRICULTURE AND MANUFACTURES

... There are many articles of manufacture which we stand absolutely in need of and shall continue to have occasion for so long as we remain an agricultural people, which will be while lands are so cheap and plenty,

*George Washington General and Commander in Chief of the American Revolution-
ary Army and first President of the United States* by Edwin after Gilbert Stuart,
[1807].

that is to say, for ages to come.

To Marquis de Lafayette, August 15, 1786   *Writings Vol. 28 p. 519*

AGRICULTURE AND SPECULATION

... an extensive speculation, a spirit of gambling, or the introduction of any thing which will divert our attention from Agriculture, must be extremely prejudicial, if not ruinous to us.

To Thomas Jefferson, January 1, 1788   *Writings Vol. 29 p. 351*

AGRICULTURE AND WAR

... for the sake of humanity it is devoutly to be wished, that the manly employment of agriculture and the humanizing benefits of commerce, would supersede the waste of war and the rage of conquest; that the swords might be turned into plough-shares, the spears into pruning hooks, and, as the Scripture expresses it, "the nations learn war no more."

To Marquis de Chastellux, April 25–May 1, 1788   *Writings Vol. 29 p. 485*

AGRICULTURE, COMMERCE, AND MANUFACTURES

... The advancement of Agriculture, Commerce and Manufactures by all proper means, will not I trust need recommendation. But I cannot forbear intimating to you the expediency of giving effectual encouragement as well to the introduction of new and useful inventions from abroad, as to the exertions of skill and genius in producing them at home.

First Annual Address, January 8, 1790   *Writings Vol. 30 p. 493*

COMMERCE AND INDUSTRY

... Commerce and industry are the best mines of a nation.

To Joseph Reed, May 28, 1780   *Writings Vol. 18 p. 437*

FOREIGN COMMERCE

... It has long been a speculative question among Philosophers and wise men, whether foreign Commerce is of real advantage to any Country; that is, whether the luxury, effeminacy, and corruptions which are introduced along with it; are counterbalanced by the convenience and wealth which it brings.

To James Warren, October 7, 1785   *Writings Vol. 28 p. 290*

... we have abundant reason to be convinced, that the spirit for Trade which pervades these States is not to be restrained; it behooves us then to establish just principles; and this, any more than other matters of national concern, cannot be done by thirteen heads differently constructed and organized. The necessity, therefore, of a controuling power is obvious; and why it should be withheld is beyond my comprehension.

To James Warren, October 7, 1785   *Writings Vol. 28 p. 290*

COMMERCE AND TRADE

... From Trade our Citizens *will not* be restrained, and therefore it behooves us to place it in the most convenient channels, under proper regulation. freed *as much as possible,* from those vices which luxury, the consequence of wealth and power, naturally introduce.

To Thomas Jefferson, March 29, 1784   *Writings Vol. 27 p. 376*

A COMMERCIAL SYSTEM

... We are either a united people under one head, and for federal purposes; or we are thirteen independent sovereignties, eternally counteracting each other: if the former, whatever such a majority of the States as the Constitution points out, conceives to be for the benefit of the whole, should, in my humble opinion, be submitted to by the minority: let the southern States always be represented; let them act more in union; let them declare freely and boldly what is for the interest of, and what is prejudicial to their constituents; and there will, there *must* be an accommodating spirit; in the establishment of a navigation act, this in a particular manner ought, and will doubtless be attended to. If the assent of nine (or as some propose, of eleven) States is necessary to give validity to a Commercial system; it insures this measure, or it cannot be obtained ....

To James McHenry, August 22, 1785   *Writings Vol. 28 p. 228*

AMERICAN COMMERCE

... The Maritime Genius of this Country is now steering our Vessels in every ocean; to the East Indies, the Northwest Coasts of America and the extremities of the Globe.

To Comte de Moustier, August 17, 1788   *Writings Vol. 30 p. 46*

... However unimportant America may be considered at present, and however Britain may affect to despise her trade, there will assuredly come a day, when this country will have some weight in the scale of Empires.

To Marquis de Lafayette, August 15, 1786   *Writings Vol. 28 p. 520*

BRITISH COMMERCE

... there are three circumstances, which are thought to give the British merchants an advantage over all others. 1st. their extensive credit: (which I confess, I wish to see abolished). 2dly. their having in one place Magazines containing all kinds of Articles that can be required: and 3rdly. their knowledge of the precise kind of merchandize and fabrics which are wanted.

To Comte de Moustier, March 26, 1788   *Writings Vol. 29 p. 448*

COMMERCIAL POLICY OF AMERICA

... Harmony, liberal intercourse with all Nations, are recommended by policy, humanity and interest. But even our Commercial policy should hold an equal and impartial hand: neither seeking nor granting exclusive favours or preferences; consulting the natural course of things; diffusing and diversifying by gentle means the streams of Commerce, but forcing nothing; establishing with Powers so disposed; in order to give trade a stable course, to define the rights of our Merchants, and to enable the Government to support them; conventional rules of intercourse, the best that present circumstances and mutual opinion will permit, but temporary, and liable to be from time to time abandoned or varied, as experience and circumstances shall dictate; constantly keeping in view, that 'tis folly in one Nation to look for disinterested favors from another; that it must pay with a portion of its Independence for whatever it may accept under that character; that by such acceptance, it may place itself in the condition of having given equivalents for nominal favours and yet of being reproached with ingratitude for not giving more. There can be no greater error than to expect, or calculate upon real favours from Nation to Nation. 'Tis an illusion which experience must cure, which a just pride ought to discard.

Farewell Address, September 19, 1796   *Writings Vol. 35 p. 235*

DOMESTIC MANUFACTURES

... Though I would not force the introduction of manufactures, by extravagant encouragements, and to the prejudice of agriculture; yet, I conceive much might be done in that way by woman, children, and others; without taking one really necessary hand from tilling the earth.

To Marquis de Lafayette, January 29, 1789   *Writings Vol. 30 p. 186*

... I have been writing to our friend Genl. Knox this day, to procure me homespun broad cloth, of the Hartford fabric, to make a suit of cloaths for myself. I hope it will not a be a great while, before it will be unfashionable for a gentleman to appear in any other dress. Indeed we have already been too long subject to British prejudices. I use no porter or cheese in my family, but such as is made in America; both those articles may now be purchased of an excellent quality.

To Marquis de Lafayette, January 29, 1789   *Writings Vol. 30 p. 187*

... The promotion of domestic manufactures will, in my conception, be among the swift consequences which may naturally be expected to flow from an energetic government. For myself having an equal regard for the prosperity of the farming, trading, and manufacturing interests, I will only observe that I cannot conceive the extension of the latter (so far as it may afford employment to a great number of hands which would be otherwise in a manner idle) can be detrimental to the former.

To the Delaware Society for Promoting Domestic Manufactures, April 19, 1789   *Writings Vol. 30 p. 289*

MANUFACTURES AND THE ARTS

... Captain Barney has just arrived here in the miniature ship called the Federalist; and has done me the honor to offer that beautiful *Curiosity* as a Present to me on your part. I pray you, Gentlemen, to accept the warmest expressions of my sensibility for this *specimen of American ingenuity:* in which the exactitude of the proportions, the neatness of the workmanship, and the elegance of the decorations (which make your Present fit to be preserved in a Cabinet of Curiosities) at the same time that they exhibit the skill and taste of the artists, demonstrate that Americans are not inferior to any people whatever in the use of mechanical instruments and the art of ship-building.

To William Smith and Others, June 8, 1788   *Writings Vol. 29 p. 516*

NATIONAL ENCOURAGEMENT OF MANUFACTURES

... Congress have repeatedly, and not without success, directed their attention to the encouragement of Manufactures. The object is of too much consequence, not to insure a continuance of their efforts, in every way which shall appear eligible.

Eighth Annual Address to Congress, December 7, 1796   *Writings Vol. 34 p. 315*

J. COMMUNICATION AND TRANSPORTATION

POST OFFICE

... I cannot forbear intimating to you the expediency of ... facilitating the intercourse between the distant parts of our Country by a due attention to the Post-Office and Post-Roads.

First Annual Address, January 8, 1790   *Writings Vol. 30 p. 493*

CIRCULATION OF POLITICAL INTELLIGENCE

... It is represented that some provisions in the law, which establishes the Post-Office, operate, in experiment, against the transmission of newspapers to distant parts of the Country. Should this, upon due inquiry, be found to be the case, a full conviction of the importance of facilitating the circulation of political intelligence and information, will, I doubt not, lead to the application of a remedy.

Fourth Annual Address to Congress, November 6, 1792 Writings Vol. 32 p. 210

PUBLIC ROADS

... It has often been understood by wise politicans and enlightened patri-ots that giving a facility to the means of travelling for Strangers and of intercourse for citizens, was an object of Legislative concern and a cir-cumstance highly beneficial to any country.

To the Secretary for Foreign Affairs, July 18, 1788   Writings Vol. 30 p. 17

NATIONAL INFLUENCE OF MAILS AND ROADS

... The importance of the Post-Office and Post-Roads, on a plan suffi-ciently liberal and comprehensive, as they respect the expedition, safety and facility of communication, is increased by the instrumentality in dif-fusing a knowledge of the laws and proceedings of the government; which, while it contributes to the security of the people, serves also to guard them against the effects of misrepresentation and misconception.

To the Senate and the House of Representatives, October 25, 1791
Writings Vol. 31 p. 403

INLAND NAVIGATION

... It gives me pleasure to find a spirit for inland navigation prevailing so generally. No country is more capable of improvements in this way than our own, none which will be more benefited by them; and to begin well, as you justly observe, is all in all ....

To Governor William Moultrie, May 25, 1786   Writings Vol. 28 p. 439

THE LAKES

... I am glad to hear the Vessels for the Lakes are going on with such Industry. Maintaining the Superiority over the Water is certainly of infi-nite Importance. I trust neither Courage nor Activity will be wanting in those to whom the Business is committed.

To Horatio Gates, August 14, 1776   Writings Vol. 5 p. 433

NAVIGATION OF THE LAKES

... I shall be mistaken if they [the New Yorkers] do not build Vessels for

the Navigation of the Lakes, which will supercede the necessity of coast-
ing on either side.

To Thomas Jefferson, March 29, 1784   *Writings Vol. 27 p. 375*

K. NATIONAL EDUCATION

POPULAR EDUCATION

. . . Promote then as an object of primary importance, Institutions for the
general diffusion of knowledge. In proportion as the structure of a government gives force to public opinion, it is essential that public opinion
should be enlightened.

Farewell Address, September 19, 1796   *Writings Vol. 35 p. 230*

EDUCATION OF ORPHANS

. . . I . . . will direct my manager Mr. Pearce to pay my annual donation for
the education of Orphan Children, or the children of indigent parents,
who are unable to be at the expence themselves. I had pleasure in appro-
priating this money to such uses, as I always shall in that of paying it.

To Reverend James Muir, February 24, 1794   *Writings Vol. 33 p. 281*

ALEXANDRIA ACADEMY

. . . To the Trustees (Governors, or by whatsoever other name they may be
designated) of the Academy in the Town of Alexandria, I give and bequeath, in Trust, four thousand dollars, or in other words twenty of the
shares which I hold in the Bank of Alexandria, towards the support of a
Free school established at, and annexed to the said Academy; for the purpose of Educating such Orphan children, or the children of such other
poor and indigent persons as are unable to accomplish it with their own
means; and who in the judgment of the Trustees of the said Seminary, are
best entitled to the benefit of this donation.

Will, July 9, 1799   *Writings Vol. 37 p. 278*

EVILS OF FOREIGN EDUCATION

. . . That as it has always been a source of serious regret with me, to see the
youth of these United States sent to foreign Countries for the purpose of
Education, often before their minds were formed, or they had imbibed
any adequate ideas of the happiness of their own; contracting, too frequently, not only habits of dissipation and extravagence, but principles

unfriendly to Republican Governmt. and to the true and genuine liberties of mankind; which, thereafter are rarely overcome.

Will, July 9, 1799   *Writings Vol. 37 p. 279*

... we ought to deprecate the hazard attending ardent and susceptible minds, from being too strongly, and too early prepossessed in favor of other political systems, before they are capable of appreciating their own.

To the Commissioners of the District of Columbia, January 28, 1795
                                                          Writings Vol. 34 p. 106

... It is with indescribable regret, that I have seen the youth of the United States migrating to foreign countries, in order to acquire the higher branches of erudition, and to obtain a knowledge of the Sciences.

To Robert Brooke, March 16, 1795   *Writings Vol. 34 p. 149*

EDUCATION OF A STUDENT AT COLLEGE

... Having once or twice of late hear you Speak highly in praise of the Jersey College, as if you had a desire of sending your Son William there (who I am told is a youth fond of study and instruction, and disposed to a sedentary studious life; in following of which he may not only promote his own happiness, but the future welfare of others) I shou'd be glad, if you have no other objection to it than what may arise from the expence, if you wou'd send him there as soon as it is convenient and depend on me for Twenty five pounds this Currency a year for his support so long as it may be necessary for the completion of his Education. If I live to see the accomplishment of this term, the sum here stipulated shall be annually paid, and if I die in the mean while, this letter shall be obligatory upon my Heirs or Executors to do it according to the true intent and meaning hereof. No other return is expected, or wished for this offer, than that you will accept it with the same freedom and good will with which it is made, and that you may not even consider it in the light of an obligation, or mention it as such; for be assur'd that from me it will never be known.

To William Ramsay, January 29, 1769   *Writings Vol. 2 p. 499*

NATIONAL UNIVERSITY

... That a National University in *this* country is a thing to be desired, has always been my decided opinion; and the appropriation of ground and funds for it in the Federal City, have long been contemplated and talked of.

To the Vice President, November 15, 1794   *Writings Vol. 34 p. 23*

... True it is, that our Country, much to its honor, contains many Seminaries of learning highly respectable and useful; but the funds upon which they rest, are too narrow, to command the ablest Professors, in the different departments of liberal knowledge, for the Institution contemplated, though they would be excellent auxiliaries.

... Amongst the motives to such an Institution, the assimilation of the principles, opinions and manners of our Country men, but the common education of a portion of our Youth from every quarter, well deserves attention. The more homogeneous our Citizens can be made in these particulars, the greater will be our prospect of permanent Union; and a primary object of such a National Institution should be, the education of our Youth in the science of *Government*. In a Republic, what species of knowledge can be equally important? and what duty, more pressing on its Legislature, than to patronize a plan for communicating it to those, who are to be the future guardians of the liberties of the Country?

Eighth Annual Address to Congress, December 7, 1796   Writings Vol. 35 p. 316

... I give and bequeath in perpetuity the fifty shares which I hold in the Potomac Company (under the aforesaid acts. of the Legislature of Virginia) towards the endowment of a UNIVERSITY to be established within the limits of the District of Columbia, under the auspices of the General Government, if that government should incline to extend a fostering hand towards it.

Will, July 9, 1799   *Writings Vol. 37 p. 280*

MILITARY EDUCATION

... I flatter myself, that, under a skilful commander, or man of sense, (whom I most sincerely wish to serve under,) with my own application and diligent study of my duty, I shall be able to conduct my steps without censure, and, in time, render myself worthy of the promotion, that I shall be favored with now.

To Richard Corbin, March 1754   *Writings Vol. 1 p. 34*

OFFICERS URGED TO GAIN KNOWLEDGE FROM BOOKS

... Remember, that it is the actions, and not the Commission, that make the Officer, and that there is more expected from him than the Title. Do not forget, that there ought to be a time appropriated to attain this knowledge; as well as to indulge pleasure. And as we now have no opportunities to improve from example; let us read, for this desirable end.

Orders, January 8, 1756   *Writings Vol. 1 p. 271*

MILITARY ACADEMY

... The Establishment of an Institution of this kind, upon a respectable and extensive basis, has ever been considered by me as an Object of primary importance to this Country; and while I was in the Chair of Government I omitted no proper opportunity of recommending it, in my public Speeches, and otherways, to the attention of the Legislature.

To Alexander Hamilton, December 12, 1799   *Writings Vol. 37 p. 473*

... The Institution of a Military Academy, is also recommended by cogent reasons. However pacific the general policy of a Nation may be, it ought never to be without an adequate stock of Military knowledge for emergencies. The first would impair the energy of its character, and both would hazard its safety, or expose it to greater evils when War could not be avoided. Besides that War, might often, not depend upon its own choice. In proportion, as the observance of pacific maxims, might exempt a Nation from the necessity of practising the rules of the Military Art, ought to be its care in preserving, and transmitting by proper establishments, the knowledge of that art. Whatever arguments may be drawn from particular examples, superficially viewed, a thorough examination of the subject will evince, that the Art of War, is at once comprehensive and complicated; that it demands much previous study; and that the possession of it, in its most improved and perfect state, is always of great moment to the security of a Nation. This, therefore, ought to be a serious care of every Government: and for this purpose, an Academy, where a regular course of Instruction is given, is an obvious expedient, which different Nations have successfully employed.

Eighth Annual Address to Congress, December 7, 1796   *Writings Vol. 35 p. 317*

THE ARTS AND SCIENCES, OF NATIONAL INTEREST

... The Arts and Sciences essential to the prosperity of the State and to the ornament and happiness of human life have a primary claim to the encouragement of every lover of his Country and mankind.

To Joseph Willard, March 22, 1781   *Writings Vol. 21 p. 352*

AMERICAN ACADEMY OF ARTS AND SCIENCES

... I shall with Zeal embrace every oppertunity of seconding their laudable views and manifesting the exalted sense I have of the institution.

To Joseph Willard, March 22, 1781   *Writings Vol. 21 p. 351*

INFLUENCE OF LEARNING

... I am not a little flattered by being considered by the Patrons of literature as one in their number. Fully apprised of the influence which sound
learning has on religion and manners, on government liberty, and laws, I
shall only lament my want of abilities to make it still more extensive.

*To the President and Faculty of the University of the State of Pennsylvania, April
20, 1789*   *Writings Vol. 30 p. 289*

IMPORTANCE OF LITERATURE, SCIENCE, AND THE ARTS

... there is nothing which can better deserve your patronage than the
promotion of Science and Literature.

First Annual Address, January 8, 1790   *Writings Vol. 30 p. 493*

... Nothing can give me more pleasure, than to patronize the essays of
Genius and a laudable cultivation of the Arts and Sciences, which had
began to flourish in so eminent a degree, before the hand of oppression
was stretched over our devoted Country. And I shall esteem myself happy,
if a Poem, which has employed the labour of Years, will derive any advantages, or bear more weight in the World, by Making its appearance under
dedication to me.

To Timothy Dwight, Junior, March 18, 1778   *Writings Vol. 11 p. 106*

COMPREHENSIVE VIEWS OF COLLEGE EDUCATION

... I confide fully in their (College of William and Mary) strenuous endeavours for placing the system of Education on such a basis, as will render it most beneficial to the State and the Republic of letters, as well as to
the more extensive interests of humanity and religion.

To Samuel Griffin, April 30, 1788   *Writings Vol. 29 p. 482*

LIBERTY HALL ACADEMY

... The hundred shares which I held in the James River Company, I have
given and now confirm in perpetuity to, and for the use and benefit of
Liberty-Hall Academy in the County of Rockbrige, in the Commonwealth
of Virga.

Will, July 9, 1799   *Writings Vol. 37 p. 281*

KNOWLEDGE AMONG THE PEOPLE

... Knowledge is in every country the surest basis of public happiness. In
one in which the measures of Government receive their impression so
immediately from the sense of the Community as in ours it is proportion-

ably essential. To the security of a free Constitution it contributes in various ways: By convincing those who are instructed with the public administration, that every valuable end of Government is best answered by the enlightened confidence of the people: and by teaching the people themselves to know and to value their own rights; to discern and provide against invasions of them; to distinguish between oppression and the necessary exercise of lawful authority; between burthens proceeding from a disregard to their convenience and those resulting from the inevitable exigencies of Society; to discriminate the spirit of Liberty from that of licentiousness, cherishing the first, avoiding the last, and uniting a speedy, but temperate vigilance against encroachments, with an inviolable respect to the Laws.   Whether this desirable object will be the best promoted by affording aids to seminaries of learning established, by the institution of a national University, or by any other expedients, will be well worthy of a place in the deliberations of the Legislature.

First Annual Address, January 8, 1790   *Writings Vol. 30 p. 494*

PERIODICAL LITERATURE

... I entertain an high idea of the utility of periodical Publications: insomuch that I could heartily desire, copies of the Museum and Magazines, as well as common Gazettes, might be spread through every city, town and village in America. I consider such easy vehicles of knowledge more happily calculated than any other, to preserve the liberty, stimulate the industry and meliorate the morals of an enlightened and free People.

To Mathew Carey, June 25, 1788   *Writings Vol. 30 p. 7*

II.
MILITARY MAXIMS

Military Maxims

———————————— ✄ ————————————

Lack of experience did not delay George Washington's early military ambitions, which were at first discouraged when Washington's mother thwarted her 14-year-old son's attempt to enlist in the British navy. In 1752, he began his military career with his appointment as Adjutant of the southern district of Virginia. The post was left vacant upon the death of George's half brother Lawrence, former Adjutant as well as captain under Admiral Edward Vernon during the Cartagena Campaign of 1740-1742, and an inspiring role model for young George. Charged with instructing and drilling the militia in his jurisdiction, Washington accepted the rank of major.

The following year Washington volunteered his services to Virginia Lieutenant Governor Dinwiddie. Dinwiddie needed a trustworthy messenger to travel to the Ohio country, which he claimed as part of the King's Colony of Virginia, to respectfully ask the French to abandon their outposts there. After receiving a polite "no" from the French, Washington returned to Williamsburg. In response, Dinwiddie raised a force of 300 men, promoted the 22-year-old George Washington to Lieutenant Colonel and sent him in advance of the expedition's commander Joshua Fry. Washington and his small force pushed toward the Ohio forks, near which the Virginia Regiment surprised and routed a French party, killing a French diplomat in the process. A month later, on July 3, 1754, Washington was, in his words, "soundly beaten" at Fort Necessity by the French. After laying down their arms, Washington and his men were allowed to return to Virginia.

During the subsequent French and Indian War, Washington served as volunteer aide-de-camp to the ill-fated General Braddock and later, appointed Colonel, he commanded the Virginia forces. In 1758, after the French abandoned Fort Duquesne at the forks, the war in Virginia was virtually ended. Washington resigned his commission and returned to Mount Vernon. In decorating his home for his new bride Martha, Washington ordered from England busts of Alexander the Great, Julius Caesar, Frederick II of Prussia, and the Duke of Marlborough, planning to surround himself with the likenesses of the world's greatest warriors.

When an agent informed him that those busts were not available, but those of Homer, Virgil, Cicero and Plato could be had, Colonel Washington cancelled his order. When Washington arrived at the Second Continental Congress in May 1775 wearing his uniform from the French and Indian War, he broadcast the strong signal that he was prepared to take up arms against Britain. Several weeks later, Congress unanimously elected Washington to lead this fight. As commander in chief of the Continental forces, Washington soon decided that the most prudent strategy was a defensive approach. It would be folly to directly challenge the King's army and navy—superior in numbers, discipline and organization. As a result, Washington's most memorable military successes (save Yorktown) were surprise attacks, such as his world-famous crossing of the Delaware on Christmas night in 1776 to overwhelm the Hessians at Trenton.

Second to the British, Washington's most significant threat was the deserting Continental soldier. Perhaps the General's finest contribution to the American effort was maintaining discipline and order in an army which, to a great extent, consisted of short-term militiamen who were often more interested in getting home in time to harvest their crops.

Persistence, too, paid off in Washington's case. In letter upon letter to Congress, Washington requested more men, more supplies, more money, and more foreign assistance. Some of his requests were finally answered, and finally, in 1781, the time was ripe for attack. With Lafayette and von Steuben resisting Cornwallis in Virginia, the British commander marched to Yorktown, hoping to combine forces with General Clinton and the British navy. While Washington and Rochambeau arrived from the north, DeGrasse's naval squadron in the Chesapeake Bay thwarted any British attempt to aid Cornwallis by sea. The British had no escape but through surrender. Two years passed before the Peace Treaty signed in Paris brought an official end to the Revolutionary War. In the meantime, Washington was forced to squelch mutinous murmurings from disgruntled officers who felt—quite literally—shortchanged by Congress. Promises of pay and land for military service were delayed, causing the idle soldiers to entertain thoughts of retaliation.

Americans learned of the Peace Treaty in October 1783. On December 23, Washington arrived at the State House in Annapolis to resign his commission before Congress. But he would don his uniform once more in 1798 when, under a threat of war with France, Washington was appointed Lieutenant General and commander in chief of the United States Army.

A. WAR

WAR, DEPRECATED AS AN EVIL

... My first wish is to see this plague to mankind banished from off the Earth, and the sons and Daughters of this world employed in more pleasing and innocent amusements, than in preparing implements and exercising them for the destruction of mankind ....

To David Humphreys, July 25, 1785   *Writings Vol. 28 p. 202*

... rather than quarrel about territory let the poor, the needy and oppressed of the Earth, and those who want Land, resort to the fertile plains of our western country, the *second Promise*, and there dwell in peace, fulfilling the first and great commandment.

To David Humphreys, July 25, 1785   *Writings Vol. 28 p. 202*

... The friends of humanity will deprecate war, wheresoever it may appear; and we have experienced enough of its evils in this Country to know, that it should not be wantonly or unnecessarily entered upon. I trust therefore, that the good Citizens of the United States will shew to the world, that they have as much wisdom in preserving peace at this critical juncture, as they have heretofore displayed valour in defending their just rights.

To the Merchants and Traders of the City of Philadelphia, May 17, 1793
                                        Writings Vol. 32 p. 460

EUROPEAN BATTLEFIELDS

... here have fallen thousands of gallant spirits to satisfy the ambition of, or to support their sovereigns perhaps in acts of oppression or injustice! melancholy reflection! For what wise purposes does Providence permit this? Is it as a scourge for mankind, or is it to prevent them from becoming too populous? If the latter, would not the fertile plains of the Western world receive the redundancy of the old.

To Marquis de Lafayette, May 10, 1786   *Writings Vol. 28 p. 420*

RESORT TO ARMS, IN DEFENSE OF FREEDOM

... At a time when our lordly Masters in Great Britain will be satisfied with nothing less than the deprication of American freedom, it seems highly necessary that some thing shou'd be done to avert the stroke and maintain the liberty which we have derived from our Ancestors; but the manner of doing it to answer the purpose effectually is the point in question. That no man shou'd scruple, or hesitate a moment to use a-ms in defence of so valuable a blessing, on which all the good and evil of life depends; is clearly my opinion; yet A-ms ... should be the last resource; the denier resort. Addresses to the Throne, and remonstrances to parliament, we have already, it is said, proved the inefficacy of; how far then their attention to our rights and priviledges is to be awakened or alarmed by starving their Trade and manufactures, remains to be tryed.

To George Mason, April 5, 1769   *Writings Vol. 2 p. 500*

THE PATRIOT'S ALTERNATIVE

... Unhappy it is though to reflect, that a Brother's Sword has been

Painted & Engraved by E. Savage

GENERAL GEORGE WASHINGTON.

General George Washington by Edward Savage. Washington's diary records three sittings with Savage in 1790 for the original painting after which this engraving was based. He wears the badge of the Society of the Cincinnati on his left lapel.

sheathed in a Brother's breast, and that, the once happy and peaceful plains of America are either to be drenched with Blood, or Inhabited by Slaves. Sad alternative! But can a virtuous Man hesitate in his choice.

To George William Fairfax, May 31, 1775　　　　　　*Writings Vol. 3 p. 292*

THE SPIRIT OF '76

... the hour is fast approaching, on which the Honor and Success of this army, and the safety of our bleeding Country depend. Remember officers and Soldiers, that you are Freemen, fighting for the blessings of Liberty— that slavery will be your portion, and that of your posterity, if you do not acquit yourselves like men ....

General Orders, August 23, 1776　　　　　　*Writings Vol. 5 p. 479*

MILITARY INFLUENCE OF CONGRESS

... if I may be allowed to speak figuratively, our Assemblies in Politics are to be compared to the Wheels of a Clock in Mechanics; the whole for the general purposes of War shd. be set in motion by the grt. Wheel (Congress) and if all will do their parts the Machine works easy; but a failure in one disorders the whole, and without the large one (wch. set the whole in motn.) nothg can be done; it is by the united wisdom and exertions of the whole, in Congress, who, I presume, do justice to all ... that we are to depend upon. without this we are no better than a rope of Sand and are as easily broken asunder.

To Archibald Cary, June 15, 1782　　　　　　*Writings Vol. 24 p. 347*

B. THE ARMY

THE SOLDIER'S DUTY

... With this hope and confidence, and that this Army will have its equal share of Honour, and Success; the General most earnestly exhorts every officer, and soldier, to pay the utmost attention to his Arms, and Health; to have the former in the best order for Action, and by Cleanliness and Care, to preserve the latter; to be exact in their discipline, obedient to their Superiors and vigilant on duty: with such preparation, and a suitable Spirit there can be no doubt, but by the blessing of Heaven, we shall repel our cruel Invaders; preserve our Country, and gain the greatest Honor.

General Orders, July 21, 1776　　　　　　*Writings Vol. 5 p. 315*

... He hopes therefore, every man's mind and arms, will be prepared for action, and when called to it, shew our enemies, and the whole world, that

Freemen contending on their own land, are superior to any mercenaries on earth.

General Orders, August 20, 1776   *Writings Vol. 5 p. 469*

... the General calls upon officers, and men, to act up to the noble cause in which they are engaged, and to support the Honor and Liberties of their Country.

General Orders, September 17, 1776   *Writings Vol. 6 p. 65*

THE ARMY, AGENTS OF CIVIL POWER

... it may be proper constantly and strongly to impress upon the Army that they are mere agents of Civil power: that out of Camp, they have no other authority than other citizens, that offences against the laws are to be examined, not by a military officer, but by a Magistrate; that they are not exempt from arrests and indictments for violations of the law.

To Daniel Morgan, March 27, 1795   *Writings Vol. 34 p. 160*

MAXIMS FOR OFFICERS

... be strict in your discipline; that is, to require nothing unreasonable of your officers and men, but see that whatever is required be punctually complied with. Reward and punish every man according to his merit, without partiality or prejudice; hear his complaints; if well founded, re-dress them; if otherwise, discourage them, in order to prevent frivolous ones. Discourage vice in every shape, and impress upon the mind of every man, from the first to the lowest, the importance of the cause, and what it is they are contending for.

To William Woodford, November 10, 1775   *Writings Vol. 4 p. 80*

... Be easy and condescending in your deportment to your officers, but not too familiar, lest you subject yourself to a want of that respect, which is necessary to support a proper command.

To William Woodford, November 10, 1775   *Writings Vol. 4 p. 81*

PATRIOT SOLDIERS

... Men, therefore, who are not employed, as mere hirelings, but have steped forth in defence of every thing that is dear and Valuable, not only to themselves but to posterity, should take uncommon pains to conduct themselves with uncommon propriety and good Order, as their honor, reputation &c. call loudly upon them for it.

To Israel Putnam, August 25, 1776   *Writings Vol. 5 p. 489*

TWO VIEWS OF DANGER

... Men who are familiarized to danger, meet it without shrinking, whereas those who have never seen Service often apprehend danger where no danger is.

To the President of Congress, February 9, 1776   *Writings Vol. 4 p. 316*

THE THREE INCENTIVES, IN BATTLE

... Three things prompt Men to a regular discharge of their Duty in time of Action: natural bravery, hope of reward, and fear of punishment....The two first (natural bravery and hope of reward) are common to the untutor'd, and the Disciplin'd Soldiers; but the latter (fear of punishment) most obviously distinguishes the one from the other.

To the President of Congress, February 9, 1776   *Writings Vol. 4 p. 316*

THE COWARD'S BRAVERY

... A Coward, when taught to believe, that if he breaks his Ranks, and abandons his Colours, will be punished with Death by his own party, will take his chance against the Enemy; but the Man who thinks little of the one, and is fearful of the other, Acts from present feelings regardless of consequences.

To the President of Congress, February 9, 1776   *Writings Vol. 4 p. 316*

RAW MILITIA

... Men just dragged from the tender Scenes of domestick life; unaccustomed to the din of Arms; totally unacquainted with every kind of Military skill, which being followed by a want of confidence in themselves, when opposed to Troops regularly train'd, disciplined, and appointed, superior in knowledge, and superior in Arms, makes them timid, and ready to fly from their own shadows.

To the President of Congress, September 24, 1776   *Writings Vol. 6 p. 110*

MILITARY RANK, THE PEOPLE'S GIFT

... I cannot conceive one more honourable, than that, which flows from the uncorrupted Choice of a brave and free People, the purest Source, and original Fountain of all Power.

To Thomas Gage, August 20, 1775   *Writings Vol. 3 p. 431*

THE FREEMAN'S HEREDITARY PRIVILEGES

... Under his Providence, those who influence the Councils of America, and all the other Inhabitants of the united Colonies at the Hazard of their

Lives are determined to hand down to Posterity those just and invaluable Privileges, which they received from their Ancestors.

To Thomas Gage, August 20, 1775   *Writings Vol. 3 p. 431*

THE SOLDIER'S MOTTO

... Perseverance and spirit have done Wonders in all Ages.

To Philip Schuyler, August 20, 1775   *Writings Vol. 3 p. 437*

SPIES

... Single men in the night will be more likely to ascertain facts than the best glasses in the day.

To Anthony Wayne, July 10, 1779   *Writings Vol. 15 p. 397*

SURPRISALS OF THE ENEMY

... The usual time for exploits of this kind is a little before day for which reason a vigilant Officer is then more on the watch I therefore recommend a midnight hour ... A Dark Night and even a Rainy one if you can find the way, will contribute to your success.

To Anthony Wayne, July 10, 1776   *Writings Vol. 15 p. 398*

REGULAR TROOPS, SUPERIOR TO MILITIA

... Regular Troops alone are equal to the exigencies of modern war, as well for defence as offence, and whenever a substitute is attempted it must prove illusory and ruinous.

To the President of Congress, September 15, 1780   *Writings Vol. 20 p. 49*

... No Militia will ever acquire the habits necessary to resist a regular force.

To the President of Congress, September 15, 1780   *Writings Vol. 20 p. 50*

... The firmness requisite for the real business of fighting is only to be attained by a constant course of discipline and service. I have never yet been witness to a single instance that can justify a different opinion; and it is most earnestly to be wished the liberties of America may no longer be trusted in any material degree to so precarious a dependence.

To the President of Congress, September 15, 1780   *Writings Vol. 20 p. 50*

MILITARY POWER

... I confess, I have felt myself greatly embarrassed with respect to a vigorous exercise of Military power. An Ill placed humanity perhaps a reluctance to give distress may have restrained me too far. But these were not all. I have been well aware of the prevalent jealousy of military power, and that this has been considered as an Evil much to be apprehended even by the best and most sensible among us. Under this Idea, I have been cautious and wished to avoid as much as possible any Act that might improve it.

To the President of Congress, December 14, 1777   *Writings Vol. 10 p. 159*

... The people at large are governed much by Custom. To Acts of Legislation or Civil Authority they have been ever taught to yield a willing obedience without reasoning about their propriety. On those of Military power, whether immediate or derived originally from another Source, they have ever looked with a jealous and suspicious Eye.

To the President of Congress, December 14, 1777   *Writings Vol. 10 p. 160*

... Extensive powers not exercised as far as was necessary, have I believe scarcely ever failed to ruin the possessor.

To Joseph Reed, July 4, 1780   *Writings Vol. 19 p. 114*

... I conceive it to be a right inherent with command to appoint particular Officers for special purposes.

To William Heath, March 21, 1781   *Writings Vol. 21 p. 344*

MILITARY DISCIPLINE

... I beg that you will be particularly careful in seeing strict order observed among the Soldiers, as that is the Life of Military discipline.

To Adam Stephen, November 18, 1755   *Writings Vol. 1 p. 235*

... do we not see that every Nation under the Sun find their acct. therein; and without, it no Order no regularity can be observed? Why then shou'd it be expected from us, (who are all young and inexperienced,) to govern, and keep up a proper spirit of Discipline with't Laws; when the best, and most Experienced, can scarcely do it with. Then if we consult our Interest, I am sure it is loudly called for.

To Robert Dinwiddie, October 11, 1755   *Writings Vol. 1 p. 202*

SUBORDINATION

... One Circumstance, in this important Business, ought to be cautiously guarded against, and that is, the Soldier and Officer being too nearly on a level. Discipline and Subordination add life and Vigour to Military movements. The person Commanded yields but a reluctant obedience to those, he conceives, are undeservedly made his Superiors. The degrees of Rank are frequently transferred from Civil life into the Departments of the

George Washington Esqr. General and Commander in Chief of the Continental Army in America. Done from an original Drawn from Life by Alexr. Campbell of Williamsburg, published by C. Shepherd, 1775. One of the several fictitious portraits of Washington that were circulated in England in the early years of the Revolution. It is believed that the artist, "Alexander Campbell," was also a fabrication of the publisher. When Washington received a copy from his aide, Joseph Reed, he wrote, "Mrs. Washington desires I well thank you for the picture you sent her. Mr. Campbell, whom I never saw to my knowledge, has made a very formidable figure of the Commander in Chief, giving him a sufficient portion of terror in his countenance."

Army. The true Criterion to judge by (when past Services do not enter into the Competition) is, to consider whether the Candidate for Office has a just pretention to the Character of a Gentleman, a proper sense of Honor, and some reputation to loose.

To Governor Patrick Henry, October 5, 1776   *Writings Vol. 6 p. 167*

... A refusal to obey the commands of a superior Officer, especially where the duty required was evidently calculated for the good of the Service, cannot be justified, without involving consequences subversive of all Military Discipline. A precedent manifestly too dangerous would be established, of dispensing with orders, and subordination would be at an end, if men's ideas were not rectified in a case of this kind, and such notice taken, as has been on my part.

To Josias Carvil Hall, April 3, 1778   *Writings Vol. 11 p. 204*

IMPRUDENT CONVERSATION OF OFFICERS

... the custom which many Officers have of speaking freely of things and reprobating measures which upon investigation may be found to be unavoidable is never productive of good, and often of very mischievous consequences.

To Charles Lee, June 15, 1778   *Writings Vol. 12 p. 62*

MUTINY

... when we consider that these Pennsylvania Levies who have now mutinyed, are Recruits and Soldiers of a day, who have not born the heat and burden of the War, and who can have in reality very few hardships to complain of, and when we at the same time recollect, that those Soldiers who have lately been furloughed from this Army, are the Veterans who have patiently endured hunger, nakedness and cold, who have suffered and bled without a murmur, and who with perfect good order have retired to their homes, without the settlement of their Accounts or a farthing of money in their pockets, we shall be as much astonished at the virtues of the latter, as we are struck with horror and detestation at the proceedings of the former; and every candid mind, without indulging ill-grounded prejudices, will undoubtedly make the proper discrimination.

To the President of Congress, June 24, 1783   *Writings Vol. 27 p. 33*

"ARMY OF THE CONSTITUTION"

... It [Pennsylvania Insurrection] has demonstrated, that our prosperity rests on solid foundations; by furnishing an additional proof, that my fellow citizens understand the true principles of government and liberty; that they feel their inseparable union: that notwithstanding all the de-

Le General Washington by Noel Le Mire after Jean Baptiste Le Paon and Charles Willson Peale, Paris, 1780. Washington owned a copy of this print and a companion engraving of General Lafayette, which he hung in the family dining room at Mount Vernon.

vices which have been used to sway them from their interest and duty, they are now as ready to maintain the authority of the laws against licentious invasions, as they were to defend their rights against usurpation. It has been a spectacle, displaying to the highest advantage, the value of Republican Government, to behold the most and least wealthy of our citizens standing in the same ranks as private soldiers; preeminently distinguished by being the army of the constitution.

Sixth Annual Address to Congress, November 19, 1794   Writings Vol. 34 p. 34

COURTS-MARTIAL

... it is recollected, to be a fundamental maxim, in our military trials, that the Judge advocate prosecutes in the name and in behalf of the United States.

To Joseph Reed, April 27, 1779   Writings Vol. 14 p. 449

MILITARY EMULATION

... I have labourd ever since I have been in the Service to discourage all kinds of local attachments, and distinctions of Country, denominating the whole by the greater name of American; but I found it impossible to overcome prejudices, and under the New Establishment I conceive it best to stir up an Emulation in order to do which, would it not be better for each State to furnish (tho not appoint) their own Brigadiers.

To the President of Congress, December 20, 1776   Writings Vol. 6 p. 405

THE SOLDIER AND THE CITIZEN

... When we assumed the Soldier, we did not lay aside the Citizen; and we shall most sincerely rejoice with you in that happy hour when the establishment of American Liberty, upon the most firm and solid foundations, shall enable us to return to our Private Stations in the bosom of a free, peaceful and happy Country.

To the New York Legislature, June 26, 1775   Writings Vol. 3 p. 305

THE FABIAN POLICY

... I am sensible a retreating Army is encircled with difficulties, that the declining an Engagement subjects a General to reproach and that the common Cause may be in some measure affected by the discouragements which it throws over the minds of many; nor am I insensible of the contrary effects, if a brilliant stroke could be made with any Probability of success, especially after our loss upon Long Island: but when the fate of America may be at stake on the Issue; when the Wisdom of cooler moments and experienced Men have decided that we should protract the

War if Possible; I cannot think it safe or wise to adopt a different System, when the season for Action draws so near a close.

To the President of Congress, September 8, 1776   *Writings Vol. 6 p. 31*

WAR OF POSTS

... on our Side the War should be defensive. It has even been called a War of Posts. That we should on all Occasions avoid a general Action, or put anything to the Risque, unless compelled by a necessity, into which we ought never to be drawn.

To the President of Congress, September 8, 1776   *Writings Vol. 6 p. 28*

IMPORTANCE OF HARMONY AMONG THE TROOPS

... Enjoin this upon the Officers, and let them inculcate, and press home to the Soldiery, the Necessity of Order and Harmony among them, who are embark'd in one common Cause, and mutually contending for all that Freeman hold dear. I am persuaded, if the Officers will but exert themselves, these Animosities, this Disorder, will in a great Measure subside, and nothing being more essential to the Service than that it should, I am hopeful nothing on their Parts will be wanting to effect it.

To Philip Schuyler, July 17, 1776   *Writings Vol. 5 p. 290*

THE ARMY, A BAND OF BROTHERS

... my first wish would be that my Military family, and the whole Army, should consider themselves as a band of brothers, willing and ready, to die for each other.

To Henry Knox, October 21, 1798   *Writings Vol. 36 p. 508*

THE BEST SOLDIER, THE BEST PATRIOT

... The General most earnestly entreats the officers, and soldiers, to consider the consequences; that they can no way assist our cruel enemies more effectually, than making division among ourselves; That, the Honor and Success of the army, and the safety of our bleeding Country, depends upon harmony and good agreement with each other; That the Provinces are all United to oppose the common enemy, and all distinctions sunk in the name of an American; to make this honorable and preserve the Liberty of our Country, ought to be our only emulation, and he will be the best Soldier, and the best Patriot, who contributes most to this glorious work, whatever his Station, or from whatever part of the Continent, he may come.

General Orders, August 1, 1776   *Writings Vol. 5 p. 361*

THE TOWNS AND THE ARMY

... I am well convinced myself, that the Enemy, long ere this, are perfectly well satisfied that the possession of our Towns, while we have an Army in the field, will avail them little. It involves *us* in difficulty, but does not, by any means, insure *them* conquest. They will know, that it is our Arms, not defenceless Towns, they have to Subdue, before they can arrive at the haven of their Wishes, and that, till this end is accomplished, the Superstructure they have been endeavouring to raise, "like the baseless fabric of a vision" falls to nothing.

To Henry Laurens, October 3, 1778   *Writings Vol. 13 p. 15*

THE ARMY AND THE PEOPLE

... I shall still continue to exert all my influence and authority to prevent the interruption of that harmony which is so essential, and which has so generally prevailed between the Army and the Inhabitants of the Country; and I need scarcely add that in doing this, I shall give every species of countenance and support to the execution of the Laws of the Land.

To Governor George Clinton, October 19, 1782   *Writings Vol. 25 p. 277*

WANTON DESTRUCTION OF PROPERTY

... it is to be hoped, that men who have property of their own, and a regard for the rights of others, will shudder at the thought of rendering any Man's Situation, to whose protection he had come, more insufferable, than his open and avowed Enemy would make it, when by duty and every rule of humanity, they ought to Aid, and not Oppress, the distressed in their habitations. The distinction between a well regulated Army, and a Mob, is the good order and discipline of the first, and the licentious and disorderly behaviour of the latter.

To Israel Putnam, August 25, 1776   *Writings Vol. 5 p. 488*

PLUNDERING

... It is our business to give protection, and support, to the poor, distressed Inhabitants; not to multiply and increase their calamities.

General Orders, January 21, 1777   *Writings Vol. 7 p. 47*

OFFICERS AND SOLDIERS; THEIR SUPPORT

... it will be of importance to conciliate the comfortable support of the Officers and Soldiers with a due regard to economy.

First Annual Address, January 8, 1790   *Writings Vol. 30 p. 492*

THE SOLDIER'S PERSONAL SACRIFICES

... When men are employed and have the incitements of military honor to engage their ambition and pride, they will cheerfully submit to inconveniences, which, in a state of tranquility would appear insupportable.

To the Committee of Conference, January 20, 1779   *Writings Vol. 14 p. 28*

... there is no set of Men in the United States (considered as a body) that have made the same sacrifices of their Interest in support of the common cause as the Officers of the American Army; that nothing but (a love of their Country,) of honor, and a desire of seeing their labours crowned with success could possibly induce them to continue one moment in Service. That no Officer can live upon his pay, that hundreds having spent their little all in addition to their scant public allowance have resigned, because they could no longer support themselves as Officers; that numbers are, at this moment, rendered unfit for duty for want of Cloathing, while the rest are wasteing their property and some of them verging fast to the gulph of poverty and distress.

To Joseph Jones, August 13, 1780   *Writings Vol. 19 p. 368*

CHARACTER AND SUFFERINGS OF THE ARMY OF THE REVOLUTION

... no Order of Men in the thirteen States have paid a more sanctimonious regard to their proceedings than the Army; and, indeed, it may be questioned, whether there has been that scrupulus adherence had to them by any other, (for without arrogance, or the smallest deviation from truth it may be said, that no history, now extant, can furnish an instance of an Army's suffering such uncommon hardships as ours have done, and bearing them with the same patience and Fortitude. To see Men without Cloaths to cover their nakedness, without Blankets to lay on, without Shoes, by which their Marches might be traced by the Blood from their feet, and almost as often without Provisions as with; Marching through frost and Snow, and at Christmas taking up their Winter Quarters within a day's March of the enemy, without a House or Hutt to cover them till they could be built and submitting to it without a murmur, is a mark of patience and obedience which in my opinion can scarce be parallel'd.)

To John Bannister, April 21, 1778   *Writings Vol. 11 p. 291*

To one well acquainted with the sufferings of the American Army as you are ... it will be sufficient to observe, the more Virtue ... the more Virtue and forbearance of it is tried the more resplendent it appears. My hopes, that the military exit of this valuable class of the community will exhibit such a proof of Amor patriae as will do them honor in the page of history.

To Marquis de Lafayette, April 5, 1783   *Writings Vol. 26 p. 300*

THE "PATRIOT ARMY"

... The glorius task for which we first fleu to Arms being thus accomplished, the liberties of our Country being fully acknowledged, and firmly secured by the smiles of heaven, on the purity of our cause, and the honest exertions of a feeble people (determined to be free) against a powerful Nation (disposed to oppress them) and the Character of those who have persevered, through every extremity of hardship; suffering and danger being immortalized by the illustrious appellation of the *patriot Army:* Nothing now remains but for the actors of this mighty Scene to preserve a perfect, unvarying, consistency of character through the very last act; to close the Drama with applause; and to retire from the Military Theatre with the same approbation of Angells and men which have crowned all their former vertuous Actions.

General Orders, April 18, 1783   *Writings Vol. 26 p. 336*

... They were indeed; at first, "a band of undisciplined Husbandmen," but it is (under God) to their bravery and attention to their duty, that I am indebted for that success which has procured me the only reward I wish to receive; the affection and esteem of my Countrymen.

To the President of Congress, April 18, 1776   *Writings Vol. 4 p. 489*

... Seconded by such a body of yeomanry as repaired to the standard of liberty, fighting in their own native land, fighting for all that freemen hold dear, and whose docility soon supplied the place of discipline, it was scarcely in human nature, under its worst character, to have abandoned them in their misfortunes: Nor is it for me to claim any singular title to merit, for having shared in a common danger, and triumphed with them, after a series of the severest toil and most accumulated distress, over a formidable foe.

South Carolina Convention, May 31, 1790   *Writings Vol. 31 p. 67*

THE CINCINNATI SOCIETY

... There is not I conceive, an unbiassed mind, that would refuse the Officers of the late Army the right of associating for the purpose of establishing a fund for the support of the poor and distressed of their fraternity, when many of them it is well known, are reduced to their last shifts by the ungenerous conduct of their Country, in not adopting more vigorous measures to render their Certificates productive. That charity is all that remains of the original Institution, none who will be at the trouble of reading it can deny.

To Samuel Vaughan, November 30, 1785   *Writings Vol. 28 p. 327*

... When this Society was first formed, I am persuaded not a member of it conceived that it would give birth to those Jealousies, or be chargeable with those dangers (real or imaginary) with which the minds of many, and some of respectable characters, were filled. The motives which induced the Officers to enter into it were, I am confident, truly and frankly recited in the Institution: one of which, indeed the principal, was to establish a charitable fund for the relief of such of their compatriots, the Widows, and descendants of them, as were fit objects for their support; and for whom no public provision had been made. But the trumpet being sounded, the alarm was spreading far and wide ....

To James Madison, December 16, 1786   *Writings Vol. 29 p. 113*

A STANDING ARMY

... I am persuaded and as fully convinced, as I am of any one fact that has happened, that our Liberties must of necessity be greatly hazarded, If not entirely lost, if their defence is left to any but a permanent standing Army, I mean one to exist during the War.

To the President of Congress, September 2, 1776   *Writings Vol. 6 p. 5*

... It becomes evidently clear then, that as this Contest is not likely to be the Work of a day; as the War must be carried on systematically, and to do it, you must have good Officers, there are, in my Judgment, no other possible means to obtain them but by establishing your Army upon a permanent footing; and giving your Officers good pay; this will induce Gentlemen, and Men of Character to engage; and till the bulk of your Officers are composed of such persons as are actuated by Principles of honour, and a spirit of enterprize, you have little to expect from them.

To the President of Congress, September 24, 1776   *Writings Vol. 6 p. 108*

... Had we kept a permanent Army on foot, the enemy would have had nothing to hope for, and would, in all probability, have listened to terms long since.

To the President of Congress, August 20, 1780   *Writings Vol. 19 p. 410*

... I most firmly believe that the Independence of the United States never will be established till there is an Army on foot for the War; that (if we are to rely on occasional or annual Levies) we must sink under the expence; and ruin must follow.

To John Mathews, October 4, 1780   *Writings Vol. 20 p. 113*

PREJUDICES AGAINST A STANDING ARMY

... the common, received Opinion, which under proper limitations is cer-

tainly true, that standing Armies are dangerous to a State, and from forming the same conclusion of the component parts of all, though they are
totally dissimilar in their Nature. The prejudices in other Countries has
only gone to them in time of *Peace,* and these from their not having in
general cases, any of the ties, the concerns or interests of Citizens or any
other dependence, than what flowed from their Military employ; in short,
from their being Mercenaries; hirelings. It is our policy to be prejudiced
against them in time of *War:* and though they are Citizens having all the
Ties, and interests of Citizens, and in most cases property totally unconnected with the Military Line. If we would pursue a right System of policy,
in my Opinion, there should be none of these distinctions. We should all
be considered, Congress, Army, &c. as one people, embarked in one
Cause, in one interest; acting on the same principle and to the same End.

To John Bannister, April 21, 1778   *Writings Vol. 11 p. 290*

. . . From long experience and fullest conviction, I have been, and now am
decidedly in favr. of a permanent force; but knowing the jealousies wch.
have been entertained on this head; Heaven knows how unjustly, (and the
cause of which could never be apprehended were a due regard had to our
local and other circumstances, even if ambitious views could be supposed
to exist); and that our political helm was in another direction, I forbore to
press my Sentiments (for a time); but at a moment when we are tottering
on the brink of a precipice, silence would have been criminal.

To John Mathews, October 4, 1780   *Writings Vol. 20 p. 115*

A TEMPORARY ARMY, INEFFECTUAL

. . . to suppose that this great revolution can be accomplished by a temporary army; that this Army will be subsisted by State supplies, and that taxation alone is adequate to our wants, is, in my Opinion absurd and as unreasonable as to expect an Inversion in the order of nature to
accommodate itself to our views.

To John Cadwalader, October 5, 1780   *Writings Vol. 20 p. 122*

THE MILITIA OF THE UNITED STATES

. . . The militia . . . is certainly an object of primary importance, whether
viewed in reference to the national security, to the satisfaction of the community, or to the preservation of order.

To the Senate and the House of Representatives, October 25, 1791

Writings Vol. 31 p. 402

PATRIOTISM AND INTEREST

. . . Men may speculate as they will; they may talk of patriotism; they may draw a few examples from ancient story, of great atchievements performed by its influence; but whoever builds upon it, as a sufficient Basis for conducting a long and bloody War, will find themselves deceived in the end .... We must take the passions of Men as Nature has given them, and those principles as a guide which are generally the rule of Action. I do not mean to exclude altogether the Idea of Patriotism. I know it exists, and I know it has done much in the present Contest. But I will venture to assert, that a great and lasting War can never be supported on this principle alone. It must be aided by a prospect of Interest or some reward. For a time, it may, of itself push Men to Action; to bear much, to encounter difficulties; but it will not endure unassisted by Interest.

To John Bannister, April 21, 1778   *Writings Vol. 11 p. 286*

MILITARY ESTABLISHMENT AND ECONOMY

... Nothing can be more obvious than a sound Military establishment and the interests of economy are the same.

To the President of Congress, October 11, 1780   *Writings Vol. 20 p. 159*

RANK, LAVISHLY BESTOWED ON FOREIGNERS

... The lavish manner, in which rank has hitherto been bestowed on these gentlemen, will certainly be productive of one or the other of these two evils, either to make it despicable in the eyes of Europe, or become a means of pouring them in upon us like a torrent, and adding to our present burden. But it is neither the expense nor the trouble of them that I most dread. There is an evil more extensive in its nature, and fatal in its consequences, to be apprehended, and that is, the driving of all our own officers out of the service, and throwing not only our army, but our military councils, entirely into the hands of foreigners.

To Gouverneur Morris, July 24, 1778   *Writings Vol. 12 p. 226*

THREE CLASSES OF FOREIGN OFFICERS

... They may be divided into three classes, namely, mere adventurers without recommendations, or recommended by persons, who do not know how else to dispose of or provide for them; men of great ambition, who would sacrifice every thing to promote their own personal glory; or mere spies, who are sent here to obtain a thorough knowledge of our situation and circumstances, in the execution of which, I am persuaded, some of them are faithful emissaries, as I do not believe a single matter escapes unnoticed, or unadvised at a foreign court.

To Gouverneur Morris, July 24, 1778   *Writings Vol. 12 p. 227*

UNDUE PROMINENCE OF FOREIGNERS

... The ambition of these men (I do not mean of the Messrs. Nevilles in particular, but of the Natives of their Country and Foreigners in general) is unlimited and unbounded; and the singular instances of rank, which have been conferred upon them, in but too many cases, have occasioned general dissatisfaction and general complaint. The feelings of our own Officers have been much hurt by it, and their ardour and love for the service greatly damped. Should a like proceeding still be practised, it is not easy to say what extensive murmurings and consequences may ensue.

To Henry Laurens, July 24, 1778   *Writings Vol. 12 p. 224*

AMERICAN NATIONAL PREDILECTIONS

... I trust you think me so much a Citizen of the World, as to believe that I am not easily warped or led away, by attachments merely local or American; Yet, I confess, I am not entirely without them, nor does it appear to me that they are unwarrantable, if confined within proper limits. Fewer promotions in the foreign line, would have been productive of more harmony, and made our warfare more agreeable to all parties. The frequency of them, is the source of jealousy and of disunion. We have many, very many, deserving Officers, who are not opposed to merit wheresoever it is found, nor insensible of the advantages derived from a long service in an experienced Army, nor to the principles of policy.   Where any of these principles mark the way to rank, I am persuaded, they yield a becoming and willing acquiescence; but where they are not the basis, they feel severely. I will dismiss the subject, knowing with you, I need not labour, either a case of Justice, or of policy.

To Henry Laurens, July 24, 1778   *Writings Vol. 12 p. 224*

THE NATIONAL POLICY AS TO FOREIGNERS

... it is not the policy of this Country to employ Aliens, where it can well be avoided, either in the Civil or Military walks of life.

To John Quincy Adams, January 20, 1799   *Writings Vol. 37 p. 99*

HIRING BRITISH DESERTERS

... I need not enlarge upon the danger of substituting as Soldiers, men who have given a glaring proof of a treacherous disposition, and who are bound to us by no motives of attachment, to Citizens, in whom the ties of Country, kindred, and some times property, are so many securities for their fidelity. The evils, with which this measure is pregnant, are obvious, and of such a serious nature, as makes it necessary not only to stop the

George Washington Esq. by David Edwin after Gilbert Stuart. Published by T. B. Freeman, Philadelphia, May 1, 1798.

farther progress of it, but likewise to apply a retrospective Remedy, and, if possible, annul it, as far as it has been carried into effect.

To James Bowdoin, March 17, 1778   *Writings Vol. 11 p. 98*

ENLISTING PRISONERS OF WAR

... in my opinion, it is neither consistent with the Rules of War, nor politic, nor can I think that because our Enemies have committed an unjustifiable action by inticing and in some instances intimidating our men into their service, we ought to follow their Example.

To the Board of War, November 30, 1776   *Writings Vol. 6 p. 317*

ENLISTING DESERTERS

... I never gave you any encouragement to inlist deserters, because I had ever found them of the greatest injury to the Service, by debauching our own Men and had therefore given positive orders to all recruiting Officers, not to inlist them upon any terms. The Congress have since made an express Resolve against it, and also against inlisting prisoners.

To Charles Armand-Tuffin, March 25, 1778   *Writings Vol. 11 p. 148*

ENLISTING FREE NEGROES

... It has been represented to me, that the free Negroes who have served in this Army, are very much disatisfied at being discarded. As it is to be apprehended that they may seek employ in the Ministerial Army, I have presumed to depart from the Resolution respecting them and have given licence for their being enlisted.

To the President of Congress, December 31, 1775   *Writings Vol. 4 p. 195*

ARMING SLAVES

... The policy of our arming Slaves is, in my opinion, a moot point, unless the enemy set the example.

To Henry Laurens, March 20, 1779   *Writings Vol. 14 p. 267*

TREATMENT OF PRISONERS

... It is not my wish that Severity should be exercised towards any, whom the fortune of War has thrown, or, shall throw into our hands. On the Contrary, It is my desire that the utmost Humanity should be shewn them. I am convinced the latter has been the prevailing line of Conduct to Prisoners. There has been instances in which some have met with less Indulgence than could have been wished, owing to a refractory conduct and a

disregard of Paroles. If there are other Instances, in which a Strict regard to propriety has not been observed, they have not come to my knowledge.
To Sir William Howe, November 9, 1776   *Writings Vol. 6 p. 260*

THE HESSIANS

... I advised the Council of Safety to separate them from their Officers, and canton them in the German Counties. If proper pains are taken to convince them, how preferable the Situation of their Countrymen, the Inhabitants of those Counties is to theirs, I think they may be sent back in the Spring, so fraught with a love of Liberty and property too, that they may create a disgust to the Service among the remainder of the foreign Troops and widen that Breach which is already opened between them and the British.
To Robert Morris, George Clymer, and George Walton, January 1, 1777
Writings Vol. 6 p. 464

... One thing I must remark in favor of the Hessians, and that is, that our people who have been prisoners generally agree that they receive much kinder treatment from them, than from the British Officers and Soldiers.
To Samuel Chase, February 5, 1777   *Writings Vol. 7 p. 108*

COMFORT OF PRISONERS

... I enjoy too much pleasure in softening the Hardships of Captivity, to with-hold any comfort from Prisoners; and beg you to do me the Justice to conclude, that no Requisition of this Nature, that should be made, will ever be denied.
To Leopold Phillip Von Heister, May 13, 1777   *Writings Vol. 8 p. 58*

... Unnecessary severity and every species of insult, I despise, and I trust none will ever have just reason to censure me in this respect.
To Sir William Howe, June 10, 1777   *Writings Vol. 8 p. 221*

EXCHANGE OF PRISONERS

... Were an Opinion once to be established, and the Enemy and their Emissaries know very well how to inculcate it, if they are furnished with a plausible Pretext, that we designedly avoided an Exchange, it would be a Cause of Dissatisfaction and Disgust to the Country and to the Army; of Resentment and Desperation to our captive Officers and Soldiers. To say nothing of the Importance of not hazarding our national Character, but upon the most solid Grounds, especially in our Embryo-state, from the Influence it may have on our Affairs abroad; it may not be a little dangerous, to beget in the minds of our own Countrymen, a Suspicion that we do not pay the strictest Observance to the Maxims of Honor and good Faith.

To the President of Congress, March 8, 1778   *Writings Vol. 11 p. 41*

... Imputations of this Nature, would have tendency to unnerve our Operations, by diminishing that Respect and Confidence, which are essential to be placed in those who are at the Head of Affairs, either in the civil or military Line. This, added to the Prospect of hopeless Captivity would be a great Discouragement to the Service. The ill Consequences of both would be immense, by increasing the Causes of Discontent in the Army, which are already too numerous, and many of which are in a great measure unavoidable, by fortifying that unwillingness, which already appears too great, towards entering into the Service, and of Course, impeding the progress both of drafting and recruiting, by dejecting the Courage of the Soldiery from an Apprehension of the Horrors of Captivity, and finally by reducing those, whose Lot it is to drink the bitter Cup, to a Despair, which can only find Relief by renouncing their Attachments and engaging with their Captors. These Effects have already been experienced in part from the Obstacles that have hitherto lain in the Way of Exchanges; but if these Obstacles were once to seem the Result of System, they would become tenfold. Nothing has operated more disagreeably upon the Minds of the Militia, than the Fear of Captivity on the Footing it has heretofore stood. What would be their Reasonings, if it should be thought to stand upon a worse.

To the President of Congress, March 8, 1778   *Writings Vol. 11 p. 42*

EXCHANGE OF OFFICERS

... I am convinced that more mischief has been done by the British Officers who have been prisoners, than by any other set of People; during their Captivity they have made Connections in the Country, they have confirmed the disaffected, converted many ignorant people, and frightened the luke warm and timid by their Stories of the power of Britain. I hope a general exchange is not far off, by which means we shall get rid of all that set of People, and I am convinced that we had better, in future, send all Officers in upon parole than keep them among us.

To John Armstrong, March 27, 1778   *Writings Vol. 11 p. 158*

C. INDIANS

THEIR CLAIM TO JUSTICE AND HUMANITY

... While the measures of Government ought to be calculated to protect its Citizens from all injury and violence, a due regard should be extended to those Indians whose happiness in the course of events so materially depends on the national justice and humanity of the United States.

To the Senate and the House of Representatives, August 7, 1789

Writings Vol. 30 p. 372

JUSTICE PLEDGED TO THEM

... the *basis* of our proceedings with the Indian Nations has been, and shall be *justice,* during the period in which I may have any thing to do in the administration of this government.

To Marquis de Lafayette, August 11, 1790   *Writings Vol. 31 p. 87*

AMICABLE INTERCOURSE WITH THEM

... It is sincerely to be desired that all need of coercion, in future, may cease; and that an intimate intercourse may succeed; calculated to advance the happiness of the Indians, and to attach them firmly to the United States. . . .That the Executive of the United States should be enabled to employ the means to which the Indians have been long accustomed for uniting their immediate Interests with the preservation of Peace. And that efficatious provision should be made for inflicting adequate penalties upon all those who, by violating their rights, shall infringe the Treaties, and endanger the peace of the Union.

Third Annual Address to Congress, October 25, 1791   *Writings Vol. 31 p. 398*

INDIAN LANGUAGES

... To know the affinity of tongues seems to be one step towards promoting the affinity of nations . . . . Should the present or any other efforts of mine to procure information respecting the different dialects of the Aborigines in America, serve to reflect a ray of light on the obscure subject of language in general, I shall be highly gratified. For I love to indulge the contemplation of human nature in a progressive state of improvement and melioration; and if the idea would not be considered visionary and chimerical, I could fondly hope, that the present plan of the great Potentate of the North* might, in some measure, lay the foundation for that assimilation of language, which, producing assimilation of manners and interests, which, should one day remove many of the causes of hostility from amongst mankind.

To Marquis de Lafayette, January 10, 1788   *Writings Vol. 29 p. 374*

---

*The Empress of Russia, Catharine the Second, who was compiling a Universal Dictionary. She obtained, through Washington, vocabularies of the Delaware and Shawnee languages.

PEACE WITH INDIANS

... A disposition to peace in these people can only be ascribed to an apprehension of danger and would last no longer than till it was over and an opportunity offered to resume their hostility with safety and success. This makes it necessary that we should endeavour to punish them severely for what has past; and by an example of rigor intimidate them in future.

To the President of Congress, May 3, 1779   *Writings Vol. 14 p. 484*

INDIAN TRADE

... a trade with the Indians should be upon such terms, and transacted by men of such principles, as would at the same time turn out to the reciprocal advantage of the colony and the Indians, and which would effectually remove those bad impressions, that the Indians received from the conduct of a set of rascally fellows, divested of all faith and honor, and give us such an early opportunity of establishing an interest with them, as would be productive of the most beneficial consequences, by getting a large share of the fur-trade, not only of the Ohio Indians, but, in time, of the numerous nations possessing the back countries westward of it. And to prevent this advantageous commerce from suffering in its infancy, by the sinister views of designing, selfish men of the different provinces, I humbly conceive it absolutely necessary that commissioners from each of the colonies be appointed to regulate the mode of that trade, and fix it on such a basis, that all the attempts of one colony undermining another, and thereby weakening and diminishing the general system might be frustrated.

To Francis Fauquier, December 2, 1758   *Writings Vol. 2 p. 313*

PURCHASE OF INDIAN LANDS

... there is nothing to be obtained by an Indian War but the Soil they live on and this can be had by purchase at less expence, and without that bloodshed, and those distresses which helpless Women and Children are made partakers of in all kinds of disputes with them.

To James Duane, September 7, 1783   *Writings Vol. 27 p. 140*

PRESENTS TO INDIANS

... the plan of annual presents in an abstract view, unaccompanied with other measures, is not the best mode of treating ignorant Savages, from whose hostile conduct we experience much distress; but it is not to be overlooked, and they, in turn, are not without serious causes of complaint, from the encroachments which are made on their lands by our people; who are not to be restrained by any law now in being, or likely to

be enacted. They, poor wretches, have no Press thro' which their griev-
ances are related; and it is well known, that when one side only of a Story
is heard, and often repeated, the human mind becomes impressed with it,
insensibly. The annual presents however, which you allude to, are not
given so much with a view to purchase peace, as by way of retribution for
injuries, not otherwise to be redressed.

To Edmund Pendleton, January 22, 1795   *Writings Vol. 34 p. 99*

... such is the nature of Indians, that nothing will prevent their going
where they have any reason to expect presents, and their cravings are in-
satiable.

To Francis Halkett, May 11, 1758   *Writings Vol. 2 p. 199*

RESIDENT INDIAN AGENTS

... To enable, by competent rewards, the employment of qualified and
trusty persons to reside among them, as agents, would also contribute to
the preservation of peace and good neighbourhood. If, in addition to
these expedients, an eligible plan could be devised for promoting civilization among the friendly tribes, and for carrying on trade with them, upon
a scale equal to their wants, and under regulations calculated to protect
them from imposition and extortion, its influence in cementing their interests with our's could not be considerable.

Fourth Annual Address to Congress, November 6, 1792 Writings Vol. 32 p. 208

INDIAN DRESS: ITS ADOPTION IN THE ARMY

... My Men are very bare of Cloaths (Regimentals I mean), and I have no
prospect of a Supply; this want, so far from my regretting during this
Campaigne, that were I left to pursue my own Inclinations I wou'd not
only order the Men to adopt the Indian dress, but cause the Officers to do
it also, and be the first to set the example myself. Nothing but the uncer-
tainty of its taking with the General causes me to hesitate a moment at
leaving my Regimentals at this place, and proceeding as light as any Indian in the Woods. 'Tis an unbecoming dress, I confess, for an officer; but
convenience rather than shew, I think shou'd be consulted. The reduction
of Bat Horses alone, is sufficient to recommend it; for nothing is more
certain than that less baggage will be requir'd and that the Publick will be
benifitted in proportion.

To Henry Bouquet, July 3, 1758   *Writings Vol. 2 p. 229*

... It is evident, Sold'rs in that trim are better able to carry their Provisions; are fitted for the active Service we must engage in; less liable to sink
under the fatiegues of a March; and by this means, get rid of much bag-

gage that wou'd consequently, if carri'd protract our line of March; this, and not whim or caprice, are really my reasons for ordering them into it.

To Henry Bouquet, July 13, 1758   *Writings Vol. 2 p. 235*

MODE OF INDIAN WARFARE

... However absurd it may appear, it is nevertheless certain, that five hundred Indians have it more in their power to annoy the inhabitants, then ten times their number of regulars. For besides the advantageous way they have of fighting in the woods, their cunning and craft are not to be equalled, neither their activity and indefatigable sufferings. They prowl about like wolves, and, like them, do their mischief by stealth. They depend upon their dexterity in hunting and upon the cattle of the inhabitants for provisions.

To Robert Dinwiddie, April 7, 1756   *Writings Vol. 1 p. 300*

THE WAR TO BE CARRIED INTO THEIR OWN COUNTRY

... My Ideas of contending with the Indians have been uniformly the same, and I am clear in opinion, that the most economical (tho' this may also be attended with great expence) as well as the most effectual mode of opposing them, where they can make incursions upon us, is to carry the war into their own Country. For supported on the one hand by, the British, and enriching themselves with the spoils of our people, they have every thing to gain and nothing to lose, while we act on the defensive, whereas the direct reverse would be the consequence of an offensive war on our part.

To James Duane, January 11, 1779   *Writings Vol. 13 p. 501*

MARKSMEN

... great Care should be observed in choosing active Marksmen; the manifest Inferiority of inactive Persons, unused to Arms, in this kind of Service, although equal in Numbers, to lively Persons who have practised Hunting is inconceivable. The Chance against them is more than two to one.

To Robert Dinwiddie, April 16, 1756   *Writings Vol. 1 p. 313*

MODE OF ATTACKING INDIANS

... I beg leave to suggest as general rules that ought to govern your operations, to make rather than receive attacks attended with as much impetuosity, shouting and noise as possible, and to make the troops act in as loose and dispersed a way as is consistent with a proper degree of government concert and mutual support. It should be previously impressed upon the minds of the men when ever they have an opportunity, to rush on with the warhoop and fixed bayonet. Nothing will disconcert and terrify the Indians more than this.

To John Sullivan, May 31, 1779   *Writings Vol. 15 p. 190*

EMPLOYMENT OF INDIANS, IN WAR

... by ... a Resolve of Congress, that I am empowered to employ a body of four hundred Indians, if they can be procured upon proper terms. Divesting them of the Savage customs exercised in their Wars against each other, I think they may be made of excellent use, as scouts and light troops, mixed with our own Parties. I propose to raise about one half the number among the Southern and the remainder among the Northern Indians. I have sent Colo Nathl. Gist, who is well acquainted with the Cherokees and their Allies, to bring as many as he can from thence, and I must depend upon you to employ suitable persons to procure the stipulated number or as near as may be from the Northern tribes. The terms made with them should be such as you think we can comply with, and persons well acquainted with their language, manners and Customs and who have gained an influence over them should accompany them.

To the Commissioners of Indian Affairs, March 13, 1778 Writings Vol. 11 p. 76

D. THE NAVY

COMMERCE AND THE NAVY

... To an active external Commerce, the protection of a Naval force is indispensable.

Eighth Annual Address to Congress, December 7, 1796   Writings Vol. 35 p. 314

SHIPS OF WAR

... Will it not then be adviseable, to begin without delay, to provide, and lay up the materials for the building and equipping of Ships of War; and to proceed in the Work by degrees, in proportion as our resources shall render it practicable without inconvenience; so that a future War of Europe, may not find our Commerce in the same unprotected state, in which it was found by the present.

Eighth Annual Address to Congress, December 7, 1796   Writings Vol. 35 p. 314

NATIONAL IMPORTANCE OF A NAVAL FORCE

... it is in our own experience, that the most sincere Neutrality is not a sufficient guard against the depredation of Nations at War. To secure re-

G. Washington after Joseph Wright, [1794]. Joseph Wright's striking profile of Washington, based on his life studies, was widely copied in prints, medallions, relief cuts and medals in America and in Europe.

spect to a Neutral Flag, requires a Naval force, organized, and ready to vindicate it, from insult or aggression. This may even prevent the necessity of going to War, by discouraging belligerent Powers from committing such violations of the rights of the Neutral party, as may first or last, leave no other option.

Eighth Annual Address to Congress, December 7, 1796   Writings Vol. 35 p. 314

A NAVAL FORCE IN THE MEDITERRANEAN

... From the best information I have been able to obtain, it would seem as if our trade to the mediterranean, without a protecting force, will always be insecure; and our Citizens exposed to the calamities from which numbers of them have but just been relieved.

Eighth Annual Address to Congress, December 7, 1796   Writings Vol. 35 p. 314

THE GRADUAL CREATION OF A NAVY

... These considerations invite the United States, to look to the means, and to set about the gradual creation of a Navy. The increasing progress of their Navigation, promises them, at no distant period, the requisite supply of Seamen; and their means, in other respects, favour the undertaking. It is an encouragement, likewise, that their particular situation, will give weight and influence to a moderate Naval force in their hands.

Eighth Annual Address to Congress, December 7, 1796   Writings Vol. 35 p. 314

E. NATIONAL DEFENSE

MEASURES FOR DEFENSE

... To be prepared for War is one of the most effectual means of preserving peace.

First Annual Address, January 8, 1790   *Writings Vol. 30 p. 491*

NATIONAL MILITARY DISCIPLINE

... A free people ought not only to be armed but disciplined; to which end a uniform and well digested plan is requisite ....

First Annual Address, January 8, 1790   *Writings Vol. 30 p. 491*

HOME MILITARY SUPPLIES

... And their safety and interest require, that they should promote such manufactories, as tend to render them independent on others for essential, particularly for military supplies.

First Annual Address, January 8, 1790   *Writings Vol. 30 p. 491*

A SYSTEM OF NATIONAL DEFENSE

... The safety of the United States, under Divine protection, ought to rest on the basis of systematic and solid arrangements; exposed as little as possible to the hazard of fortuitous circumstances.

To the Senate and the House of Representatives, October 25, 1791

Writings Vol. 31 p. 403

A CONDITION OF DEFENSE

... I cannot recommend to your notice measures for the fulfilment of *our* duties to the rest of the world, without again pressing upon you the necessity of placing ourselves in a condition of compleat defence, and of exacting from *them* the fulfilment of *their* duties toward *us*.

Fifth Annual Address to Congress, December 3, 1793   Writings Vol. 33 p. 165

READINESS FOR WAR

... The United States ought not to endulge a persuasion, that, contrary to the order of human events, they will for ever keep at a distance those painful appeals to arms, with which the history of every other nation abounds. There is a rank due to the United States among Nations, which will be withheld, if not absolutely lost, by the reputation of weakness. If we desire to avoid insult, we must be able to repel it; if we desire to secure peace, one of the most powerful instruments of our rising prosperity, it must be known, that we are at all times ready for War.

Fifth Annual Address to Congress, December 3, 1793   Writings Vol. 33 p. 165

OFFENSIVE OPERATIONS

... offensive operations, often times is the *surest,* if not the *only* (in some cases), means of defence.

To John Trumbull, June 25, 1799   *Writings Vol. 37 p. 250*

ATTACK, OFTEN THE BEST DEFENSE

... It has been very properly the policy of our Government to cultivate peace. But in contemplating the possibility of our being driven to unqualified War, it will be wise to anticipate, that frequently the most effectual way to defend is to attack.

To the Secretary of War, December 13, 1798   *Writings Vol. 37 p. 37*

III.
Social Maxims

SOCIAL MAXIMS

———————————— ⇒⇐ ————————————

Sometime before his 16th birthday, young George Washington copied down 110 "Rules of Civility and Decent Behaviour in Company and Conversation" as part of a school exercise. Washington, who did not enjoy the social advantages which came with English schooling, was a self-taught Virginia gentleman. His half brother Lawrence had attended Appleby School in England and married into the socially prominent Fairfax family of Belvoir. As a teenager, George was an attentive student of the proper social graces he saw exhibited at various Fairfax gatherings and no doubt received useful instruction from his adored sibling.

The period from George and Martha Washington's wedding in 1759 until the First Continental Congress in 1774 has been referred to as the "golden years" at Mount Vernon. During this time George Washington was relatively free from public commitments. Aside from trips to Williamsburg where he represented his constituents as a member of the House of Burgesses, he could play the part of the gentleman farmer. His diaries illustrate, in Washington's words, "where and how my time is spent." During the 1760s, particularly, there are numerous entries describing fox hunting (his favorite pastime), card playing, and dining at Mount Vernon with fellow members of his social stature. Among other entertainments, Washington also frequented balls and attended the theatre.

Mount Vernon's hospitality was known far and wide. The Washingtons, who gained a reputation as ever-gracious and amiable hosts, seldom allowed loss of privacy or expenditure of personal funds to restrict their entertainment of guests. In 1786, Washington recorded in his diary that he had welcomed over 300 visitors that year to Mount Vernon, which he later described as a "well resorted tavern." This hospitality continued during the presidency, although for practical purposes, the Washington's open-door policy was somewhat more restrained. Martha Washington, for instance, held levees (receptions) on Friday evenings when "respectable" ladies and gentlemen would visit with the First Lady. Occasionally, the President would attend as well.

Despite the glamour that may have accompanied a man in Washington's position, the master of Mount Vernon much preferred life at home over the battlefield or the seat of government. "Under the shadow of my own Vine and my own Fig-tree," wrote Washington, did he find his greatest satisfaction. He called the life of a farmer "the most delectable," riding daily to oversee the management of the five farms which made up the Mount Vernon estate. His "rural amusements" included experimenting with over 60 crops in his lifetime, harvesting herring and shad from the abundant Potomac River, and then, as many a self-sufficient Virginia farmer, packing and shipping his products to domestic and foreign markets. Unfortunately, public duty prevented Washington from fully enjoying the tranquil domestic life offered at Mount Vernon. From the time he first settled at his Potomac estate in 1754 until his death in 1799, Washington spent nearly 20 of these years away from home tending to military or political obligations.

A. FRIENDSHIP

LOVE AND GRATITUDE OF A FRIEND

... Your forward zeal in the cause of liberty; Your singular attachment to this infant World; Your ardent and persevering efforts, not only in America but since your return to France to serve the United States; Your polite attention to Americans, and your strict and uniform friendship for *me*, has ripened the first impressions of esteem and attachment which I imbibed for you into such perfect love and gratitude that neither time nor absence can impair.

To Marquis de Lafayette, September 30, 1779   *Writings Vol. 16 p. 369*

PARTING EMOTIONS

... In the moment of our separation upon the road as I travelled, and every hour since, I felt all that love, respect and attachment for you, with which length of years, close connexion and your merits have inspired me. I often asked myself, as our carriages distended, whether that was the last sight, I ever should have of you? And tho' I wished to say no, my fears answered yes. I called to mind the days of my youth, and found they had long since fled to return no more; that I was now descending the hill, I had been 52 years climbing, and that tho' I was blessed with a good constitution, I was of a short lived family, and might soon expect to be entombed in the dreary mansions of my father's. These things darkened the shades and gave a gloom to the picture, consequently to my prospects of seeing you again: but I will not repine, I have had my day.

To Marquis de Lafayette, December 8, 1784   *Writings Vol. 28 p. 7*

PERPETUITY OF FRIENDSHIP

... it is my wish, the mutual friendship and esteem which have been planted and fostered in the tumult of public life, may not wither and die in the serenity of retirement ... we shou'd rather amuse our evening hours of Life in cultivating the tender plants, and bringing them to perfection, before they are transplanted to a happier clime.

To Jonathan Trumbull, Junior, January 5, 1784   *Writings Vol. 27 p. 294*

FRIENDLY ADVICE

... the opinion and advice of my friends I receive at all times as a proof of their friendship and am thankful when they are offered.

To Robert R. Livingston, June 29, 1780   *Writings Vol. 19 p. 91*

NATURE OF TRUE FRIENDSHIP

... true friendship is a plant of slow growth, and must undergo and withstand the shock of adversity before it is entitled to the appellation.

To Bushrod Washington, January 15, 1783   *Writings Vol. 26 p. 39*

ACTIONS, NOT WORDS

... A slender acquaintance with the world must convince every man that actions, not words are the true criterion of the attachment of his friends, and that the most liberal professions of good-will are very far from being the surest marks of it, I should be happy that my own experience had afforded fewer examples of the little dependance to be placed on them.

To John Sullivan, December 15, 1779   *Writings Vol. 17 p. 266*

PROFESSIONS OF FRIENDSHIP

... the arts of dissimulation. These I despise, and my feelings will not permit me to make professions of friendship to the man I deem my Enemy, and whose system of conduct forbids it.

To the President of Congress, January 2, 1778   *Writings Vol. 10 p. 249*

LETTERS OF FRIENDSHIP

... It is not the letters from my friends which give me trouble, or adds ought to my perplexity ... to corrispond with those I love is among my highest gratifications.

To Henry Knox, January 5, 1785   *Writings Vol. 28 p. 23*

... Letters of friendship require no study, the communications are easy, and allowances are expected, and made.

To Henry Knox, January 5, 1785   *Writings Vol. 28 p. 24*

Sacred to Patriotism, engraving on linen after Cornelius Tiebout and Charles Buxton, Glasgow, Scotland, 1819. The background depicts Bowling Green, New York at the time of the British evacuation, with an empty pedestal where a statue of George III formerly stood. Washington stands on a pedestal in the foreground as a symbolic replacement for the king, surrounded by symbols of his military and political achievements.

HOSPITALITY OF FRIENDSHIP

... If the assurances of the sincerest esteem and affection: if the varieties of uncultivated nature; the novelty of exchanging the gay and delightful scenes of Paris with which you are surrounded, for the rural amusements of a country in its infancy; if the warbling notes of the feathered songsters on our Lawns and Meads, can for a moment make you forget the melody of the Opera, and the pleasure of the Court, these, all invite you to give us this honour, and the opportunity of expressing to you personally, those sentiments of attachment and love with which you have inspired us.

To Marchionesse de la Lafayette, May 10, 1786   Writings Vol. 28 p. 418

... I will only repeat to you the assurances of my friendship, and of the pleasure I shou'd feel in seeing you in the shade of those trees which my hands have planted, and which by their rapid growth, at once indicate a knowledge of my declination, and their disposition to spread their mantles over me, before I go hence to return no more, for this, their gratitude, I will nurture them while I stay.

To Chevalier de Chastellux, June 2, 1784   *Writings Vol. 27 p. 413*

FRIENDSHIP IN ADVERSITY

... My friendship for his father [Lafayette] so far from being diminshd has encreased in the ratio of his misfortunes.

To George Cabot, September 7, 1795   *Writings Vol. 34 p. 300*

RENEWAL OF FRIENDSHIP'S COVENANT

... The friendship I have conceived for you will not be impaired by absence, but it may be no unpleasing circumstance to brighten the Chain, by a renewal of the Covenant.

To Henry Knox, February 20, 1784   *Writings Vol. 27 p. 341*

PERSONAL FRIENDSHIP AND POLITICAL DISAGREEMENT

... The friendship I ever professed, and felt for you, met with no diminution from the difference in our political Sentiments. I know the rectitude of my own intentions, and believing in the sincerity of yours, lamented, though I did not condemn, your renunciation of the creed I had adopted. Nor do I think any person, or power, ought to do it, whilst your conduct is not opposed to the general Interest of the people and the measures they are pursuing; the latter, that is our actions, depending upon ourselves, may be controuled, while the powers of thinking originating in higher causes, cannot always be moulded to our wishes.

To Bryan Fairfax, March 1, 1778   *Writings Vol. 11 p. 2*

B. BENEVOLENCE

SOCIAL COURTESY

... Be courteous to all, but intimate with few, and let those few be well tried before you give them your confidence.

To Bushrod Washington, January 15, 1783   *Writings Vol. 26 p. 39*

COMPANY

... the Company in which you will improve most, will be least expensive to you.

To Bushrod Washington, January 15, 1783   *Writings Vol. 26 p. 39*

SHAKING OFF ACQUAINTANCES

... It is easy to make acquaintances, but very difficult to shake them off, however irksome and unprofitable they are found after we have once committed ourselves to them.

To Bushrod Washington, January 15, 1783   *Writings Vol. 26 p. 39*

DIFFIDENCE

... submit your sentiments with diffidence. A dictorial Stile, although it may carry conviction, is always accompanied with disgust.

To Bushrod Washington, November 10, 1787   *Writings Vol. 29 p. 313*

THE GOLDEN RULE

... it is a maxim with me not to ask what under similar circumstances, I would not grant.

To the Emperor of Germany, May 15, 1796   *Writings Vol. 35 p. 45*

DEVOTION TO THE PEOPLE

... There is nothing I have more at Heart, than to discharge the great duties incumbent on me with the strictest Attention to the Ease and Convenience of the People.

To Thomas Wharton, Junior, March 7, 1778   *Writings Vol. 11 p. 45*

NATIONAL, DISTINGUISHED FROM PERSONAL, HOSTILITY

... I was opposed to the policy of G: B; and became an enemy to her measures; but I always distinguished between a Cause and Individuals; and while the latter supported their opinion upon liberal and generous grounds, personally, I never could be an enemy to them.

To John Joiner Ellis, July 10, 1783   *Writings Vol. 27 p. 56*

DIFFERENCE OF OPINION, NO CRIME

... Men's minds are as varient as their faces, and, where the motives to their actions are pure, the operation of the former is no more to be imputed to them as a crime, than the appearance of the latter; for both, being the work of nature, are equally unavoidable.

To Benjamin Harrison, March 9, 1789   *Writings Vol. 30 p. 223*

... A difference of opinion on political points is not to be imputed to Freemen as a fault; since it is to be presumed that they are all actuated by an equally laudable and sacred regard for the liberties of their Country. If the mind is so formed in different persons as to consider the same object to be somewhat different in its nature and consequences as it happens to be placed in different points of view; and if the oldest, the ablest, and the most virtuous Statesmen have often differed in judgment, as to the best forms of Government, we ought, indeed rather to rejoice that so much has been effected, than to regret that more could not all at once be accomplished.

To the Governor and Council of North Carolina, June 19, 1789

Writings Vol. 30 p. 347

DUTIES OF THE MINORITY

... To be disgusted at the decision of questions because they are not consonant to your own ideas, and to withdraw ourselves from public assemblies, or to neglect our attendance at them upon suspicion that there is a party formed who are enimical to our Cause, and to the true interest of our Country is wrong because these things may originate in a difference of opinion; but supposing the fact is otherwise and that our suspicions are well founded it is the indispensable duty of every patriot to counteract them by the most steady and uniform opposition.

To John Parke Custis, February 28, 1781   *Writings Vol. 21 p. 318*

CHARITY

... Let your *heart* feel for the affliction, and distresses of every one; let your *hand* give in proportion to your purse; remembering always, the estimation of the Widows mite. But, that it is not every one who asketh, that deserveth charity; all however are worthy of the enquiry, or the deserving may suffer.

To Bushrod Washington, January 15, 1783   *Writings Vol. 26 p. 40*

... Let the Hospitality of the House, with respect to the poor, be kept up; Let no one go hungry away. If any of these kind of People should be in want of Corn, supply their necessities, provided it does not encourage them in idleness; and I have no objection to your giving my Money in Charity, to the Amount of forty or fifty Pounds a Year, when you think it well bestowed. What I mean, by having no objection, is, that it is my desire that it should be done. You are to consider that neither myself or Wife are now in the way to do these good Offices. In all other respects, I recommend it to you, and have no doubts, of your observing the greatest Economy and frugality; as I suppose you know that I do not get a farthing for my services here more than my Expenses; It becomes necessary, therefore, for me to be saving at home.

To Lund Washington, November 26, 1775   *Writings Vol. 4 p. 115*

COMPASSION FOR MAN AND BEAST

... they (the soldiers) have been (two or three times), days together, without Provisions; and once Six days without any of the Meat kind; could the poor Horses tell their tale, it would be in a strain still more lamentable, as numbers have actually died from pure want.

To John Cadwalader, March 20, 1778   *Writings Vol. 11 p. 117*

SUFFERERS IN THE INDIAN WARS

... The supplicating tears of the women, and moving petitions from the men, melt me into such deadly sorrow, that I solemnly declare, if I know my own mind, I could offer myself a willing sacrifice to the butchering enemy, provided that would contribute to the people's ease.

To Robert Dinwiddie, April 22, 1756   *Writings Vol. 1 p. 325*

WOMEN, CHILDREN, AND THE INFIRM

... When I consider that the City of New York, will in all human probability very soon be the Scene of a bloody Conflict; I cannot but view the great Numbers of Women, Children and infirm Persons remaining in it, with the most melancholy concern. ... It would relieve me from great anxiety, if your Honble. Body would Immediately deliberate upon it and form and execute some plan for their removal and relief; In which I will cooperate and assist to the utmost of my Power.

To the New York Legislature, August 17, 1776   *Writings Vol. 5 p. 444*

WIDOWS AND ORPHANS

... I am at a loss, however, for whose benefits to apply the little I can give, and into whose hands to place it; whether for the use of the fatherless

children and widows (made so by the late calamity) who may find it difficult, whilst Provisions, Wood and other necessaries are so dear, to support themselves; or to other and better purpose (if any) I know not and
therefore have taken the liberty of asking your advice.

To Reverend William White, December 31, 1793   *Writings Vol. 33 p. 221*

THE SICK

... The case of our Sick is also worthy of much consideration, their number by the returns form at least 1/4th. of the Army: Policy and humanity
require they should be made as comfortable as possible.

To the President of Congress, September 8, 1776   *Writings Vol. 6 p. 30*

KINDNESS TO PRISONERS OF WAR

... I have shew'd all the respect I co'd to them here, and have given some
necessary cloathing, by which I have disfurnish'd myself, for having
brought no more than two or three Shirts from Will's C'k that we might be
light I was ill provided to furnish them.

To Robert Dinwiddie, May 29, 1754   *Writings Vol. 1 p. 67*

... If Lord Chatham's Son should be in Canada and in any Way in your
Power, you are enjoined to treat him with all possible Deference and Respect. You cannot err in paying too much Honour to the Son of so illustrious a Character and so true a Friend to America. Any other Prisoners who
may fall into your Hands, you will treat with as much Humanity and kindness, as may be consistent with your own Safety and the public Interest.

Instructions to Colonel Benedict Arnold, September 14, 1775

Writings Vol. 3 p. 494

... Be very particular in restraining not only your own Troops, but the
Indians from all Acts of Cruelty and Insult, which will disgrace the American Arms, and irritate our Fellow Subjects against us.

Instructions to Colonel Benedict Arnold, September 14, 1775

Writings Vol. 3 p. 495

RETALIATION AND HUMANITY

... I really know not what to say on the subject of Retaliation. Congress
have it under consideration and we must await their determination. Of
this I am convinced, that of all Laws it is the most difficult to execute,
where you have not the transgressor himself in your possession. Humanity will ever interfere and plead strongly against the sacrifice of an innocent person for the guilt of another.

To Nathanael Greene, December 15, 1781   *Writings Vol. 23 p. 391*

PARDON OF CRIMINALS

... As your Honor were pleased to leave to my discretion to punish or pardon the criminals, I have resolved on the latter, since I find examples of so little weight, and since those poor unhappy criminals have undergone no small pain of body and mind, in a dark room, closely ironed!

To Robert Dinwiddie, August 27, 1757   *Writings Vol. 2 p. 122*

PUNCTILIOS OF HONOR

... Trifling punctilios should have no influence upon a man's conduct in such a case, and at such a time as this. ... If smaller matters do not yield to greater, If trifles, light as Air in comparison of what we are contending for, can withdraw or withhold Gentlemen from Service, when our all is at Stake and a single cast of the die may turn the tables, what are we to expect! It is not a common contest we are engaged in, every thing valuable to us depends upon the success of it, and the success upon a Steady and Vigorous exertion.

To William Woodford, March 3, 1777   *Writings Vol. 7 p. 240*

DUELING CONDEMNED

... The generous Spirit of Chivalry, exploded by the rest of the World, finds a refuge, My dear friend, in the sensibility of your Nation *only*. But it is in vain to cherish it, unless you can find Antagonists to support it; and however well adapted it might have been to the times in which it existed, in our days it is to be feared that your opponent, sheltering himself behind Modern opinion, and under his present public Character of Commissioner, would turn a virtue of such ancient date, into ridicule. Besides, supposing his Lordship accepted your terms, experience has proved, that chance is as often, as much concerned in deciding these matters as bravery, and always more than the justice of the Cause; I would not therefore have your life, by the remotest possibility, exposed, when it may be reserved for so many greater occasions. His Excellency the Admiral I flatter myself, will be in Sentimt. with me; and, as soon as he can spare you, send you to head Quarters, where I anticipate the pleasure of seeing you.

To Marquis de Lafayette, October 4, 1778   *Writings Vol. 13 p. 20*

... The coincidence between Your Excellency's sentiments, respecting the Marquis de la fayette's Cartel communicated in the letter with which you honored me the 20th. and those which I expressed to him on the same subject, are peculiarly flattering to me. I am happy to find that my disapporbation of this measure was founded on the same arguments which in Your Excellency's hands acquire new force and persuasion. I omitted neither serious reasoning nor pleasantry to divert him from a Scheme in which he could be so easily foiled, without having any credit given him by his antagonist for his generosity and sensibility. He intimated that Your Excellency did not discountenance it, and that he had pledged himself to the principal Officers of the french Squadron to carry it into execution; the charms of vindicating the honor of his country were irresistible; but besides he had in a manner committed himself and could not decently retract; I however continued to lay my friendly commands upon him to renounce his project; but I was well assured that if he determined to persevere in it, neither authority nor vigilance would be of any avail to prevent his message to Lord Carlisle. And though his ardour was an overmatch for my advice and influence, I console myself with the reflexion that his Ldship will not accept the challenge, and that while our friend gains all the applause which is due to him for wishing to become the Champion of his Country, he will be secure from the possibility of such dangers as my fears wd otherwise create for him, by those powerful barriers which shelter his ldship and which I am persuaded he will not in the present instance violate.

To Comte D'Estaing, October 24, 1778   *Writings Vol. 13 p. 142*

FELLOWSHIP OF THE FREE

... the Cause of Virtue and Liberty is Confined to no Continent or Climate, it comprehends within its capacious Limits, the Wise and good, however dispersed and seperated in Space or distance.

To the Inhabitants of the Island of Bermuda, September 6, 1775

Writings Vol. 3 p. 475

COMPREHENSIVE BENEVOLENCE

... we do not wish to be the only people who may taste the sweets of an equal and good government; we look with an anxious eye to the time, when happiness and tranquility shall prevail in your country, and when all Europe shall be freed from commotions, tumults, and alarms.

To Marquis de Lafayette, July 28, 1791   *Writings Vol. 31 p. 326*

C. DOMESTIC LIFE

THE HUSBANDMAN

... the life of a Husbandman of all others is the most delectable. It is honorable. It is amusing, and, with judicious management, it is profitable.

To Alexander Spotswood, February 13, 1788   *Writings Vol. 29 p. 414*

AT MOUNT VERNON, JUST AFTER HIS MARRIAGE

. . . I am now I believe fixd at this Seat with an agreeable Consort* for Life and hope to find more happiness in retirement than I ever experienc'd amidst a wide and bustling World.

To Richard Washington, September 20, 1759   *Writings Vol. 2 p. 337*

HOME

. . . I can truly say I had rather be at Mount Vernon with a friend or two about me, than to be attended at the Seat of Government by the Officers of State and the Representatives of every Power in Europe.

To David Stuart, June 15, 1790   *Writings Vol. 31 p. 54*

CONJUGAL AFFECTION

. . . I retain an unalterable affection for you which neither time or distance can change.

To Martha Washington, June 23, 1775   *Writings Vol. 3 p. 301*

. . . You may believe me, my dear Patsy, when I assure you, in the most solemn manner that, so far from seeking this appointment [commander in chief], I have used every endeavor in my power to avoid it, not only from my unwillingness to part with you and the family, but from a consciousness of its being a trust too great for my capacity, and that I should enjoy more real happiness in one month with you at home, than I have the most distant prospect of finding abroad, if my stay were to be seven times seven years.

To Martha Washington, June 18, 1775   *Writings Vol. 3 p. 293*

. . . I shall rely therefore, confidently on that Providence, which has heretofore preserved and been bountiful to me, not doubting but that I shall return safe to you in the fall. I shall feel no pain from the toil or the danger of the campaign; my unhappiness will flow from the uneasiness I know you will feel from being left alone.

To Martha Washington, June 18, 1775   *Writings Vol. 3 p. 294*

. . . I shall hope that my Friends will visit and endeavor to keep up the spirits of my Wife as much as they can, as my departure will, I know, be a cutting stroke upon her.

To John Augustine Washington, June 20, 1775   *Writings Vol. 3 p. 300*

*Washington married, on the sixth of January 1759, Mrs. Martha Dandridge Custis.

Washington in 1772 Aetatis 40 by J. W. Steel after Anson Dickinson, 1833. This portrait is based on the earliest known portrait of George Washington by Charles Willson Peale, now in the collection of Washington and Lee University.

PROVISION FOR HIS WIFE, IN CASE OF HIS DEATH

... To my dearly [be]loved wife Martha Washington [I] give and bequeath the use, profit [an]d benefit of my whole Estate, real and p[e]rsonal, for the term of her natural li[fe;] except such parts thereof as are s[pec]ifically disposed of hereafter ....

Will, July 9, 1799   *Writings Vol. 37 p. 275*

ADOPTION OF HIS WIFE'S GRANDCHILDREN

... it has always been my intention, since my expectation of having Issue has ceased, to consider the Grand children of my wife in the same light as I do my own relations, and to act a friendly part by them; more especially by the two whom we have reared from their earliest infancy.

Will, July 9, 1799   *Writings Vol. 37 p. 290*

FILIAL LOVE

... I am, Hon'd Madam Yr. most dutiful Son.

To Mary Ball Washington, July 18, 1755   *Writings Vol. 1 p. 152*

... If it is in my power to avoid going to the Ohio again, I shall, but if the Command is press'd upon me by the genl. voice of the Country, and offer'd upon such terms as can't be objected against, it wou'd reflect eternal dishonour upon me to refuse it; and that, I am sure must, or ought, to give you greater cause of uneasiness than my going in an honourable Com'd.

To Mary Ball Washington, August 14, 1755   *Writings Vol. 1 p. 159*

ELEGANT SIMPLICITY IN DOMESTIC LIFE

... Her [Mrs. Washington] wishes coincide with my own as to simplicity of dress, and everything which can tend to support propriety of character without partaking of the follies of luxury and ostentation.

To Catherine Macaulay Graham, January 9, 1790   *Writings Vol. 30 p. 498*

HIS PORTRAIT

... In for a penny, in for a pound is an old adage. I am so hackneyed to the touches of the Painters pencil, that I am now altogether at their beck, and sit like patience on a Monument whilst they are delineating the lines of my face. It is proof among many others of what habit and custom can effect. At first I was as impatient at the request, and as restive under the operation, as a Colt is of the Saddle. The next time, I submitted very reluctantly, but with less flouncing. Now, no dray moves more readily to the Thill, than I do to the Painters Chair.

To Francis Hopkinson, May 16, 1785   *Writings Vol. 28 p. 140*

ANNIVERSARY OF HIS BIRTHDAY

The flattering distinction paid to the anniversary of my birthday is an honor for which I dare not attempt to express my gratitude. I confide in your Excellency's sensibility to interpret my feelings for this, and for the obliging manner in which you are pleased to announce it.

To Comte de Rochambeau, February 24, 1781　　　　　*Writings Vol. 21 p. 286*

THE PROPOSED MARRIAGE OF HIS WARD

... his [John Parke Custis'] youth, inexperience, and unripened Education, is, and will be insuperable obstacles in my eye, to the completion of the Marriage. As his Guardian, I conceive it to be my indispensable duty (to endeavor) to carry him through a regular course of Education, many branches of which, sorry I am to add, he is totally deficient of; and to guard his youth to a more advanced age before an Event, on which his own Peace and the happiness of another is to depend, takes place; not that I have any doubt of the warmth of his Affections, nor, I hope I may add, any fears of a change in them; but at present, I do not conceive that he is capable of bestowing that due attention to the Important consequences of a marriage State, which is necessary to be done by those, who are Inclin'd to enter into it; and of course, am unwilling he should do it till he is. If the Affection which they have avowd for each other is fixd upon a Solid Basis, it will receive no diminution in the course of two or three years, in which time he may prosecute his Studies, and thereby render himself more deserving of the Lady, and useful to Society; If unfortunately, (as they are both young) there should be an abatement of Affection on either side, or both, it had better precede, than follow after, Marriage. Delivering my Sentiments thus, will not, I hope, lead you into a belief that I am desirous of breaking off the Match; to postpone it, is all I have in view; for I shall recommend it to the young Gentleman with the warmth that becomes a man of honour, (notwithstanding he did not vouchsafe to consult either his Mother or me, on the occasion) to consider himself as much engaged to your Daughter as if the indissoluble Knot was tied; and, as the surest means of effecting this, to stick close to his Studies, (in which I flatter myself you will join me) by which he will, in a great measure, avoid those little Flirtations with other Girls which may, by dividing the Attention, contribute not a little to divide the Affection.

To Benedict Calvert, April 3, 1773　　　　　*Writings Vol. 3 p. 130*

ADVICE ON MATRIMONY

... if this should be the case, and she wants advice upon it; a Father and Mother, who are at hand, and competent to give it, are at the same time most proper to be consulted on so interesting an event. For my own part,

I never did, nor do I believe I ever shall give advice to a woman who is setting out on a matrimonial voyage; first, because I never could advise one to marry without her own consent; and secondly, because I know it is to no purpose to advise her to refrain, when she has obtained it. A woman very rarely asks an opinion or requires advice on such an occasion, 'till her resolution is formed; and then it is with the hope and expectation of obtaining a sanction, not that she means to be governed by your disapprobation, that she applies. In a word, the plain english of the application may be summed up in these words; "I wish you to think as I do; but if unhappily you differ from me in opinion, my heart, I must confess is fixed, and I have gone too far *now* to retract." . . . I will give her my opinion of the *measure*, not of the *man*, with candour, and to the following effect. I never expected you would spend the residue of your days in widowhood; but in a matter so important, and so interesting to yourself, children and connexions; I wish you would make a prudent choice; to do which, many considerations are necessary; such as the family and connexions of the man, his fortune (which is not the *most* essential in my eye), the line of conduct he has observed, and disposition and frame of his mind. You should consider, what prospect there is of his proving kind and affectionate to you; just, generous and attentive to your children; and, how far his connexions will be agreeable to you; for when they are once formed, agreeable or not, the die being cast, your fate is fixed.

To Lund Washington, September 20, 1783   *Writings Vol. 27 p. 157*

CONNUBIAL LIFE

. . . in my estimation more permanent and genuine happiness is to be found in the sequestered walks of connubial life, than in the giddy rounds of promiscuous pleasure, or the more tumultuous and imposing scenes of successful ambition.

To Charles Armand-Tuffin, August 10, 1786   *Writings Vol. 28 p. 514*

THE PRIVATE CITIZEN

. . . the great Searcher of human hearts is my witness, that I have no wish, which aspires beyond the humble and happy lot of living and dying a private citizen on my own farm.

To Charles Pettit, August 16, 1788   *Writings Vol. 30 p. 42*

DOMESTIC RETIREMENT

. . . As Peace and retirement are my ultimate aim, and the most pleasing and flattering hope of my Soul, every thing advansive of this end, contributes to my satisfaction, however difficult, and inconvenient in the attainment; and will reconcile any place and all circumstances to my feelings whilst I continue in Service.

To Joseph Reed, December 12, 1778   *Writings Vol. 13 p. 385*

. . . The great object for which I had the honor to hold an appointment in the Service of my Country, being accomplished, I am now preparing to resign it into the hands of Congress, and to return to that domestic retirement, which, it is well known, I left with the greatest reluctance, a Retirement, for which I have never ceased to sigh through a long and painful absence, and in which (remote from the noise and trouble of the World) I meditate to pass the remainder of life in a state of undisturbed repose.

Circular to the States, June 8, 1783   *Writings Vol. 26 p. 483*

. . . the hour of my resignation is fixed at twelve this day; after which I shall become a private Citizen on the Banks of the Potomack.

To Baron Steuben, December 23, 1783   *Writings Vol. 27 p. 283*

. . . The scene is at last closed. I feel myself eased of a load of public Care. I hope to spend the remainder of my Days in cultivating the affections of good men, and in the practice of the domestic Virtues.

To George Clinton, December 28, 1783   *Writings Vol. 27 p. 288*

DOMESTIC EASE

. . . From the clangor of arms and the bustle of a camp, freed from the cares of public employment, and the responsibility of office, I am now enjoying domestic ease under the shadow of my own Vine, and my own Fig tree; and in a small Villa, with the implements of Husbandry, and Lambkins around me, I expect to glide gently down the stream of life, 'till I am entombed in the dreary mansions of my Fathers.

To Marchioness de Lafayette, April 4, 1784   *Writings Vol. 27 p. 385*

. . . A month from this day, if I live to see the completion of it, will place me on the wrong (perhaps it would be better to say, on the advanced) side of my grand climacteric; and altho' I have no cause to complain of the want of health, I can religiously aver that no man was ever more tired of public life, or more devoutly wished for retirement, than I do.

To Edmund Pendleton, January 22, 1795   *Writings Vol. 34 p. 98*

TRANQUILITY

. . . under the shadow of my own Vine and my own Fig-tree, free from the bustle of a camp and the busy scenes of public life, I am solacing myself with those tranquil enjoyments, of which the Soldier who is ever in pursuit of fame, the Statesman, whose watchful days and sleepless nights are spent in devising schemes to promote the welfare of his own, perhaps the ruin of other countries, as if this globe was insufficient for us all, and the Courtier, who is always watching the countenance of his Prince, in hopes of catching a gracious smile, can have very little conception. I am not only retired from all public employments, but I am retiring within myself; and shall be able to view the solitary walk, and tread the paths of private life with heartfelt satisfaction. Envious of none, I am determined to be pleased with all; and this my dear friend, being the order for my march, I will move gently down the stream of life, until I sleep with my Fathers.

To Marquis de Lafayette, February 1, 1784   *Writings Vol. 27 p. 317*

THE GOOD CITIZEN

... No wish in my retirement can exceed that of seeing our Country happy; and I can entertain no doubt of its being so, if all of us act the part of good Citizens; contributing our best endeavours to maintain the Constitution, support the laws, and guard our Independence against all assaults from whatsoever quarter they may come. clouds may and doubtless often will in the vicissitudes of events, hover over our political concerns, but a steady adherence to these principles will not only dispel them but render our prospects the brighter by such temporary obscurities.

To the Citizens of Alexandria and its Neighborhood, March 23, 1797
Writings Vol. 35 p. 423

AGREEABLE RECOLLECTIONS

... the affection and attachment of my fellow citizens, through the whole period of my public employments, will be the subject of my most agreeable recollections: while the belief, which the affecting sentiments of the people of Massachusetts, expressed by their Senate and House of Representatives, with those of my fellow citizens in general, have inspired, that I have been the happy instrument of much good to my country and to mankind will be a source of unceasing gratitude to Heaven.

To the Massachusetts Senators, February 24, 1797   *Writings Vol. 35 p. 398*

RURAL EMPLOYMENTS

... My time is now occupied by rural amusements, in which I have great satisfaction; and my first wish is, altho' it is against the profession of arms and would clip the wings of some of you young soldiers who are soaring after glory, to see the whole world in peace, and the Inhabitants of it as one band of brothers, striving who should contribute most to the happiness of mankind.

To Charles Armand-Tuffin, October 7, 1785   *Writings Vol. 28 p. 289*

GEN. WASHINGTON takes Command of the
American Army at Cambridge July 3d 1775.

Genl. Washington by Tisdale for C. Smith, New York [1797].

... Rural employments while I am spared (which in the natural course of things cannot be long) will now take place of toil, responsibility, and the sollicitudes attending the walks of public life; and with vows for the peace, the happiness, and prosperity of a country in whose service the prime of my life hath been spent, and with best wishes for the tranquillity of all Nations, and all men, the scene will close; grateful to that Providence which has directed my steps, and shielded me in the various changes and chances, through which I have passed, from my youth to the present moment.

To Reverend William Gordon, October 15, 1797   *Writings Vol. 36 p. 49*

THE PATRIOT, AT HOME

... every day the encreasing weight of years admonishes me more and more, that the shade of retirement is as necessary to me as it will be welcome. Satisfied that if any circumstances have given peculiar value to my services, they were temporary, I have the consolation to believe, that while choice and prudence invite me to quit the political scene, patriotism does not forbid it.

Farewell Address, September 19, 1796   *Writings Vol. 35 p. 216*

... To have finished my public career to the satisfaction of my fellow-citizens, will, to my latest moments, be matter of pleasing reflection; and to find an evidence of this approbation among my neighbours and friends (some of whom have been the companions of my Juvenile years) will contribute not a little to highten the enjoyment.

To the Citizens of Alexandria and its Neighborhood, March 23, 1797

Writings Vol. 35 p. 423

IV.
Moral Maxims

Moral Maxims

To possess and retain the favorable opinion of his countrymen remained of utmost importance to George Washington. When he spoke of "reputation," Washington referred to his standing as a duty-bound citizen in the eyes of his fellow Americans.

At least twice in his career, Washington, in his mind, was forced to risk his reputation for the sake of the larger cause. When the General resigned his commission after the Revolutionary War in 1783, he vowed to "take my leave of all the employments of public life." However, just four years later his fellow statesmen were urging him to come out of retirement to serve as a delegate to the Constitutional Convention in Philadelphia. Even when his contemporaries argued that Washington's presence at the convention was vital to its success, Washington hesitated. As a duty-bound citizen, the retired general wanted to do what was best for the country. He felt that the challenge of formulating a new Constitution could be better handled by energetic young statesmen such as Alexander Hamilton and James Madison. Washington was also concerned that his reemergence in Philadelphia might well be viewed as inconsistent, since he had already declared his retirement from public life. Yet, when the delegates convened in Philadelphia in May 1787, Washington not only attended but also served as president of the Convention.

Two years later, when Washington was elected President, his reservations over his abilities to carry out the duties of chief executive caused him great concern. A lifelong commitment to duty—would it be washed away in a calamitous beginning to the new government? Despite his misgivings, Washington's dedication to duty superseded the preservation of his own reputation at these most critical junctures in early American history, as it had throughout his life.

As devotion to duty perched high on Washington's list of moral maxims, so did justice and temperance. As commander in chief of the Continental Army, Washington led by example. Even his critics admitted that Washington's renown as an equitable man was indisputable. Although punishments were meted out, Washington insisted that even the contemptible traitor's account be heard.

The General's men could also count on Washington's strict orders restricting gambling, drunkenness and profane language. In private life, no one enjoyed a fine glass of Madeira after dinner or betting a few pounds on cards more than Washington. Yet even at Mount Vernon, restraint was advisable. In the field, it was absolutely necessary.

Whether he was called upon to lead his nation's army or serve as head of its new government, Washington endeavored to "promote the progress" of human happiness by "inculcating the practice" of moral duty. One elusive issue, however, that continued to frustrate Washington until his dying days, was that of slavery. Even though the plantation economy dictated the use of slave labor, Washington, over the course of his life, realized that slavery was a moral wrong. His personal solution was to free his own slaves, which he provided for in his will. When addressing the broader issue, Washington believed that legislation should be passed authorizing the gradual emancipation of the slave population.

A. VIRTUE AND VICE

VIRTUE AND HAPPINESS

... since there is no truth more thoroughly established, than that there exists in the economy and course of nature, an indissoluble union between virtue and happiness, between duty and advantage, between the genuine maxims of an honest and magnanimous policy, and the solid rewards of public prosperity and felicity.

The First Inaugural Address, April 30, 1789   *Writings Vol. 30 p. 294*

HUMAN HAPPINESS AND MORAL DUTY

... the consideration that human happiness and moral duty are inseparably connected, will always continue to prompt me to promote the progress of the former, by inculcating the practice of the latter.

To the Bishops, Clergy, and Laity of the Protestant Episcopal Church in New York,
August 1789   *Writings Vol. 30 p. 383*

MORALITY AND CIVIL GOVERNMENT

... 'Tis substantially true, that virtue or morality is a necessary spring of popular government.

Farewell Address, September 19, 1796   *Writings Vol. 35 p. 229*

... Your love of liberty — your respect for the laws — your habits of industry — and your practice of the moral and religious obligations, are the strongest claims to national and individual happiness.

To the Inhabitants of the Town of Boston, October 27, 1789
                                              Writings Vol. 30 p. 453

TALENTS, WITHOUT VIRTUE

... without Virtue and without integrity the finest talents of the most brilliant accomplishments can never gain the respect or conciliate the esteem

Genl. George Washington. An early fictitious image published in William Russell's *The History of America from the Discovery of Columbus to the Conclusion of the Late War* (London, 1779).

of the truly valuable part of mankind.

To Bartholomew Dandridge, March 8, 1797   *Writings Vol. 35 p. 422*

IGNORANCE AND WICKEDNESS

... there is more wickedness than ignorance mixed in our Councils. ...
Ignorance and design are difficult to combat. Out of these proceed illiberal sentiments, *improper* jealousies, and a train of evil which oftentimes, in republican governments, must be sorely felt before they can be removed ... ignorance, being a fit soil for the latter to work in, tools are employed by them which a generous mind would disdain to use; and which nothing but time, and their own puerile or wicked productions can show the inefficacy and dangerous tendency of. I think often of our situation and view it with concern.

To the Secretary for Foreign Affairs, May 18, 1786   *Writings Vol. 28 p. 431*

GOOD SENSE AND HONESTY

... these are qualities too rare and too precious not to merit one's particular esteem.

To Marquis de Lafayette, February 7, 1788   *Writings Vol. 29 p. 409*

THE MOST ENVIABLE OF TITLES

... I hope I shall always possess firmness and virtue enough to maintain (what I consider the most enviable of all titles) the character of *an honest man.*

To Alexander Hamilton, August 28, 1788   *Writings Vol. 30 p. 67*

COMMON SENSE AND COMMON HONESTY

... It appears to me, that little more than common sense and common honesty, in the transactions of the community at large, would be necessary to make us a great and happy Nation. For it the general Government, lately adopted, shall be arranged and administered in such a manner as to acquire the full confidence of the American People, I sincerely believe, they will have greater advantages, from their Natual, moral and political circumstances, for public felicity, than any other People ever possessed.

To the Citizens of Baltimore, April 17, 1789   *Writings Vol. 30 p. 288*

POLITICAL EQUITY

... in all matters of great national moment, the only true line of conduct, in my opinion, is, dispassionately to compare the advantages and disadvantages of the measure proposed, and decide from the balance.

To Henry Lee, October 31, 1786   *Writings Vol. 29 p. 35*

CONVENIENCE AND FRIENDSHIP

... I can never think of promoting my convenience at the expense of your interest and inclination.

To Joseph Reed, November 20, 1775   *Writings Vol. 4 p. 104*

CONVENIENCE AND DUTY

... I shall never suffer private convenience to interfere with what I conceive to be my official duties.

To the Secretary of State, July 29, 1795   *Writings Vol. 34 p. 255*

HUMAN IMPERFECTION

... It is to be lamented however that great characters are seldom without a blot.

To Marquis de Lafayette, May 10, 1786   *Writings Vol. 28 p. 420*

... If the enlightened, and virtuous part of the Community will make allowances for my involuntary errors I will promise they shall have no cause to accuse me of wilful ones.

To Oliver Wolcott, February 1, 1796   *Writings Vol. 34 p. 447*

SENSE OF HONOR

... I feel every thing that hurts the Sensibility of a Gentleman.

To Marquis de Lafayette, September 1, 1778   *Writings Vol. 12 p. 382*

TREASON

... This [Arnold's treason] is an event that occasions me equal regret and mortification; but traitors are the growth of every country and in a revolution of the present nature, it is more to be wondered at, that the catalogue is so small than that there have been found a few.

To Comte de Rochambeau, September 27, 1780   *Writings Vol. 20 p. 97*

THE TRIAL OF VIRTUE

... Few men have virtue to withstand the highest bidder.

To Robert Howe, August 17, 1779   *Writings Vol. 16 p. 119*

DECEPTION

... I hate deception, even where the imagination only is concerned.

To Doctor John Cochran, August 16, 1779   *Writings Vol. 16 p. 116*

PALLIATING FAULTS

... I shall never attempt to paliate my own faults by exposing those of another.

To Joseph Reed, August 22, 1779   *Writings Vol. 16 p. 151*

INGRATITUDE

... nothing is a greater stranger to my Breast, or a Sin that my Soul ab-hors, than that black and detestable one Ingratitude.

To Robert Dinwiddie, May 29, 1754   *Writings Vol. 1 p. 60*

... ingratitude, which I hope will never constitute a part of my character, nor find a place in my bosom.

To Landon Carter, May 30, 1778   *Writings Vol. 11 p. 492*

SECRECY AND DISPATCH

... Secrecy and Dispatch must prove the Soul of success to Enterprise.

To David Cobb, June 30, 1781   *Writings Vol. 22 p. 292*

PRIVATE VIRTUE, AND MILITARY GLORY

... the private virtues of economy, prudence, and industry, will not be less amiable in civil life, than the more splendid qualities of valour, persever-ance, and enterprise were in the Field.

Farewell Orders to the Armies of the United States, November 2, 1783
Writings Vol. 27 p. 225

THE PASSIONS

... The various passions and motives, by which men are influenced are concomitants of fallibility, engrafted into our nature.

To Edmund Randolph, January 8, 1788   *Writings Vol. 29 p. 357*

BIDING THE TIME

... Time may unfold more, than prudence ought to disclose.

To Henry Lee, July 21, 1793   *Writings Vol. 33 p. 24*

MORAL CHARACTER

... a good moral character is the first essential in a man. ....It is therefore highly important that you should endeavor not only to be learned but virtuous.

To George Steptoe Washington, December 5, 1790   *Writings Vol. 31 p. 163*

B. APPROBATION AND CENSURE

APPROBATION OF THE WISE AND GOOD

... nothing in human life, can afford a liberal Mind, more rational and exquisite satisfaction, than the approbation of a Wise, a great and virtuous Man.

To Sarah Bache, January 15, 1781   *Writings Vol. 21 p. 102*

REPUTATION

... the good opinion of honest men, friends to freedom and well-wishers to mankind, wherever they may be born or happen to reside, is the only kind of reputation a wise man would ever desire.

To Edward Pemberton, June 20, 1788   *Writings Vol. 30 p. 1*

POPULAR FAVOR

... The accounts which you have given of the sentiments of the people respecting my conduct, is extremely flattering. Pray God, I may continue to deserve them, in the perplexed and intricate situation I stand in.

To Joseph Reed, December 15, 1775   *Writings Vol. 4 p. 166*

... To stand well in the estimation of ones Country, is a happiness that no rational creature can be insensible of.

To Joseph Reed, July 29, 1779   *Writings Vol. 16 p. 8*

DESERT, DISTINGUISHED FROM SUCCESS

... it will be a consolation to you to reflect that the thinking part of Mankind do not form their judgment from events; and that their equity will ever attach equal glory to those actions which deserve success, as to those which have been crowned with it. It is in the trying circumstances to which your Excellency has been exposed, that the virtues of a great Mind are displayed in their brightest lustre; and that the General's Character is better known than in the moment of Victory; it was yours, by every title which can give it, and the adverse element which robbed you of your prize, can never deprive you of the Glory due to you. Tho your success has not been equal to your expectations yet you have the satisfaction of reflecting that you have rendered essential Services to the common cause.

To Comte D'Estaing, September 11, 1778   *Writings Vol. 12 p. 423*

TRIUMPH OF PRINCIPLE

... In times of turbulence, when the passions are afloat, calm reason is swallowed up in the extremes to wch. measures are attempted to be carried; but when those subside and the empire of it is resumed, the man who acts from principle, who pursues the paths of truth, moderation and justice, will regain his influence.

To John Luzac, December 2, 1797   *Writings Vol. 36 p. 84*

DUTY AND VIRTUE, BEFORE POPULARITY

... Though I prize, as I ought, the good opinion of my fellow citizens; yet, if I know myself, I would not seek or retain popularity at the expense of one social duty or moral virtue.

To Henry Lee, September 22, 1788   *Writings Vol. 30 p. 97*

CONSCIOUS RECTITUDE

... I have happily had but few differences with those with whom I have the honor of being connected in the Service; with whom, and of what nature these have been, you know. I bore much for the sake of peace and the public good. My conscience tells me I acted rightly in these transactions, and should they ever come to the knowledge of the world I trust I shall stand acquitted.

To Nathanael Greene, October 6, 1781   *Writings Vol. 23 p. 190*

... conscious integrity has been my unceasing support; and while it gave me confidence in the measures I pursued, the belief of it, by acquiring to me the confidence of my fellow-citizens, ensured the success which they have had. This consciousness will accompany me in my retirement: without it, public applauses could be viewed only as proofs of public error, and felt as the upbraidings of personal demerit.

To the Pennsylvania Senate, January 13, 1797   *Writings Vol. 35 p. 366*

THE GOOD CITIZEN'S TWO-FOLD MOTIVE

... Next to the approbation of my own mind, arising from a consciousness of having uniformly, diligently and sincerely aimed, by doing my duty, to promote the true interests of my country, the approbation of my fellow citizens is dear to my heart. In a free country, such approbation *should* be a citizen's best reward; and so it *would* be, if Truth and Candour were always to estimate the conduct of public men. But the reverse is so often the case, that he who, wishing to serve his country, is not influenced by higher motives, runs the risk of being miserably disappointed. Under such discouragements, the good citizen will look beyond the applauses and reproaches of men, and persevering in his duty, stand firm in conscious rectitude, and in the hope of [an] approving Heaven.

To the Citizens of Frederick County, Virginia, December 16, 1795
       Writings Vol. 34 p. 395

DICTATES OF CONSCIENCE

... While I feel the most lively gratitude for the many instances of approbation from my country; I can no otherwise deserve it, than by obeying the dictates of my conscience.

To the Boston Selectmen, July 28, 1795   *Writings Vol. 34 p. 254*

PUBLIC OBSERVATION

... the eyes of Argus are upon me; and no slip will pass unnoticed.

To Bushrod Washington, July 27, 1789   *Writings Vol. 30 p. 366*

ENMITY AND DETRACTION

... It is a tax, however, severe, which all those must pay, who are called to eminent stations of trust, not only to be held up as conspicuous marks to the enmity of the Public adversaries to their country, but the malice of secret traitors and the *envious intrigues* of false friends and factions.

To William Livingston, February 2, 1778   *Writings Vol. 10 p. 415*

MAKING ENEMIES

... Among Individuals, the most certain way to make a Man your Enemy, is to tell him, you esteem him such; so with public bodies.

To John Bannister, April 21, 1778   *Writings Vol. 11 p. 291*

ANTIDOTE TO SLANDER

... So far as these attacks are aimed at me, *personally,* it is, I can assure you, Sir, a misconception if it be supposed I feel the venom of the darts. Within me, I have a consolation which proves an antidote agt. their utmost malignity, rendering my mind in the retirement I have long panted after perfectly tranquil.

To John Langhorne, October 15, 1797   *Writings Vol. 36 p. 53*

THE DISCONTENTED

... Against the malignancy of the discontented, the turbulant, and the vicious, no abilities; no exertions; nor the most unshaken integrity, are any safeguard.

To John Jay, November 1–5, 1794   *Writings Vol. 34 p. 16*

... It is much easier to avoid disagreements than to remove discontents.

To John Sullivan, May 11, 1781   *Writings Vol. 22 p. 70*

Portrait of Washington by Benoit Louis Prevost after Pierre Eugene Du Simitiere, 1781. As part of a series of portraits of leaders of the American Revolution, Washington sat for Du Simitiere, a Swiss artist, in Philadelphia in 1779.

RASH JUDGMENTS

... It is the Nature of Man to be displeased with every thing that disappoints a favourite hope, or flattering project; and it is the folly of too many of them, to condemn without investigating circumstances.

To Marquis de Lafayette, September 1, 1778   *Writings Vol. 12 p. 383*

GRATUITOUS CENSURE

... I have studiously avoided in all letters intended for the public eye, I mean for that of the Congress, every expression that could give pain or uneasiness; and I shall observe the same rule with respect to private letters, further than appears absolutely necessary for the elucidation of facts.

To Joseph Reed, December 15, 1775   *Writings Vol. 4 p. 165*

FRIENDLY MONITIONS

... The hints you have communicated from time to time not only deserve, but do most sincerely and cordially meet with my thanks. You cannot render a more acceptable service, nor in my estimation give a more convincing proof of your friendship, than by a free, open and undisguised account of every matter relative to myself or conduct. I can bear to hear of imputed or real errors. The man, who wishes to stand well in the opinion of others, must do this; because he is thereby enabled to correct his faults, or remove prejudices which are imbibed against him. For this reason, I shall thank you for giving me the opinions of the world, upon such points as you know me to be interested in; for, as I have but one capital object in view, I could wish to make my conduct coincide with the wishes of mankind, as far as I can consistently; I mean, without departing from that great line of duty, which, though hid under a cloud for some time, from a peculiarity of circumstances, may nevertheless bear a scrutiny.

To Joseph Reed, January 14, 1776   *Writings Vol. 4 p. 240*

OPINION OF THE WORLD

... nothing would give more real satisfaction, than to know the sentiments, which are entertained of me by the public, whether they be favorable or otherwise .... the man, who wished to steer clear of shelves and rocks, must know where they lay I know — but to declare it, unless to a friend, may be an argument of vanity — the integrity of my own heart. I know the unhappy predicament I stand in; I know that much is expected of me; I know, that without men, without arms, without ammunition, without any thing fit for the accommodation of a soldier, little is to be done; and, which is mortifying, I know, that I cannot stand justified to the world without exposing my own weakness, and injuring the cause, by declaring my wants, which I am determined not to do, further than unavoidable necessity brings every man acquainted with them.

If, under these disadvantages, I am able to keep above water, (as it were) in the esteem of mankind, I shall feel myself happy; but if, from the unknown peculiarity of my circumstances, I suffer in the opinion of the world, I shall not think you take the freedom of a friend, if you conceal the reflections that may be cast upon my conduct. My own situation feels so irksome to me at times, that, if I did not consult the public good, more than my own tranquillity, I should long ere this have put every thing to the cast of a Dye.

To Joseph Reed, February 10, 1776   *Writings Vol. 4 p. 319*

THE BEST ANSWER TO CALUMNY

... to persevere in one's duty and be silent, is the best answer to calumny.

To William Livingston, December 7, 1779   *Writings Vol. 17 p. 225*

EVIL REPORTS

... I never suffer reports, unsupported by proofs, to have weight in my Mind.

To Richard Henry Lee, July 15, 1781   *Writings Vol. 22 p. 382*

VANITY

... Do not conceive that fine Clothes make fine Men, any more than fine feathers make fine Birds. A plain genteel dress is more admired and obtains more credit than lace and embroidery in the Eyes of the judicious and sensible.

To Bushrod Washington, January 15, 1783   *Writings Vol. 26 p. 40*

VERBIAGE OF VANITY

... there is no restraining men's tongues, or pens, when charged with a little vanity.

To Joseph Reed, December 15, 1775   *Writings Vol. 4 p. 166*

IDLE FORMS

... Every one who has any knowledge of my manner of acting in public life, will be persuaded that I am not accustomed to impede the despatch or frustrate the success of business, by a ceremonious attention to idle forms.

To Comte de Moustier, May 25, 1789   *Writings Vol. 30 p. 334*

CEREMONIOUS CIVILITY, AND INCIVILITY

... I cannot charge myself with incivility, or, what in my opinion is tantamount, ceremonious civility.

To Joseph Reed, December 15, 1775   *Writings Vol. 4 p. 165*

ON MEMOIRS

... any memoirs of my life, distinct and unconnected with the general history of the war, would rather hurt my feelings than tickle my pride whilst I lived. I had rather glide gently down the stream of life, leaving it to posterity to think and say what they please of me, than by any act of mine to have vanity or ostentation imputed to me. . . . I do not think vanity is a trait of my character.

To Doctor James Craik, March 25, 1784   *Writings Vol. 27 p. 371*

THE CITIZEN'S REWARD

... The confidence and affection of his fellow Citizens is the most valuable and agreeable reward a Citizen can receive. Next to the happiness of my Country, this is the most powerful inducement I can have to exert my self in its Service.

To the Inhabitants of Providence March 14, 1781   *Writings Vol. 21 p. 337*

CAVILLERS

... with those who are disposed to cavil, or who have the itch of writing strongly upon them, nothing can be made to suit their palates: the best way therefore to disconcert and defeat them, is to take no notice of their pubications; all else is but food for declamation.

To Samuel Vaughan, November 30, 1785   *Writings Vol. 28 p. 327*

RECRIMINATION

... should any thing present itself in this or any other publication, I shall never undertake the painful task of recrimination, nor do I know that I should ever enter upon my justification.

To William Goddard, June 11, 1785   *Writings Vol. 28 p. 162*

CENSURE, THE SHADOW OF MERIT

... why should I expect to be exempt from censure; the unfailing lot of an elevated station? Merits and talents, with which I can have no pretensions of rivalship, have ever been subject to it.

To Henry Laurens, January 31, 1778   *Writings Vol. 10 p. 411*

His Excellency George Washington Esq. Captain General of all the American Forces by an unidentified artist, published in *An Impartial History of the War in America between Great Britain and Her Colonies . . .* (London & Carlisle, 1780).

UNJUST CENSURE, TO BE DESPISED

... While doing what my conscience informed me was right, as it re-spected my God, my Country and myself, I could despise all the party clamor and unjust censure, which must be expected from some, whose personal enmity might be occasioned by their hostility to the govern-ment.

To Henry Lee, September 22, 1788   *Writings Vol. 30 p. 98*

CENSURE AND DUTY

... I am resolved that no mis-representations, falsehoods or calumny; shall make me swerve from what I conceive to be the strict line of my duty.

To John Eager Howard, November 30, 1795   *Writings Vol. 34 p. 380*

MEN MUST BE TOUCHED, TO BE MOVED

... unfortunately, the nature of man is such, that the experience of others is not attended to as it ought to be: we must *feel ourselves*, before we can think, or perceive the danger which threatens.

To John Marshall, December 4, 1797   *Writings Vol. 36 p. 93*

UNAVAILING COMPLAINTS AND PRESENT DUTY

... We ought not to look back, unless it is to derive useful lessons from past errors, and for the purpose of profiting by dear bought experience. To enveigh against things that are past and irremediable, is unpleasing; but to steer clear of the shelves and rocks we have struck upon, is the part of wisdom, equally incumbent on political, as other men, who have their own little bark, or that of others to navigate through the intricate paths of life, or the trackless Ocean to the haven of secury. and rest.

To John Armstrong, March 26, 1781   *Writings Vol. 21 p. 378*

SENSIBILITY TO PUBLIC APPROBATION

... For having performed duties, (which I conceive every Country has a right to require of its citizens) I claim no merit; but no man can feel more sensibly the reward of approbation for such services, than I do.

To the Earl of Radnor, July 8, 1797   *Writings Vol. 35 p. 493*

APPEAL TO THE ARCHIVES

... I appeal to the Archives of Congress, and call on those sacred deposits to witness for me.

To the President of Congress, March 18, 1783   *Writings Vol. 26 p. 230*

C. INTEMPERANCE AND GAMING

USE OF WINES AND SPIRITUOUS LIQUORS

... my greatest reason for supposing the trade to be detrimental to us was, that Rum, the principal article received from thence, is, in my opinion, the bane of morals and the parent of idleness....I could wish to see the direct commerce with France encouraged to the greatest degree; and that almost all the foreign spirits which we consumed should consist of the Wines and Brandies made in that Country. The use of those liquors would at least be more innocent to the health and morals of the people, than the thousands of Hogsheads of poisonous Rum which are annually consumed in the United States.

To Comte de Moustier, December 15, 1788   *Writings Vol. 30 p. 162*

IMMORALITY, DISCOUNTENANCED

... *this* I am certain of, and can call my conscience, and what, I suppose, will still be a more demonstrable proof in the eyes of the world, my orders, to witness how much I have, both by threats and persuasive means, endeavoured to discountenance gaming, drinking, swearing, and irregularities of every other kind; while I have, on the other hand, practised every artifice to inspire a laudable emulation in the officers for the service of their country, and to encourage the soldiers in the unerring exercise of their duty.

To Robert Dinwiddie, April 18, 1756   *Writings Vol. 1 p. 317*

TIPPLING-HOUSES

... I apprehend it will be thought advisable to keep a garrison always at Fort Loudoun; for which reason I would beg leave to represent the great nuisance the number of tippling-houses in Winchester are of to the soldiers, who, by this means, in despite of the utmost care and vigilance, are, so long as their pay holds good, incessantly drunk, and unfit for service.

To Robert Dinwiddie, September 23, 1756   *Writings Vol. 1 p. 470*

PROFANITY AND DRUNKENNESS

... The General most earnestly requires, and expects, a due observance of those articles of war, established for the Government of the army, which forbid profane cursing, swearing and drunkenness.

General Orders, July 4, 1775   *Writings Vol. 3 p. 309*

EVILS OF RUM, IN THE ARMY

... The quantity of spirituous liquors, which is a component part of the ration, is so large as to endanger, where they might not before exist, habits of intemperance, alike fatal to health and discipline. Experience has repeatedly shown, that many soldiers will exchange their rum for other articles; which is productive of the double mischief of subjecting those with whom the exchange is made, to the loss of what is far more necessary and to all the consequences of brutal intoxication. The step having been once taken, a change is delicate; but it is believed to be indispensable, and that the temporary evils of a change can bear no proportion to the permanent and immense evils of a continuance of the error.

To the Secretary of War, December 13, 1798   *Writings Vol. 37 p. 55*

GAMES OF CHANCE

... All Officers, non-commissioned Officers and Soldiers are positively forbid playing at Cards, and other Games of Chance. At this time of public distress, men may find enough to do in the service of their God, and their Country, without abandoning themselves to vice and immorality.

General Orders, February 26, 1776   *Writings Vol. 4 p. 347*

... Gaming of every kind is expressly forbid, as the foundation of evil, and the cause of many Gallant and Brave Officer's Ruin. Games of exercise, for amusement, may not only be permitted but encouraged.

To William Smallwood, May 26, 1777   *Writings Vol. 8 p. 129*

... avoid Gaming. This is a vice which is productive of every possible evil. equally injurious to the morals and health of its votaries. It is the child of Avarice, the brother of inequity, and father of Mischief. It has been the ruin of many worthy familys; the loss of many a man's honor; and the cause of Suicide. To all those who enter the list, it is equally fascinating; the Successful gamester pushes his good fortune till it is over taken by a reverse; the loosing gamester, in hopes of retrieving past misfortunes, goes on from bad to worse; till grown desperate, he pushes at every thing; and looses his all.... few gain by this abominable practice (the profit, if any, being diffused) while thousands are injured.

To Bushrod Washington, January 15, 1783   *Writings Vol. 26 p. 40*

D. PUNISHMENTS

MODERATION AND TENDERNESS

... though I shall always think it a sacred duty, to exercise with firmness and energy, the Constitutional powers with which I am vested, yet it appears to me no less consistent with the public good, than it is with my personal feelings, to mingle in the operations of government, every degree of moderation and tenderness, which the national justice, dignity and safety may permit.

Seventh Annual Address, December 8, 1795   *Writings Vol. 34 p. 390*

EFFECT OF LENITY

... Lenity will operate with greater force, in such Instances, than rigour; 'tis therefore my first wish to have our whole conduct distinguished by it.

To Thomas Mifflin, February 14, 1777   *Writings Vol. 7 p. 151*

SEVERITIES, NOT TO BE UNDUE

... It is not my wish that Severity should be exercised towards any, whom the fortune of War has thrown, or, shall throw into our hands.

To Sir William Howe, November 9, 1776   *Writings Vol. 6 p. 260*

LENITY TO TORIES

... in behalf of the United States, by virtue of the powers committed to me by Congress, ... granting full Liberty to all such as prefer the interest and protection of Great-Britain to the freedom and happiness of their country, forthwith to withdraw themselves and families within the enemy's lines.

Proclamation, January 25, 1777   *Writings Vol. 7 p. 62*

RULE OF LENITY

... Where acts of providence interfere to disable a Tenant, I would be lenient in the exaction of rent; but when the cases are otherwise, I will not be put off; because it is on these my own expenditures depend, and because an accumulation of undischarged rents is a real injury to the Tenant.

To Thomas Freeman, September 23, 1784   *Writings Vol. 27 p. 470*

MILD MEASURES, RECOMMENDED

... With respect to the Tory, who was tried and executed by your order, though his crime was heinous enough to deserve the fate he met with, and though I am convinced you acted in the affair with a good intention, yet I cannot but wish it had not happened. In the first place, it was a matter that did not come within the jurisdiction of martial law, and therefore the whole proceeding was irregular and illegal, and will have a tendency to excite discontent, jealousy and murmurs among the people. In the Second, if the trial could properly have been made by a Court Martial, as the

G. Washington by Jacques Le Roy after John Trumbull, Brussels, 1781.

Division you command is only a detachment from the Army, and you cannot have been considered as in a Separate Department, there is none of our articles of War that will justify your inflicting a *Capital* punishment, even on a Soldier, much less a Citizen. I mention these things for your future Government, as what is past cannot be recalled. The temper of the Americans and the principles on which the present contest turns, will not countenance proceedings of this nature.

To Preudhomme de Borre, August 3, 1777   *Writings Vol. 9 p. 7*

EXEMPLARY PUNISHMENT

... severe examples should, in my judgment, be made of those who were forgiven former offences and again in Arms against us.

To Henry Laurens, March 20, 1779   *Writings Vol. 14 p. 266*

RETALIATION

... Retaliation is certainly just and sometimes necessary, even where attended with the severest penalties; But when the Evils which may and must result from it, exceed those intended to be redressed, prudence and policy require that it should be avoided.

To the President of Congress, March 1, 1777   *Writings Vol. 7 p. 211*

... Americans have the feelings of Sympathy, as well as other men. A series of injuries may exhaust their patience, and it is natural that the sufferings of their Friends in Captivity, should at length irritate them into resentment and to Acts of retaliation.

To Sir William Howe, January 20, 1778   *Writings Vol. 10 p. 323*

E. SLAVERY

EMANCIPATION OF SLAVES

... The scheme, my dear Marqs. which you propose as a precedent, to encourage the emancipation of the black people of this Country from that state of Bondage in wch. they are held, is a striking evidence of the benevolence of your Heart. I shall be happy to join you in so laudable a work.

To Marquis de Lafayette, April 5, 1785   *Writings Vol. 26 p. 300*

ABOLITION OF SLAVERY

... there is not a man living who wishes more sincerely than I do, to see a plan adopted for the abolition of it; but there is only one proper and effectual mode by which it can be accomplished, and that is by Legislative authority; and this, as far as my suffrage will go, shall never be wanting. But when slaves who are happy and contented with their present masters, are tampered with and seduced to leave them; when masters are taken unawares by these practices; when a conduct of this sort begets discontent on one side and resentment on the other, and when it happens to fall on a man, whose purse will not measure with that of the Society, and he looses his property for want of means to defend it; it is oppression in the latter case, and not humanity in any; because it introduces more evils than it can cure.

To Robert Morris, April 12, 1786   *Writings Vol. 28 p. 408*

... I wish from my soul that the legislature of this State could see a policy of a gradual Abolition of Slavery.

To Lawrence Lewis, August 4, 1797   *Writings Vol. 36 p. 2*

... With respect to the other species of property ... I shall frankly declare to you that I do not like to even think, much less talk of it. However, as you have put the question I shall, in a few words, give you *my ideas* of it. Were it not then, that I am principled agt. selling negroes, as you would do cattle in the market, I would not, in twelve months from this date, be possessed of one, as a slave.

To Alexander Spotswood, November 23, 1794   *Writings Vol. 34 p. 47*

LAFAYETTE'S ABOLITION SCHEME

... your late purchase of an estate in the colony of Cayenne, with a view to emancipating the slaves on it, is a generous and noble proof of your humanity. Would to God a like spirit would diffuse itself generally into the minds of the people of this country; but I despair of seeing it. Some petitions were presented to the Assembly, at its last Session, for the abolition of slavery, but they could scarcely obtain a reading. To set them afloat at once would, I really believe, be productive of much inconvenience and mischief; but by degrees it certainly might, and assuredly ought to be effected; and that too by Legislative authority.

To Marquis de Lafayette, May 10, 1786   *Writings Vol. 28 p. 424*

MODE OF ABOLISHING SLAVERY

... I never mean (unless some particular circumstance should compel me to it) to possess another slave by purchase; it being among my first wishes to see some plan adopted, by which slavery in this country may be abolished by slow, sure, and imperceptible degrees.

To John Francis Mercer, September 9, 1786   *Writings Vol. 29 p. 5*

PROPOSED LIBERATION OF SLAVES

... I have no scruple to disclose to you, that my motives to these sales (as hath been, in part, expressed to Mr. Young) are to reduce my income, be it more or less, to specialties, that the remainder of my days may, thereby, be more tranquil and freer from cares; and that I may be enabled (knowing precisely my dependence) to do as much good with it as the resource will admit; for although, in the estimation of the world I possess a good, and clear estate, yet, so unproductive is it, that I am oftentimes ashamed to refuse aids which I cannot afford unless I was to sell part of it to answer the purpose. (Private) Besides these, I have another motive which makes me earnestly wish for the accomplishment of these things, it is indeed more powerful than all the rest. namely to liberate a certain species of property which I possess, very repugnantly to my own feelings; but which imperious necessity compels; and until I can substitute some other expedient, by which expences not in my power to avoid (however well disposed I may be to do it) can be defrayed.

To Tobias Lear, May 6, 1794   *Writings Vol. 33 p. 358*

SLAVES LIBERATED

... Upon the decease [of] my wife, it is my Will and desire, th[at] all the Slaves which I hold in [my] *own right,* shall receive their free[dom.] To emancipate them during [her] life, would, tho' earnestly wish[ed by] me, be attended with such insu[perab]le difficulties, on account of thei[r intermi]ixture by Marriages with the [Dow]er Negroes, as to excite the most pa[i]nful sensations, if not disagreeabl[e c]onsequences from the latter, while [both] descriptions are in the occupancy [of] the same Proprietor; it not being [in] my power, under the tenure by whic[h t]he Dower Negroes are held, to man[umi]t them.

Will, July 9, 1799   *Writings Vol. 37 p. 276*

... I am principled against this kind of traffic in the human species. . .and to disperse the families I have an aversion.

To Robert Lewis, August 18, 1799   *Writings Vol. 37 pp. 338–339*

PROVISION FOR AGED, INFIRM, AND INFANT SLAVES

... And whereas among [thos]e who will receive freedom ac[cor]ding to this devise, there may b[e so]me, who from old age or bodily infi[rm]ities, and others who on account of [thei]r infancy, that will be unable to [su]pport themselves; it is [my] Will a[nd de]sire that all who [come under the first] and second descrip[tion shall be comfor]tably cloathed and [fed by my heirs while] they live; and that such of the latter description as have no parents living, or if living are unable, or unwilling to provide for them, shall be bound by the Court until they shall arrive at the age of twenty five years; and in cases where no record can be produced, whereby their ages can be ascertained, the judgment of the Court upon its own view of the subject, shall be adequate and final.

Will, July 9, 1799   *Writings Vol. 37 p. 276*

NEGROES, TO BE TAUGHT TO READ AND WRITE

... The Negros thus bound, are (by their Masters or Mistresses) to be taught to read and write; and to be brought up to some useful occupation, agreeably to the Laws of the Commonwealth of Virginia, providing for the support of Orphan and other poor Children.

Will, July 9, 1799   *Writings Vol. 37 p. 277*

PERMANENT FUND FOR AGED AND INFIRM NEGROES

... I do moreover most pointedly, and most solemnly enjoin it upon my Executors hereafter named, or the Survivors of them, to see that *this* [cl]ause respecting Slaves, and every part thereof be religiously fulfilled at the Epoch at which it is directed to take place; without evasion, neglect or delay, after the Crops which may then by on the ground are harvested, particularly as it respects aged and infirm; seeing that a regular and permanent fund be established for their support so long as there are subjects requiring it; not trusting to the uncertain provision to be made by individuals.

Will, July 9, 1799   *Writings Vol. 37 p. 277*

WILLIAM LEE'S IMMEDIATE FREEDOM

... to my Mulatto man William (calling himself William Lee) I give immediate freedom; or if he should prefer it (on account of the accidents which have befallen him, and which have rendered him incapable of walking or of any active employment) to remain in the situation he now is, it shall be optional in him to do so; In either case however, I allow him an annuity of thirty dollars during his natural life, which shall be independent of victuals and cloaths he has been accustomed to receive, if he chuses the last alternative; but in full, with his freedom, if he prefers the first; and this I give him as a testimony of my sense of his attachment to me, and for his faithful services during the Revolutionary War.

Will, July 9, 1799   *Writings Vol. 37 p. 277*

FREEDOM OF THE DANDRIDGE SLAVES

... the Negros, (then thirty three in number) formerly belonging to the said estate, who were taken in execution, sold, and purchased in, on my

Event of the 19th of Octr 1781, at *YORKTOWN* in *VIRGINIA*.

GEN^l. WASHINGTON.

Genl. Washington, with a vignette showing the British surrender at Yorktown, October 19, 1781, published by T. Holloway, May 21, 1794.

account in the year and ever since have remained in the possession, and to the use of Mary, Widow of the said Bartholomew Dandridge with their increase, it is my Will and desire shall continue, and be in her possession, without paying hire, or making compensation for the same for the time past or to come, during her natural life; at the expiration of which, I direct that all of them who are forty years old and upwards, shall receive their freedom; all under that age and above sixteen, shall serve seven years and no longer; and all under sixteen years, shall serve until they are twenty five years of age, and then be free. And to avoid disputes respecting the ages of any of these Negros, they are to be taken to the Court of the County in which they reside, and the judgment thereof, in its relation, shall be final; and a record thereof made; which may be adduced as evidence at any time thereafter, if disputes should arise concerning the same.

Will, July 9, 1799   *Writings Vol. 37 p. 282*

V.
Religious Maxims

RELIGIOUS MAXIMS

———————————— ❧ ————————————

When George Washington settled in as the master of Mount Vernon in 1759, most Virginia planters were members of the Anglican Church of England. In a colony that provided a fertile bed for evangelical sects, such as the Baptists and Methodists, Washington remained affiliated with the established church.

Like his father Augustine, George Washington served Truro Parish as a vestryman, one of 12 men who managed the affairs of the church and enjoyed considerable influence in choosing the rector. He worshipped at Pohick Church where he was named warden in 1763. Later in life the General also attended Christ Church in Alexandria.

A product of the Enlightenment, Washington's terms for God included "Divine Author of our blessed Religion," "Divine Providence," and "the Almighty Being who rules over the Universe." Like many Deists, Washington viewed the supreme being as an overseer and protector of all men, not simply the God of Presbyterians, Episcopalians or Baptists. As such, his political stance on separating church and state was probably a personal one as well. As both President and Virginia planter, Washington believed in freedom of religion. Just as he was careful to act non-partisan in political matters, Washington strove to be non-sectarian in religious affairs.

Throughout the Revolutionary War and his presidency, Washington periodically proclaimed days of thanksgiving. As commander in chief, Washington called on army chaplains to prepare discourses and hold services on selected days in order to acknowledge the blessings bestowed by Divine Providence upon America and her military forces. On October 3, 1789, the establishment of the new government prompted President Washington to announce the first national day of thanksgiving. Americans had much to be grateful for, and the Thanksgiving Proclamation reflected this sentiment.

Washington believed that one should not fear death, but accept it as an end to the natural course of life. In a broader sense, his view of death reflected his view of life: that Providence's hand would lead man from birth to "that country from whence no Traveller returns." The best one could do is to faithfully discharge the duties presented him throughout the interim.

A. GOD

THE AUTHOR OF ALL GOOD

... that great and glorious Being, who is the beneficent Author of all the good that was, that is, or that will be.

Thanksgiving Proclamation, October 3, 1789   *Writings Vol. 30 p. 427*

THE SOURCE OF ALL BLESSINGS

... The sentiments we have mutually expressed of profound gratitude to the source of those numerous blessings — the author of all good — are pledges of our obligations to unite our sincere and zealous endeavours, as the instruments of divine providence, to preserve and perpetuate them.

To the House of Representatives, December 17, 1795   *Writings Vol. 34 p. 393*

THE DISPOSER OF EVENTS; ALL-POWERFUL, AND ALL-WISE

... I feel now, however, as I conceive a wearied Traveller must do, who, after treading many a painful step, with a heavy burden on his shoulders, is eased of the latter, having reached the Goal to which all the former were directed; and from his House top is looking back, and tracing with a grateful eye the Meanders by which he escaped the quicksands and Mires which lay in his way; and into which none but the All-powerful guide, and great disposer of human Events could have prevented his falling.

To Henry Knox, February 20, 1784   *Writings Vol. 27 p. 340*

... as the allwise disposer of events has hitherto watched over my steps, I trust that in the important one I may soon be called upon to take, he will mark the course so plainly, as that I cannot mistake the way.

To the Attorney General, August 26, 1792   *Writings Vol. 32 p. 136*

DIVINE WISDOM AND GOODNESS

... I flatter myself that a Superintending Providence is ordering everything for the best and that, in due time, all will end well.

To Landon Carter, October 27, 1777   *Writings Vol. 9 p. 453*

... The determinations of Providence are all ways wise; often inscrutable, and though its decrees appear to bear hard upon us at times is nevertheless meant for gracious purposes.

To Bryan Fairfax, March 1, 1778   *Writings Vol. 11 p. 3*

DIVINE MUNIFICENCE

... When I contemplate the interposition of Providence, as it was visibly manifested, in guiding us through the Revolution, in preparing us for the reception of a general government, and in conciliating the good will of the People of America towards one another after its' adoption, I feel myself oppressed and almost overwhelmed with a sense of the divine munificence.

To the Mayor, Recorder, Alderman, and Common Council of Philadelphia, April 20, 1789   *Writings Vol. 30 p. 289*

... I have lately made a tour through the Lakes George and Champlain as far as Crown point; then returning to Schenectady, I proceeded up the Mohawk river to Fort Schuyler (formerly Fort Stanwix), and crossed over to the Wood Creek which empties into the Oneida Lake, and affords the water communication with Ontario. I then traversed the country to the head of the Eastern Branch of the Susquehanna and viewed the Lake Otsego, and the portage between that lake and the Mohawk river at Canajohario. Prompted by these actual observations, I could not help taking a more contemplative and extensive view of the vast inland navigation of these United States, from maps and the information of others; and could not but be struck with the immense diffusion and importance of it; and with the goodness of that Providence which has dealt her favors to us with so profuse a hand. Would to God we may have wisdom enough to improve them.

To Chevalier de Chastellux, October 12, 1783   *Writings Vol. 27 p. 189*

GOD, OUR PRESERVER

... we may, with a kind of grateful and pious exultation, trace the finger of Providence through those dark and mysterious events, which first induced the States to appoint a general Convention and then led them one after another (by such steps as were best calculated to effect the object) into an adoption of the system recommended by that general Convention; thereby, in all human probability, laying a lasting foundation for tranquillity and happiness; when we had but too much reason to fear that confusion and misery were coming rapidly upon us. That the same good Providence may still continue to protect us and prevent us from dashing the cup of national felicity just as it has been lifted to our lips, is the earnest prayer of My Dear Sir, your faithful friend, &c.

To Jonathan Trumbull, July 20, 1788   *Writings Vol. 30 p. 22*

... The great Director of events has carried us thro' a variety of Scenes during this long and bloody contest in which we have been for Seven

Campaigns, most nobly struggling.

To William Ramsay, John Fitzgerald, Robert Hooe, and the other Inhabitants of Alexandria, November 10, 1781   *Writings Vol. 23 p. 356*

THE OMNIPOTENT, OUR GUARDIAN

... I earnestly pray that the Omnipotent Being who has not deserted the cause of America in the hour of its extremest hazard, will never yield so fair a heritage of freedom a prey to *Anarchy* or *Despotism.*

To the Secretary at War, July 31, 1788   *Writings Vol. 31 p. 30*

... Satisfied therefore, that you have sincerely wished and endeavoured to avert war, and exhausted to the last drop, the cup of reconciliation, we can with pure hearts appeal to Heaven for the justice of our cause, and may confidently trust the final result to that kind Providence who has heretofore and so often, signally favoured the People of these United States.

To the President of the United States, July 13, 1798   *Writings Vol. 36 p. 328*

... the great Ruler of events will not permit the happiness of so many millions to be destroyed; and to his keeping I resign you.

To Marquis de Lafayette, September 10, 1791   *Writings Vol. 31 p. 363*

THE DIVINE DELIVERER

... Our affairs are brought to an awful crisis, that the hand of Providence, I trust, may be more conspicuous in our deliverance. The many remarkable interpositions of the divine governmt. in the hours of our deepest distress and darkness, have been too luminous to suffer me to doubt the happy issue of the present contest.

To John Armstrong, March 26, 1781   *Writings Vol. 21 p. 378*

DIVINE PROTECTION

... by the miraculous care of Providence, that protected me beyond all human expectation; I had 4 Bullets through my Coat, and two Horses shot under me, and yet escaped unhurt.

To John Augustine Washington, July 18, 1755   *Writings Vol. 1 p. 152*

... I go fully trusting in that Providence, which has been more bountiful to me than I deserve, & in full confidence of a happy meeting sometime in the Fall.

To Martha Washington, June 23, 1775   *Writings Vol 3. p. 301*

... Providence has heretofore taken us up when all other means and hope seemed to be departing from us, in this I will confide.

To Benjamin Harrison, December 18–30, 1778   *Writings Vol. 13 p. 468*

... I consider it an indispensable duty to close this last solemn act of my Official life, by commending the Interest of our dearest Country to the protection of Almighty God, and those who have the superintendence of them, to his holy keeping.

Address to Congress on Resigning his Commission, December 23, 1783
Writings Vol. 27 p. 285

THE SUPREME RULER OF THE UNIVERSE

... The situation in which I now stand, for the last time, in the midst of the Representatives of the People of the United States, naturally recalls the period when the Administration of the present form of Government commenced; and I cannot omit the occasion, to congratulate you and my Country, on the success of the experiment; nor to repeat my fervent supplications to the Supreme Ruler of the Universe, and Sovereign Arbiter of Nations, that his Providential care may still be extended to the United States; that the virtue and happiness of the People, may be preserved; and that the Government, which they have instituted, for the protection of their liberties, may be perpetual.

To the Senate and the House of Representatives, December 7, 1796
Writings Vol. 35 p. 319

THE RULER OF NATIONS

... Let us unite, therefore, in imploring the Supreme Ruler of nations, to spread his holy protection over these United States: to turn the machinations of the wicked to the confirming of our constitution: to enable us at all times to root out internal sedition, and put invasion to flight: to perpetuate to our country that prosperity, which his goodness has already conferred, and to verify the anticipation of this government being a safe guard to human rights.

To the Senate and the House of Representatives, November 19, 1794
Writings Vol. 34 p. 37

... we may then unite in most humbly offering our prayers and supplications to the great Lord and Ruler of Nations and beseech him to pardon our national and other transgressions, to enable us all, whether in public or private stations, to perform our several and relative duties properly and punctually, to render our national government a blessing to all the People, by constantly being a government of wise, just and constitutional

General Washington's Resignation by Alexander Lawson after a design by John James Barralet, published in the *Philadelphia Magazine and Review,* January 1799. Washington addresses the Goddess of Peace, having laid down symbols of his military career, and gestures toward his home, Mount Vernon.

laws, discreetly and faithfully executed and obeyed, to protect and guide all Sovereigns and Nations (especially such as have shown kindness unto us) and to bless them with good government, peace, and concord.

Thanksgiving Proclamation, October 3, 1789   *Writings Vol. 30 p. 428*

THE FATE OF NATIONS, SUSPENDED ON GOD'S WILL

... I humbly implore that Being, on whose Will the fate of Nations depends, to crown with success our mutual endeavours for the general happiness.

Fifth Annual Address to Congress, December 3, 1793   *Writings Vol. 33 p. 164*

THE GOD OF ARMIES

... the vicissitudes of War being in the hands of the Supreme Director, where no controul is.

To the Secretary of State, July 11, 1798   *Writings Vol. 36 p. 323*

NATIONAL RIGHTEOUSNESS, AND THE DIVINE FAVOR

... the propitious smiles of Heaven, can never be expected on a nation that disregards the eternal rules of order and right, which Heaven itself has ordained ....

The First Inaugural Address April 30, 1789   *Writings Vol. 30 p. 294*

REMARKABLE INSTANCES OF THE PROVIDENCE OF GOD

... In no instance since the commencement of the War has the interposition of Providence appeared more conspicuous than in the rescue of the Post and Garrison of West point from Arnolds villainous perfidy.

To John Laurens, October 13, 1780   *Writings Vol. 20 p. 173*

... I most devoutly congratulate you, my Country, and every well wisher to the Cause on this Signal Stroke of Providence.

To John Augustine Washington, October 18, 1777   *Writings Vol. 9 p. 399*

... the interposing Hand of Heaven in the various Instances of our extensive Preparations for this Operation, has been most conspicuous and remarkable.

To Thomas McKean, November 15, 1781   *Writings Vol. 23 p. 343*

GOD, OUR BENIGN PARENT

... Having thus imported to you my sentiments, as they have been awakened by the occasion which brings us together, I shall take my present leave; but not without resorting once more to the benign parent of the human race, in humble supplication that since he has been pleased to favour the American people, with opportunities for deliberating in perfect tranquility, and dispositions for deciding with unparellelled unanimity on a form of Government, for the security of their Union, and the advancement of their happiness; so his divine blessing may be equally *conspicuous* in the enlarged views, the temperate consultations, and the wise measures on which the success of this Government must depend.

The First Inaugural Address, April 30, 1789   *Writings Vol. 30 p. 296*

B. RELIGION AND THE STATE

MUTUAL INFLUENCE OF GOVERNMENT AND RELIGION

... while just government protects all in their religious rights, true religion affords to government its surest support.

To the Synod of the Dutch Reformed Church in North America, October 9, 1789   *Writings Vol. 30 p. 432*

RELIGIOUS INFLUENCE OF THE UNION

... I believe it's mild, yet efficient, operations will tend to remove every remaining apprehension of those with whose opinions it may not entirely coincide, as well as to confirm the hopes of it's numerous friends; and because the moderation, patriotism, and wisdom of the present federal Legislature, seem to promise the restoration of Order, and our ancient virtues; the extension of genuine religion, and the consequent advancement of our respectability abroad, and of our substantial happiness at home.

To the general convention of Bishops, Clergy, and Laity of the Protestant Episcopal Church in New York, New Jersey, Pennsylvania, Delaware, Maryland, Virginia, and North Carolina, August 19, 1789   *Writings Vol. 30 p. 383*

NATIONAL JUSTICE AND BENEVOLENCE

... Observe good faith and justice towds. all Nations. Cultivate peace and harmony with all. Religion and morality enjoin this conduct; and can it be that good policy does not equally enjoin it? It will be worthy of a free, enlightened, and, at no distant period, a great Nation, to give to mankind the magnanimous and too novel example of a People always guided by an exalted justice and benevolence. Who can doubt that in the course of time and things the fruits of such a plan would richly repay any temporary advantages wch. might be lost by a steady adherence to it? Can it be, that

Providence has not connected the permanent felicity of a Nation with its virtue? The experiment, at least, is recommended by every sentiment which ennobles human Nature.

Farewell Address, September 19, 1796   *Writings Vol. 35 p. 231*

RELIGION AND MORALITY, THE PILLARS OF HUMAN HAPPINESS

... Of all the dispositions and habits which lead to political prosperity, Religion and morality are indispensable supports. In vain would that man claim the tribute of Patriotism, who should labour to subvert these great Pillars of human happiness, these firmest props of the duties of Men and citizens. The mere Politician, equally with the pious man ought to respect and to cherish them. A volume could not trace all their connections with private and public felicity. Let it simply be asked where is the security for property, for reputation, for life, if the sense of religious obligation *desert* the oaths, which are the instruments of investigation in Courts of Justice?

Farewell Address, September 19, 1796   *Writings Vol. 35 p. 229*

RELIGION, DISTINGUISHED FROM MORALITY

... let us with caution indulge the supposition, that morality can be maintained without religion. Whatever may be conceded to the influence of refined education on minds of peculiar structure, reason and experience both forbid us to expect that National morality can prevail in exclusion of religious principle.

Farewell Address, September 19, 1796   *Writings Vol. 35 p. 229*

RELIGIOUS DUTIES OF NATIONS

... it is the duty of all Nations to acknowledge the providence of Almighty God, to obey his will, to be grateful for his benefits, and humbly to implore his protection and favor.

Thanksgiving Proclamation, October 3, 1789   *Writings Vol. 30 p. 427*

NATIONAL HOMAGE TO GOD

... it would be peculiarly improper to omit in this first official Act, my fervent supplications to that Almighty Being who rules over the Universe, who presides in the Councils of Nations, and whose providential aids can supply every human defect, that his benediction may consecrate to the liberties and happiness of the People of the United States, a Government instituted by themselves for these essential purposes: and may enable every instrument employed in its administration to execute with success, the functions allotted to his charge. In tending this homage to the Great Author of every public and private good, I assure myself that it expresses your sentiments not less than my own; nor those of my fellow-citizens at large, less than either. No People can be bound to acknowledge and adore the invisible hand, which conducts the Affairs of men more than the People of the United States. Every step, by which they have advanced to the character of an independent nation, seems to have been distinguished by some token of providential agency.

The First Inaugural Address, April 30, 1789   *Writings Vol. 30 p. 292*

... It always affords me satisfaction, when I find a concurrence in sentiment and practice between all conscientious men in acknowledgements of homage to the great Governor of the Universe and in professions of support to a just civil government.

To the Bishops of the Methodist Episcopal Church, May 29, 1789
Writings Vol. 30 p. 339

NATIONAL RELIGIOUS THANKSGIVING

... It having pleased the Almighty ruler of the Universe propitiously to defend the Cause of the United American-States and finally by raising us up a powerful Friend among the Princes of the Earth to establish our liberty and Independence upon lasting foundations, it becomes us to set apart a day for gratefully acknowledging the divine Goodness and celebrating the important Event which we owe to his benign Interposition.

After Orders, May 5, 1778   *Writings Vol. 11 p. 354*

C. RELIGIOUS ACTS AND EMOTIONS

DEPENDENCE ON GOD

... it will ever be the first wish of my heart to aid your pious endeavours to inculcate a due sense of the dependance we ought to place in that all wise and powerful Being on whom alone our success depends.

To Reverend Israel Evans, March 13, 1778   *Writings Vol. 11 p. 78*

... We have ... abundant reason to thank providence for its many favourable interpositions in our behalf. It has, at times been my only dependence for all other resources seemed to have fail'd us.

To Reverend William Gordon, March 9, 1781   *Writings Vol. 21 p. 332*

... If I should (unluckily for me) be reduced to the necessity of giving an answer to the question, which you suppose will certainly be put to me, I would fain do what is in all respects best. But how can I know what is best, or what I shall determine? May Heaven assist me in forming a judgment: for at present I see nothing but clouds and darkness before me.

To Jonathan Trumbull, December 4, 1788   *Writings Vol. 30 p. 149*

FAITH AND EFFORT

... To trust altogether in the justice of our cause, without our own utmost exertions, would be tempting Providence.

To Jonathan Trumbull, August 7, 1776   *Writings Vol. 5 p. 390*

... Liberty, Honor, and Safety are all at stake, and I trust Providence will smile upon our Efforts, and establish us once more, the Inhabitants of a free and happy Country.

To the Officers and Soldiers of the Pennsylvania Associators, August 8, 1776
Writings Vol. 5 p. 398

... The Honor and safety of our bleeding Country, and every other motive that can influence the brave and heroic Patriot, call loudly upon us, to acquit ourselves with Spirit. In short, we must now determine to be enslaved or free. If we make Freedom our choice, we must obtain it, by the Blessings of Heaven on our United and Vigorous Efforts.

To the Officers and Soldiers of the Pennsylvania Associators, August 8, 1776
Writings Vol. 5 p. 398

RELIGIOUS GRATITUDE

... It is not a little pleasing, nor less wonderful to contemplate, that after two years Manoeuvring and undergoing the strangest vicissitudes that perhaps ever attended any one contest since the creation both Armies are brought back to the very point they set out from and, that that, which was the offending party in the beginning is now reduced to the use of the spade and pick axe for defence. The hand of Providence has been so conspicuous in all this, that he must be worse than an infidel that lacks faith, and more than wicked, that has not gratitude enough to acknowledge his obligations.

To Thomas Nelson, August 20, 1778   *Writings Vol. 12 p. 343*

... My friends therefore may believe me sincere in my professions of attachment to them, whilst Providence has a joint claim to my humble and grateful thanks, for its protection and direction of me, through the many difficult and intricate scenes, which this contest hath produced; and for the constant interposition in our behalf, when the clouds were heaviest and seemed ready to burst upon us. To paint the distresses and perilous situation of this army in the course of last winter, for want of cloaths, provisions, and almost every other necessary, essential to the well-being,

WASHINGTON.

Rare, primitive American print of Washington, after Gilbert Stuart's "Lansdowne Portrait," date unknown.

(I may say existence,) of an army, would require more time and an abler pen than mine; nor, since our prospects have so miraculously brightened, shall I attempt it, or even bear it in remembrance, further than as a memento of what is due to the great Author of all the care and good, that have been extended in relieving us in difficulties and distress.

To Landon Carter, May 30, 1778   *Writings Vol. 11 p. 492*

... Although guided by our excellent constitution, in the discharge of official duties, and actuated through the whole course of my public life, solely by a wish to promote the best interests of our Country; yet, without the beneficient interposition of the Supreme Ruler of the Universe we could not have reached the distinguished situation which we have attained with such unprecedented rapidity. To him, therefore, should we bow with gratitude and reverence, and endeavour to merit a continuance of his special favors.

To the General Assembly of Rhode Island, April 3, 1797   Writings Vol. 35 p. 431

RELIANCE ON THE PROVIDENCE OF GOD

May that being, who is powerful to save, and in whose hands is the fate of nations, look down with an eye of tender pity and compassion upon the whole of the United Colonies; may He continue to smile upon their counsels and arms, and crown them with success, whilst employed in the cause of virtue and mankind. May this distressed colony and its capital, and every part of this wide extended continent, through His divine favor, be restored to more than their former lustre and once happy state, and have peace, liberty, and safety secured upon a solid, permanent, and lasting foundation.

Answer to an Address from the Massachusetts Legislature, March 1776
                                  Writings Vol. 4 p. 441–442

TRUST IN GOD

... Should providence be pleased to crown our Arms in the course of the Campaign, with one more fortunate stroke, I think we shall have no great cause for anxiety respecting the future designs of Britain. I trust all will be well in his good time.

To Israel Putnam, October 19, 1777   *Writings Vol. 9 p. 400*

... It is indeed a pleasure, from the walks of private life to view in retrospect, all the meanderings of our past labors, the difficulties through which we have waded, and the fortunate Haven to which the Ship has been brought! Is it possible after this that it should founder? Will not the All Wise, and all powerfull director of human events, preserve it? I think he will, he may however (for wise purposes not discoverable by finite minds) suffer our indiscretions and folly to place our national character low in the political Scale; and this, unless more wisdom and less prejudice take the lead in our governments, will most assuredly be the case.

To Jonathan Trumbull, May 15, 1784   *Writings Vol. 27 p. 399*

THE DESIGN OF GOD, IN OUR TRIALS

. . . ours is a kind of struggle designed I dare say by Providence to try the patience, fortitude and virtue of Men; none therefore that are engaged in it, will suffer themselves, I trust, to sink under difficulties, or be discouraged by hardships.

To Andrew Lewis, October 15, 1778   *Writings Vol. 13 p. 79*

SUBMISSION

. . . the ways of Providence are unscrutable, and Mortals must submit.

To Thaddeus Kosciuszko, August 31, 1797   *Writings Vol. 36 p. 22*

GLORY AND PRAISE ASCRIBED TO GOD

. . . If such talents as I possess have been called into action by great events, and those events have terminated happily for our country, the glory should be ascribed to the manifest interposition of an overruling Providence.

To the Synod of the Reformed Dutch Church in North America, October 9, 1789   *Writings Vol. 30 p. 432*

. . . I was but the humble Agent of favouring Heaven, whose benign interference was so often manifested in our behalf, and to whom the praise of victory alone is due.

To the Legislature of the State of Connecticut, October 17, 1789
                                         Writings Vol. 30 p. 453

D. CHRISTIANITY

THE PURE AND BENIGN LIGHT OF REVELATION

. . . the free cultivation of Letters, the unbounded extension of Commerce, the progressive refinement of Manners, the growing liberality of sentiment, and above all, the pure and benign light of Revelation, have had a meliorating influence on mankind and increased the blessings of Society.

Circular to the States, June 8, 1783   *Writings Vol. 26 p. 485*

SPIRIT OF CHRISTIANITY

... it would ill become me to conceal the joy I have felt in perceiving the fraternal affection which appears to encrease every day among the friends of genuine religion. It affords edifying prospects indeed to see Christians of different denominations dwell together in more charity, and conduct themselves in respect to each other with a more christian-like spirit than ever they have done in any former age, or in any other Nation.

To the Bishops, Clergy, and Laity of the Protestant Episcopal Church in New York, New Jersey, Pennsylvania, Delaware, Maryland, Virginia, and North Carolina, August 1789   *Writings Vol. 30 p. 383*

EXAMPLE OF ITS DIVINE AUTHOR

... I now make it my earnest prayer, that God would have you, and the State over which you preside, in his holy protection, that he would incline the hearts of the Citizens to cultivate a spirit of subordination and obedience to Government, to entertain a brotherly affection and love for one another, for their fellow Citizens of the United States at large, and particularly for their brethren who have served in the Field, and finally, that he would most graciously be pleased to dispose us all, to do Justice, to love mercy, and to demean ourselves with that Charity, humility and pacific temper of mind, which were the Characteristicks of the Divine Author of our blessed Religion, and without an humble imitation of whose example in these things, we can never hope to be a happy Nation.

Circular to the States, June 8, 1783   *Writings Vol. 26 p. 496*

CHRISTIAN MORALS

... While I reiterate the profession of my dependence upon Heaven as the source of all public and private blessings; I will observe that the general prevalence of piety, philanthropy, honesty, industry and economy seems, in the ordinary course of human affairs, particularly necessary for advancing and confirming the happiness of our country. While all men within our territories are protected in worshipping the Deity according to the dictates of their consciences; it is rationally to be expected from them in return, that they will be emulous of evincing the sanctity of their professions by the innocence of their lives, and the beneficence of their actions: for no man, who is profligate in his morals, or a bad member of the civil community, can possibly be a true Christian, or a credit to his own religious society.

To the General Assembly of the Presbyterian Church in the United States, May 26, 1780   *Writings Vol. 30 p. 336*

... The General hopes and trusts, that every officer and man, will endeavour so to live, and act, as becomes a Christian Soldier defending the dearest Rights and Liberties of his country.

General Orders, July 9, 1776   *Writings Vol. 5 p. 245*

CONSTITUTIONAL PROVISIONS

... Government being, among other purposes, instituted to protect the persons and consciences of men from oppression, it certainly is the duty of Rulers, not only to abstain from it themselves, but according to their stations, to prevent it in others.

To the Religious Society called Quakers, September 28, 1789
Writings Vol. 30 p. 416

... If I could have entertained the slightest apprehension, that the constitution framed in the convention, where I had the honor to preside, might possibly endanger the religious rights of any ecclesiastical society, certainly I would never have placed my signature to it. . . .if I could conceive that the general government might ever be so administered as to render the liberty of conscience insecure, I beg you will be persuaded, that no one would be more zealous than myself to establish effectual barriers against the horrors of spiritual tyranny, and every species of religious persecution.

To the United Baptist Churches in Virginia, May 10, 1789
Writings Vol. 30 p. 321

RELIGIOUS TOLERATION

... Being no bigot myself to any mode of worship, I am disposed to indulge the professors of Christianity in the church, that road to Heaven, which to them shall seem the most direct plainest easiest and least liable to exception.

To Marquis de Lafayette, August 15, 1787   *Writings Vol. 29 p. 259*

... As mankind become more liberal, they will be more apt to allow, that all those, who conduct themselves as worthy members of the community are equally entitled to the protection of civil government. I hope ever to see America among the foremost nations in examples of justice and liberality.

To a Committee of Roman Catholics, March 15, 1790   *Writings Vol. 31 p. 22*

... I trust the people of every denomination, who demean themselves as good citizens, will have occasion to be convinced, that I shall always strive to prove a faithful and impartial Patron of genuine, vital religion.

To the Bishops of the Methodist Episcopal Church, May 29, 1789
Writings Vol. 30 p. 339

RELIGIOUS TENETS AND CIVIL RIGHTS

... We have abundant reason to rejoice that in this Land the light of truth
and reason has triumphed over the power of bigotry and superstition,
and that every person may here worship God according to the dictates of
his own heart. In this enlightened Age and in this Land of equal liberty it
is our boast, that a man's religious tenets will not forfeit the protection of
the Laws, nor deprive him of the right of attaining and holding the highest Offices that are known in the United States.

To the Members of the New Church in Baltimore, January 27, 1793

Writings Vol. 32 p. 315

CIVIL AND RELIGIOUS LIBERTY

... It shall still be my endeavor to manifest, by overt acts, the purity of my
inclination for promoting the happiness of mankind, as well as the sincerity of my desires to contribute whatever may be in my power towards the
preservation of the civil and religious liberties of the American People.

To the Bishops of the Methodist Episcopal Church, May 29, 1789

Writings Vol. 30 p. 339

... The liberty enjoyed by the people of these States of worshipping Almighty God agreeable to their consciences is not only among the choicest
of their *blessings* but also of their *rights*.

To the Religious Society called Quakers, September 28, 1789

Writings Vol. 30 p. 416

... While men perform their social duties faithfully, they do all that society or the state can with propriety demand or expect; and remain responsible only to their Maker for the religion, or modes of faith, which they
may prefer or profess.

To the Religious Society called Quakers, September 28, 1789

Writings Vol. 30 p. 416

RELIGIOUS DISPUTES

... Of all the animosities which have existed among mankind, those
which are caused by a difference of sentiments in religion appear to be
the most inveterate and distressing, and ought most to be deprecated. I
was in hopes, that the enlightened and liberal policy, which has marked
the present age, would at least have reconciled *Christians* of every denomination so far, that we should never again see their religious disputes carried to such a pitch as to endanger the peace of Society.

To Sir Edward Newenham, October 20, 1792   *Writings Vol. 32 p. 190*

TOLERATION OF THE JEWS

... May the same wonder-working Deity, who long since delivering the Hebrews from their Egyptian Oppressors planted them in the promised land — whose providential agency has largely been conspicuous in establishing these United States as an independent Nation — still continue to water them with the dews of Heaven and to make the inhabitants of every denomination participate in the temporal and spiritual blessings of that people whose God is Jehovah.

To the Hebrew Congregation of the City of Savannah, May, 1790
Writings Vol. 31 p. 42

REGARD TO CONSCIENTIOUS SCRUPLES

... in my opinion the conscientious scruples of all men should be treated with great delicacy and tenderness, and it is my wish and desire that the laws may always be as extensively accommodated to them, as a due regard to the Protection and essential interests of the nation may justify and permit.

To the Religious Society called Quakers, September 28, 1789
Writings Vol. 30 p. 416

RELIGIOUS DIFFERENCES AND POLITICAL UNITY

... It gives me the most sensible pleasure to find, that, in our nation, however different are the sentiments of citizens on religious doctrines, they generally concur in one thing, for their political professions and practices are almost universally friendly to the order and happiness of our civil institutions.

To the Convention of the Universalist Church, lately assembled in Philadelphia,
July 1790   *Writings Vol. 31 p. 73*

RIGHTS OF CONSCIENCE

... As the Contempt of the Religion of a Country by ridiculing any of its Ceremonies or affronting its Ministers or Votaries has ever been deeply resented, you are to be particularly careful to restrain every Officer and Soldier from such Imprudence and Folly and to punish every Instance of it. On the other Hand, as far as lays in your power, you are to protect and support the free Exercise of the Religion of the Country and the undisturbed Enjoyment of the rights of Conscience in religious Matters, with your utmost Influence and Authority.

Instructions to Colonel Benedict Arnold, September 14, 1775
Writings Vol. 3 p. 495

. . . avoid all Disrespect to or Contempt of the Religion of the Country and its Ceremonies. Prudence, Policy, and a true Christian Spirit, will lead us to look with Compassion upon their Errors without insulting them. While we are contending for our own Liberty, we should be very cautious of violating the Rights of Conscience in others, ever considering that God alone is the Judge of the Hearts of Men, and to him only in this Case, they are answerable.

Instructions to Colonel Benedict Arnold, September 14, 1775

Writings Vol. 3 p. 492

UNIVERSAL RELIGIOUS LIBERTY

. . . I have often expressed my sentiments, that every man, conducting himself as a good citizen, and being accountable to God alone for his religious opinions, ought to be protected in worshipping the Deity according to the dictates of his own conscience.

To the General Committee of the United Baptist Churches in Virginia, May 1789   *Writings Vol. 30 p. 321*

THE CHRISTIAN MINISTRY

. . . The want of a chaplain does, I humbly conceive, reflect dishonor upon the regiment, as all other officers are allowed. The gentlemen of the corps are sensible of this, and did propose to support one at their private expense. But I think it would have been a more graceful appearance were he appointed as others are.

To Robert Dinwiddie, September 23, 1756   *Writings Vol. 1 p. 470*

. . . Believing, as I do, that *Religion* and *Morality* are the essential pillars of Civil society, I view, with unspeakable pleasure, that harmony and brotherly love which characterizes the Clergy of different denominations, as well in this, as in other parts of the United States; exhibiting to the world a new and interesting spectacle, at once the pride of our Country and the surest basis of universal Harmony.

To the Clergy of Different Denominations Residing in and near the City of Philadelphia, March 3, 1797   *Writings Vol. 35 p. 416*

. . . Common decency, Sir, in a camp calls for the services of a divine, and which ought not to be dispensed with, altho' the world should be so uncharitable as to think us void of religion, and incapable of good instructions.

To John Blair, April 17, 1758   *Writings Vol. 2 p. 178*

PUBLIC AND PRIVATE WORSHIP

... The General most earnestly requires, and expects, a due observance of those articles of war, established for the Government of the army, which forbid profane cursing, swearing and drunkeness; And in like manner requires and expects, of all Officers, and Soldiers, not engaged on actual duty, a punctual attendance on divine Service, to implore the blessings of heaven upon the means used for our safety and defence.

General Orders, July 4, 1775   *Writings Vol. 3 p. 309*

... The Continental Congress having ordered, Friday the 17th. Instant to be observed as a day of "fasting, humiliation and prayer, humbly to supplicate the mercy of Almighty God, that it would please him to pardon all our manifold sins and transgressions, and to prosper the Arms of the United Colonies, and finally, establish the peace and freedom of America, upon a solid and lasting foundation" — The General commands all officers, and soldiers, to pay strict obedience to the Orders of the Continental Congress, and by their unfeigned, and pious observance of their religious duties, incline the Lord, and Giver of Victory, to prosper our arms.

General Orders, May 15, 1776   *Writings Vol. 5 p. 43*

... That the Troops may have an opportunity of attending public worship, as well as take some rest after the great fatigue they have gone through; The General in future excuses them from fatigue duty on Sundays (except at the Ship Yards, or special occasions) until further orders.

General Orders, August 3, 1776   *Writings Vol. 5 p. 367*

... as a Chaplain is allowed to each Regiment, see that the Men regularly attend divine Worship.

To William Smallwood, May 26, 1777   *Writings Vol. 8 p. 129*

... To morrow being the day set apart by the Honorable Congress for public Thanksgiving and Praise; and duty calling us devoutly to express our grateful acknowledgements to God for the manifold blessings he has granted us. The General directs that the army remain in it's present quarters, and that the Chaplains perform divine service with their several Corps and brigades. And earnestly exhorts, all officers and soldiers, whose absence is not indispensibly necessary, to attend with reverence the solemnities of the day.

General Orders, December 17, 1777   *Writings Vol. 10 p. 168*

Geo: Washington, artist unknown. Engraved for the *Ladies Magazine,* London, June 1795.

... Divine Service is to be performed tomorrow in the several Brigades or Divisions. The Commander in Chief earnestly recommends that the troops not on duty should universally attend with that seriousness of Deportment and gratitude of Heart which the recognition of such reiterated and astonishing interpositions of Providence demand of us.

After Orders, October 20, 1781   *Writings Vol. 23 p. 247*

GENEROUS FORGIVENESS OF ENEMIES

... I am told ... that if they [the Tories] could have thought that the most abject submission would have procured peace for them, they would have humbled themselves in the dust, and kissed the rod that should be held out for chastisement. Unhappy wretches! Deluded mortals! Would it not be good policy to grant a generous amnesty, and conquer these people by a generous forgiveness?

To Joseph Reed, April 1, 1776   *Writings Vol. 4 p. 455*

MISSIONS AMONG THE INDIANS

... A System corrisponding with the mild principles of Religion and Philanthropy towards an unenlightened race of Men, whose happiness materially depends on the conduct of the United States, would be as honorable to the national character as conformable to the dictates of sound policy.

Third Annual Address to Congress, October 25, 1791   Writings Vol. 31 p. 399

... I am clearly in sentiment with her Ladyship, that christianity will never make any progress among the Indians, or work any considerable reformation in their principles, until they are brought to a state of greater civilization; and the mode by which she means to attempt this, as far as I have been able to give it consideration, is as likely to succeed as any other that could have been devised, and may in time effect the great and benevolent object of her Ladyships wishes: but that love of ease, impatience under any sort of controul, and disinclination to every kind of pursuit but those of hunting and war, would discourage any person possessed of less piety, zeal and philanthrophy than are characteristick of Lady Huntington.

To Sir James Jay, January 25, 1785   *Writings Vol. 28 p. 41*

... In proportion as the general Government of the United States shall acquire strength by duration, it is probable they may have it in their power to extend a salutary influence to the Aborigines in the extremities of their Territory. In the meantime, it will be a desirable thing for the protection of the Union to cooperate, as far as circumstances may conveniently admit, with the disinterested endeavours of your Society to civilize and Christianize the Savages of the Wilderness.

To the Society of United Brethren for Propagating the Gospel among the Heathen, July 10, 1789   *Writings Vol. 30 p. 355*

... if an event so long and so earnestly desired as that of converting the Indians to Christianity and consequently to civilization, can be effected, the Society of Bethlehem bids fair to bear a very considerable part in it.

To Reverend John Ettwein, May 2, 1788   *Writings Vol. 29 p. 489*

... Impressed as I am with an opinion, that the most effectual means of securing the permanent attachment of our savage neighbors, is to convince them that we are just, and to shew them that a proper and friendly intercourse with us would be for our mutual advantage: I cannot conclude without giving you my thanks for your pious and benevolent wishes to effect this desirable end, upon the mild principles of Religion and Philanthropy. And when a proper occasion shall offer, I have no doubt but such measures will be pursued as may seem best calculated to communicate liberal instruction, and the blessings of society, to their untutored minds.

To Reverend John Carroll, April 10, 1792   *Writings Vol. 32 p. 20*

PUBLIC BENEFICENCE

... if it should please the General Assembly to permit me to turn the destination of the fund vested in me, from my private emolument, to objects of a public nature, it will be my study in selecting these to prove the sincerity of my gratitude for the honor conferred on me, by preferring such as may appear most subservient to the enlightened and patriotic views of the Legislature.

To Patrick Henry, October 29, 1785   *Writings Vol. 28 p. 304*

RECONCILIATION

... every exertion of my worthy Colleagues and myself will be equally extended to the re-establishment of Peace and Harmony between the Mother Country and the Colonies, as to the fatal, but necessary, operations of War.

To the New York Legislature, June 26, 1775   *Writings Vol. 3 p. 305*

THE CAUSE OF THE OPPRESSED

... my anxious recollections, my sympathetic feelings, and my best wishes are irresistibly excited, whensoever, in any country, I see an oppressed nation unfurl the banners of Freedom.

Reply to the French Minister, January 1, 1796   *Writings Vol. 34 p. 413*

... our citizen-soldiers impressed an useful lesson of patriotism on mankind.

To the People of the State of South Carolina, May 1790   *Writings Vol. 31 p. 67*

UNIVERSAL SYMPATHY

... the voice of mankind is with me.

To Bryan Fairfax, July 20, 1774   *Writings Vol. 3 p. 234*

... My Policy in our foreign transactions has been, to cultivate peace with all the world.

The Sixth Annual Address, November 19, 1794   *Writings Vol. 34 p. 37*

... For me to express my sentiment with respect to the Administration of the concerns of another government, might incur a charge of stepping beyond the line of prudence; but the principles of humanity, will justify an avowal of my regret, and I do regret exceedingly, that any causes whatever, should have produced, and continued until this time a war more bloody, more expensive, more calamitous, and more pregnant of events, than modern, or perhaps any other time, can furnish an example. And I most sincerely and devoutly wish that your exertions, and those of others having the same object in view, may effect what human nature cries aloud for, a General Peace.

To Thomas Erskine, July 7, 1797   *Writings Vol. 35 p. 490*

THE CAUSE OF SUFFERING HUMANITY

... I observe, with singular satisfaction, the cases in which your benevolent Instutition has been instrumental in recalling some of our Fellow creatures (as it were) from beyond the gates of Eternity, and has given occasion for the hearts of parents and friends to leap for joy. The provision made for the preservation of shipwrecked Mariners is also highly estimable in the view of every philanthropic mind and greatly consolatory to that suffering part of the Community. These things will draw upon you the blessings of those, who were nigh to perish. These works of charity and good-will towards me reflect, in my estimation, great lustre upon the authors and presage an era of still farther improvements. How pitiful, in the eye of reason and religion, is that false ambition which desolates the world with fire and sword for the purposes of conquest and fame; when compared to the milder virtues of making our neighbours and our fellow men as happy as their frail conditions and perishable natures will permit *them to be!*

To Reverend John Lathrop, June 22, 1788   *Writings Vol. 30 p. 5*

THE BROTHERHOOD OF MAN

... as the member of an infant empire, as a Philanthropist by character, and (if I may be allowed the expression) as a Citizen of the great republic of humanity at large; I cannot help turning my attention sometimes to this subject. I would be understood to mean, I cannot avoid reflecting with pleasure on the probable influence that commerce may hereafter have on human manners and society in general. On these occasions I consider how mankind may be connected like one great family in fraternal ties. I indulge a fond, perhaps an enthusiastic idea, that as the world is evidently much less barbarous than it has been, its melioration must still be progressive; that nations are becoming more humanized in their policy, that the subjects of ambition and causes for hostility are daily diminishing, and, in fine, that the period is not very remote, when the benefits of a liberal and free commerce will, pretty generally, succeed to the devastations and horrors of war.

To Marquis de Lafayette, August 15, 1786   *Writings Vol. 28 p. 520*

E. DEATH

BEREAVEMENT

... I am extremely sorry for the death of Mrs. Putnam and Sympathise with you upon the occasion. Remembering that all must die, and that she had lived to an honourable age, I hope you will bear the misfortune with that fortitude and complacency of mind, that become a Man and a Christian.

To Israel Putnam, October 19, 1777   *Writings Vol. 9 p. 401*

MOURNING

... Nature, no doubt, must feel severely before *calm* resignation will over come it.

To Henry Knox, August 19, 1787   *Writings Vol. 29 p. 261*

DEATH OF SEVERAL REVOLUTIONARY WORTHIES

... Thus some of the pillars of the revolution fall. Others are mouldering by insensible degrees. May our Country never want props to support the glorious fabrick!

To Thomas Jefferson, August 1, 1786   *Writings Vol. 28 p. 506*

CHRISTIAN FORTITUDE

... Time *alone* can blunt the keen edge of afflictions; Philosophy and our Religion holds out to us such hopes as will, upon proper reflection, enable us to bear with fortitude the most calamitous incidents of life and these are all that can be expected from the feelings of humanity.

To Benjamin Lincoln, February 11, 1788   *Writings Vol. 29 p. 413*

RESIGNATION

... is not for man to scan the wisdom of Providence. The best he can do, is to submit to its decrees. Reason, religion and Philosophy, teaches us to do this, but 'tis time alone that can ameliorate the pangs of humanity, and soften its woes.

To Henry Knox, March 2, 1797   *Writings Vol. 35 p. 409*

HIS MOTHER'S DEATH

... Awful, and affecting as the death of a Parent is, there is consolation in knowing, that Heaven has spared ours to an age, beyond which few attain, and favored her with the full enjoyment of her mental faculties, and as much bodily strength as usually falls to the lot of fourscore. Under these considerations and a hope that she is translated to a happier place, it is the duty of her relatives to yield due submission to the decrees of the Creator.

To Betty Washington Lewis, September 13, 1789   *Writings Vol. 30 p. 399*

CARES OF LIFE

... Life and the concerns of this world, one would think, are so uncertain, and so full of disappointments, that nothing is to be counted upon from human actions.

To Henry Lee, July 26, 1786   *Writings Vol. 28 p. 485*

... It is in vain, I perceive, to look for ease and happiness in a world of troubles.

To Henry Knox, July 16, 1798   *Writings Vol. 36 p. 345*

CONSOLATION

... In looking forward to that awful moment, when I must bid adieu to Sublunary Scenes, I anticipate the consolation of leaving our Country in a

George Washington Esqr. Obt. Decbr. 14th 1799 AE 68 by William Hamlin after Edward Savage.

prosperous condition. And, while the curtain of seperation shall be drawing, my last breath will, I trust, expire in a prayer for the temporal and eternal felicity of those, who have not only endeavoured to gild the evening of my days with unclouded serenity, but extended their desires to my happiness hereafter in a brighter world.

To the General Assembly of Virginia, April 27, 1790   *Writings Vol. 31 p. 39*

CALM VIEWS OF DEATH

... The want of regular exercise, with the cares of office, will, I have no doubt hasten my departure for that country from whence no Traveller returns; but a faithful discharge of whatsoever trust I accept, as it ever has, so it always will be the primary consideration in every transaction of my life be the consequences what they may.

To Doctor James Craik, September 8, 1789   *Writings Vol. 30 p. 396*

THE FAMILY VAULT

... The family Vault at Mount Vernon requiring repairs, and being improperly situated besides, I desire that a new one of Brick, and upon a larger Scale, may be built at the foot of what is commonly called the Vineyard Inclosure, on the ground which is marked out. In which my remains, with those of my deceased relatives (now in the old Vault) and such others of my family as may chuse to be entombed there, may be deposited. And it is my express desire that my Corpse may be Interred in a private manner, without parade, or funeral Oration.

Will, July 9, 1799   *Writings Vol. 37 p. 293*

Tributes and Quotations
About George Washington

—— ❧ ——

I should be happy to see your Excellency in Europe. Here you would know, and enjoy, what posterity will say of Washington. At present, I enjoy that pleasure for you; as I frequently hear the old generals of this martial country, who study the maps of America, and mark upon them all your operations, speak with sincere approbation and great applause of your conduct; and join in giving you the character of *One of the Greatest Captains of the Age.*

BENJAMIN FRANKLIN
Passy, France, March 5, 1780

Every mark of friendship I receive from you, adds to my happiness, as I love you with all the sincerity and warmth of my heart; and the sentiment I feel for you goes to the very extent of my affections.

LAFAYETTE
May 1781

After such services, which consecrate your name to all posterity, with what home-felt satisfaction must your future days be blest! Heaven Crown them with every favor! May you live long, my dear General, and long have they joy to see the increasing splendor and prosperity of a rising nation, aided by your counsels, and defended by your sword! Indulge me the pleasure to believe, that I have a place in your recollections, and still honor and make me happy in your friendship.

JOHN HANCOCK
October 15, 1783

You have wisely retired from public employments, and calmly view, from the temple of Fame, the various exertions of that sovereignty and independence, which Providence has enabled you to be so greatly and gloriously instrumental in securing to your country. Yet, I am persuaded, that you cannot view them with the eye of an unconcerned spectator.

JOHN JAY
1786

If we look over the catalogue of the first magistrates of nations, whether they have been denominated Presidents or Consuls, Kings or Princes, where shall we find one, whose commanding talents, virtues whose overruling good fortune, has so completely united all hearts and voices in his favor! who enjoyed the esteem and admiration of foreign nations, and fellow citizens, with equal unanimity! qualities so uncommon are no common blessings to the country that possesses them. By these great qualities, and their benign effects, has Providence marked out the head of this Nation, with the hand so distinctly visible, as to have been seen by all men, and mistaken by none.

JOHN ADAMS
April 21, 1789

In war, your fame is immortal as the hero of liberty. In peace, you are the patron and the firmest supporter of her rights. Your greatest admirers, and even your best friends, have now but one wish left for you: that you may long enjoy health and your present happiness.

JOHN PAUL JONES
December 20, 1789

He is polite with dignity, affable without familiarity, distant without Haughtyness, Grave without Austerity, Modest, wise & Good. These are traits in his Character which peculiarly fit him for the exalted station he holds, and God Grant that he may Hold it with the same applause & universal satisfaction for many years, as it is my firm opinion that no other man could rule over this great people & consolidate them into one mighty Empire but He who is set over us. . . .

ABIGAIL ADAMS
January 5, 1790

Give me leave, my dear General, to present you with a picture of the Bastille, just as it looked a few days after I had ordered its demolition,— with *the main key* of the fortress of despotism. It is a tribute, which I owe, as a son to my adoptive father, as an Aide-de-camp to my General, as a Missionary of liberty to its Patriarch.

LAFAYETTE
March 17, 1790

George Washington, Commander of the American armies, who, like Joshua of old, commanded the sun and the moon to stand still, and they obeyed him.

BENJAMIN FRANKLIN

America lamenting her Loss at the Tomb of General Washington by James Akin
and William Harrison. This memorial print was published in Philadelphia, January 20, 1800, less than seven weeks after George Washington's
death.

Oh, Washington! thou hero, patriot sage, Friend of all climes, and pride of every age!

THOMAS PAINE

I cannot, indeed, help admiring the wisdom and fortune of this great man. By the phrase, "fortune," I mean not in the smallest degrees to derogate from his merit. But, notwithstanding his extraordinary talents and exalted integrity, it must be considered as singularly fortunate, that he should have experienced a lot, which so seldom falls to the portion of humanity, and have passed through such a variety of scenes, without stain and without reproach. It must, indeed, create astonishment, that placed in circumstances so critical, and filling for a series of years a station so conspicuous, his character should never once have been called in question; that he should in no one instance have been accused either of improper insolence, or of mean submission, in his transactions with foreign nations. For him it has been reserved, to run the race of glory, without experiencing the smallest interruption to the brilliancy of his career.

CHARLES FOX
January 31, 1794

No American who has not been in England, can have a just idea of the admiration, expressed among all parties, of General Washington.

RUFUS KING
February 6, 1797

I take the liberty to introduce your august and immortal name in a short sentence, which will be found in the book I send you. I have a large acquaintance among the most valuable and exalted classes of men; but you are the only human being for whom I ever felt an awful reverence. I sincerely pray God, to grant a long and serene evening to a life so gloriously devoted to the universal happiness of the world.

LORD ERSKINE
1797

A citizen, first in war, first in peace, and first in the hearts of his countrymen.

HENRY (LIGHT-HORSE HARRY) LEE
December 26, 1799

His example is complete; and it will teach wisdom and virtue to Magistrates, Citizens, and Men, not only in the present age, but in future generations.

JOHN ADAMS
December 23, 1799

To his equals he was condescending, to his inferiors kind, and to the dear object of his affections exemplarily tender.

HENRY (LIGHT-HORSE HARRY) LEE
December 26, 1799

In mourning the loss of the Man of the Age, I equally mourn that of the long-tried patron, — the kind and unchanging friend.

ALEXANDER HAMILTON
December 1799

Vice shuddered at his presence, and Virtue always felt his fostering hand.

HENRY (LIGHT-HORSE HARRY) LEE
December 26, 1799

The virtues of our departed friend were crowned by piety. He is known to have been habitually devout. To Christian institutions he gave the countenance of his example; and no one could express, more fully, his sense of the Providence of God, and the dependence of man.

REVEREND J. T. KIRKLAND
December 29, 1799

There was a gravity and reserve, indeed, in his countenance and deportment, partly natural, and partly the effect of habitual cares for the public weal; but these were wholly unmixed with the least austerity or moroseness. True native dignity was happily blended with the most placid mildness and condescension.

J. M. SEWALL
December 31, 1799

Enemies he had, but they were few, and chiefly of the same family with the man, who could not bear to hear Aristides always called the just. Among them all *I have never heard of one who charged him with any habitual vice, or even foible.*

DAVID RAMSAY, M.D.
January 15, 1800

Memorial engraving, *Pater Patriae* by Enoch G. Gridley after John Coles, Jr. and Edward Savage, c. 1800. Surrounding Washington's image are the figures of Columbia, Minerva, Mars, Fame, Liberty and Truth. The war veteran in the foreground represents the "Grief of all the Army of America for the loss of their beloved General and Commander in Chief."

His course he finished, in the peaceful retreat of his own election, in the arms of a dutiful and affectionate wife, and bedewed with the tears of surrounding relatives and friends, with the unspeakably superior advantage to that of a Roman general, in the hopes afforded by the Gospel of pardon and peace!

THE EARL OF BUCHAN
January 28, 1800

This great man fought against tyranny; he established the liberty of its country. His memory will always be dear to the French people, as it will be to all freemen of the two worlds.

NAPOLEON BONAPARTE,
February 9, 1800

Neither in the parade of military life, nor in the cares of civil administration, neither in a state of depression, nor amidst the intoxicating sweets of power and adulation; did he forget to pay homage to the "Most High, who doeth according to his will in the army of heaven, and among the inhabitants of the earth."

WILLIAM LINN, D.D.
February 22, 1800

He had all the genuine mildness of Christianity, with all its force. He was neither ostentatious nor ashamed of his Christian profession.

J. SMITH
February 22, 1800

Above all, he was influenced by the more permanent and operative principle of religion; by the firm and active persuasion of an All-seeing, All-powerful Deity; by the high consciousness of future accountability, and the assured hope and prospect of immortality.

JOHN DAVIS
1800

The character of Washington is worthy of the best days of antiquity....It seems as if we had recovered a lost life of some of those illustrious men, whose portraits Plutarch has so well delineated.

M. FONTANES
1800

He was, in every sense of the words, a wise, a good, and a great man...
The whole of his character was in its mass perfect, in nothing bad in a few

points indifferent. And it may be truly said, that never did nature and fortune combine more perfectly to make a man great, and to place him in the same constellation with whatever worthies have merited from man an everlasting remembrance. . . .

THOMAS JEFFERSON
January 2, 1814

He did the two greatest things which, in politics, man can have the privilege of attempting. He maintained, by peace, that independence of his country, which he had acquired by war. He funded a free government, in the name of the principles of order, and by re-establishing their sway.

M. GUIZOT

If the title of Great Man ought to be reserved for him who cannot be charged with an indiscretion or a vice, who spent his life in establishing the independence, the glory, and durable prosperity of his country; who succeeded in all that he undertook, and whose successes were never won at expense of honor, justice, integrity, or by the sacrifice of a single principle, — this title will not be denied to Washington.

JARED SPARKS

War was not a game in which he sought amusement at the expense of others, but a Last Resort, in whose dangers and toils he always bore his full share, and from which he sought release, as soon as conscience and honor would permit. *The spirit in which he contended* was that which *secured favor of a righteous Providence, and the approbation of all good men.*

E. C. M'GUIRE, D.D.

To him belonged the proud distinction of being the leader in a revolution, without awakening one doubt or solicitude, as to the spotless purity of his purpose. His was the glory of being the brightest manifestation of the spirit which reigned in this country; and in this way he became a source of energy, a bond of union, the centre of an enlightened people's confidence. By an instinct which is unerring, we call Washington, with grateful reverence, the *Father of His Country*, but not its *Saviour*. A people which wants a Saviour, which does not possess an earnest and pledge of freedom in its own heart, is not yet ready to be free.

WILLIAM E. CHANNING

The admiration with which Washington is regarded by all civilized nations, shows him to be one of the few among mankind, to whom is given an immortality more durable than brass or marble, and whose spot-less and beneficent memory is cherished by the latest posterity.

FREDERICK VON RAUMER

Amid all the tumult of the camp, and all the excesses inseparable from civil war, humanity took refuge under his tent, and never was re-pelled from it. In triumphs and in adversity, he was ever tranquil as wis-dom, and simple as virtue. The gentle affections abode in the depths of his heart, even in those moments when the claims of his own cause seemed to sanction in a manner the laws of vengeance.

M. FONTANES

Perhaps there never was another man, whose personal character and conduct exercised an influence, so powerful and so beneficial, on the des-tiny of a great nation.

JAMES GRAHAME

Can tyrants but by tyrants conquered be,
And freedom find no champion and no child,
Such as Columbia saw arise, when she
Sprung forth a Pallas, arm'd and undefil'd?
Or must such minds be nourish'd in the wild,
Deep in the unpruned forest, 'midst the roar
Of cataracts, where nursing nature smiled
On infant Washington? Has earth no more
Such seeds within her breast, or Europe no such shore?

LORD BYRON

He was one of those virtuous citizens, to whom the world refuses the credit of genius, because they are not beset with a destructive restlessness, nor devoured with the ambition of domineering over mankind; but who really deserve the name of GREAT, better than many others, because their number is rare.

FELIX BODIN

He changed mankind's ideas of political greatness.

FISHER AMES

Favored of heaven, he was blest in the most endearing relation of human society. The amiable and much respected partner of his happiness, enjoyed his affection and esteem, and was worthy to participate the honors of his exalted station.

WILLIAM JACKSON

He deserved and enjoyed both success and repose. Of all great men, he was the most virtuous and most fortunate. In this world, God has no higher favor to bestow.

M. GUIZOT

On no occasion is there the least authority for supposing he ever transcended the bounds of moderation in the enjoyments of life, or the indulgence of those passions universally implanted in the nature of man. He consequently escaped all the delusions of excess, which consist in false, misty, and exaggerated views or designs, stimulated into action by artificial excitement, and misleading the judgment, while they aggravate the passions and madden imagination. Thus, his intellect was always clear, and the admirable physical powers bestowed upon him by nature were never debased to bad purposes, or weakened by licentious indulgence.

JAMES K. PAULDING

By an instinct which is unerring we call Washington, with grateful reverence, — *The Father of His Country.*

WILLIAM E. CHANNING, D.D.

The most humble citizen of the United States may copy his private virtues, and the most lofty and magnanimous spirit cannot propose to itself a more noble object of ambition, than to aspire to an imitation of his public services. In contemplating such a character, our children will equally acquire a reverence for virtue, and a sacred devotion to the obligations of citizens of a free state.

JAMES K. PAULDING

Without making ostentatious professions of religion, he was a sincere believer in the Christian faith, and a truly devout man.

JOHN MARSHALL

His hopes for his country, were always founded on the righteousness of the cause, and the blessing of Heaven. His was the belief of Reason and Revelation; and that belief was illustrated and exemplified in all his actions.

JAMES K. PAULDING

To Christian institutions he gave the countenance of his example.

REVEREND J. T. KIRKLAND

Washington — a fixed star in the firmament of great names, shining without twinkling or obscuration, with clear, beneficent light.

DANIEL WEBSTER
August 2, 1826

Washington is the mightiest name of earth — long since mightiest in the cause of civil liberty, still mightiest in moral reformation. On that name no eulogy is expected. It cannot be. To add brightness to the sun or glory to the name of Washington is alike impossible. Let none attempt it. In solemn awe pronounce the name, and in its naked deathless splendor leave it shining on.

ABRAHAM LINCOLN
February 22, 1842

America has furnished to the world the character of Washington. And if our American institutions had done nothing else, that alone would have entitled them to the respect of mankind.

DANIEL WEBSTER
June 17, 1843

The character, the counsels, and example of our Washington. . .will guide us through the doubts and difficulties that beset us; they will guide our children and our children's children in the paths of prosperity and peace, while America shall hold her place in the family of nations.

EDWARD EVERETT
July 5, 1858

CHRONOLOGY

———————————— ❊ ————————————

1732

February 22   (February 11, 1731/32 Old-Style Calendar) George, first child of Augustine Washington and his second wife, Mary Ball Washington, born at family home on Popes Creek, Westmoreland County, Virginia.

1743

April 12   Death of father, Augustine.

1752

July 26   Death of older half brother, Lawrence.

November 6   Appointed major in Virginia militia.

1753

October 31   Sent by Governor Dinwiddie on important mission to Ohio territory to deliver ultimatum to French.

1754

March 20   Assumed command of forces sent on mission to Fort Duquesne.

July 4   Surrendered to French at Fort Necessity.

December 17   Signed lease with Ann Fairfax Washington Lee, widow of Lawrence Washington, to rent Mount Vernon for the sum of 15,000 pounds of tobacco or cash equivalent per year.

1755

May 10   Appointed volunteer aide-de-camp to General Braddock.

July 9   Braddock's army defeated, the General is killed; Washington praised for his courage.

August 14   Appointed Colonel and Commander of Virginia Regiment.

1758

July 24   Elected Burgess for Frederick County, Virginia.

November 23   Fort Duquesne abandoned by French; Washington resigned commission.

1759

January 6   Married Martha Dandridge Custis, a widow with two children, John Parke Custis and Martha Parke Custis.

1761

March 14   Death of Ann Fairfax Washington Lee, widow of Lawrence Washington; Washington officially inherited Mount Vernon according to the terms of his half brother's will.

May 18   Re-elected to House of Burgesses.

1762

October 25   Appointed vestryman of Truro Parish, Fairfax County.

1763

October 3   Appointed warden of Pohick Church, Truro Parish.

1765

July 16   Elected to the Virginia House of Burgesses for Fairfax County (re-elected 1768, 1769, 1771, 1774).

1769

May 18   Created and signed articles of non-importation association with George Mason as co-author.

1770

October 5   Departed on trip to explore Ohio Territory.

1773

June 19   Death of stepdaughter, Martha Parke Custis.

1774

August 1   Elected to attend First Continental Congress.

September-October   First Continental Congress meets in Philadelphia.

1775

May-June   Delegate at Second Continental Congress.

June 16   Elected General and Commander in Chief of Continental forces.

July 3   Took command of forces at Cambridge, Massachusetts.

1776

March 16   Washington's troops occupied Boston.

July 4   Declaration of Independence.

August 27-29   Battle of Long Island; Americans retreat to Manhattan.

December 25-26   Continental Army re-crossed Delaware River; victory over Hessians.

1777

January 3   Battle of Trenton; British defeated. Established headquarters at Morristown, New Jersey.

September 11   Americans defeated at Brandywine.

October 4   Americans defeated at Germantown.

October 17   Surrender of Burgoyne at Saratoga.

1777–1778   Winter at Valley Forge.

1778

June 18   British evacuate Philadelphia.

June 28   British defeated at Battle of Monmouth.

1780

July 11   Arrival of French fleet and army under command of Rochambeau at Newport, Rhode Island.

1781

September 9-12   Brief stop at Mount Vernon for the first time since 1775.

October 19   Battle of Yorktown, Cornwallis surrenders.

November 5   Death of stepson John Parke Custis. The Washingtons decide to take in Custis' two youngest children and raise them at Mount Vernon.

1783

March 15   Newburgh Address.

June 8   Circular Letter to the States.

June 19   Elected president of the Society of the Cincinnati.

November 2   Farewell to army.

December 4   Farewell to his officers at Fraunces' Tavern, New York City.

December 23   Resigned commission to Congress at Annapolis.

December 24   Returned to Mount Vernon after eight-year absence.

1785

March 25-28   Hosted Mount Vernon Conference, which results in Mount Vernon Compact between Maryland and Virginia.

May 17   Elected president of the Potomac Company.

1786

September 14   Annapolis Convention.

1787

May-September   Served as President of Constitutional Convention in Philadelphia.

September 17   Draft of Constitution signed; convention adjourned.

1788

June 21   New Hampshire ratifies the Constitution, became ninth and deciding state.

June 25   Virginia ratifies the Constitution.

1789

February 4   Unanimously elected President of the United States.

April 14   Officially informed of election results at Mount Vernon by Secretary of Congress, Charles Thomson.

April 16   Departed Mount Vernon for New York, location of the first capital.

April 30   Inaugurated President at Federal Hall in New York City.

August 25   Death of Washington's mother, Mary Ball Washington, at Fredericksburg, Virginia.

October-November   Presidential tour of New England (excluding Rhode Island).

1790

August   Presidential visit to Rhode Island.

September   Arrived in Philadelphia, new temporary capital of the United States.

1791

April-June   Presidential tour of southern states.

December 15   Bill of Rights ratified.

1792

December 5   Unanimously re-elected president.

1793

March 4   Inaugurated president for second term at Independence Hall, Philadelphia.

April 22   Issued proclamation of neutrality.

September 18   Laid cornerstone of Capitol in Federal City (Washington, D.C.).

December 31   Resignation of Thomas Jefferson as Secretary of State.

G. WASHINGTON.

G. Washington by B. Tanner after Gilbert Stuart.

1794

November Declared suppression of Whiskey Rebellion.

1795

January 31 Resignation of Alexander Hamilton as Secretary of the Treasury.

August 14 Signed Jay Treaty.

1796

September 19 Farewell Address published in Philadelphia's *American Daily Advertiser.*

1797

March 4 Returned to Mount Vernon after two terms as President of the United States.

1798

July 4 Appointed Lieutenant General and Commander in Chief of the Armies of the United States.

1799

December 14 Died at Mount Vernon.

December 18 Buried in family vault at Mount Vernon.

INDEX

Life, liberty and property secured, 3, 6
Lincoln, Abraham, 203
Lincoln, Benjamin, 189
Linn, William, 199
Literature, 50, 78–79, 177
Livingston, Robert R., 118
Livingston, William, 146, 149
Local prejudices, 29–32, 40, 94, 95
Luxury goods, 69–70, 129. *See also*
    Simplicity in dress and character
Luzac, John, 145

M

MacKenzie, Robert, 6
Madison, James, 5, 29, 37, 38, 39, 99
Manufactures
  advanced by inventions, 69
  American quality of, 71–72
  British, 9, 70–71
  cloth, 71
  domestic, encouragement of, 63, 66, 69,
    71–72, 113
  employment in, not detrimental to
    agriculture, 71–72
  made prosperous by neutrality, 47
  needed by farmers, 67
Marksmen, 110
Marriage, readiness for, 130–131
Marriage of Negroes, 159
Marshall, John, 152, 202
Martial law, 87, 94, 155–157. *See also*
    Courts-martial
Mason, George, 84
Massachusetts Legislature, 12, 13, 133, 176
Massachusetts Senate, 18, 133
Masses, influences upon and of the, 43–44
Mathews, John, 25, 99, 100
McHenry, James, 58, 70. *See also* Secretary
    of War
McKean, Thomas, 25, 170
Memoirs, 150
Mercenary soldiers, 87, 100
Mercer, John Francis, 158
Methodist Episcopal Church, 173, 179, 180
M'Guire, E. C., 200
Mifflin, Thomas, 155
Military Academy, U.S., 77
Military establishment, 101. *See also*
    Standing Army
Military power, 89–90
Military supplies, 113
Militia, 88, 89, 99–100, 106
Mint, U.S., 66–67
Monarchy and titles proposed for the U.S.,
    5, 18–19
Monroe, James, 55
Moral character, 143
Morality, 172, 178, 182

Moravian church (United Brethren),
    185–186
Morgan, Col. Daniel, 87
Morris, Gouverneur, 6, 54, 61, 64, 65, 101
Morris, Robert, 105, 158
Moultrie, William, 73
Mourning, 188–189
Moustier, Comte de, 3, 61, 62, 70, 71, 149,
    153
Muir, James, 74
Murray, William Vans, 56
Mutiny of the Pennsylvania troops, 92

N

National candor and honesty, 62
National character, 29, 38, 39, 44, 54, 56,
    170–171, 177
National debt, 55, 63, 64
National defense, 58, 113–114. *See also*
    Standing Army
National education, 74–79
National government necessary for foreign
    trade, 69–70
National morality, 172
National policy, 17, 43, 52–59. *See also*
    Constitution of the U.S.; Federal
    Union
National prosperity, 47–52
National reputation, 50
National revolutions, 4
National sentiments, 62
National University, 75–76
Natural rights, defense of, 8, 10, 17, 18, 24.
    See also Human rights; Religion
Navigation, 70, 73–74, 111–113
Navy, U.S., 111–113
Negroes, 104, 157–162
Nelson, Thomas, 34, 174
Neutrality, 47, 49, 52, 55, 56, 59, 111–113
Neville, Mssrs., 102
New Hampshire Executive, 11
New Jersey Legislature, 16
New York Legislature, 94, 123, 186
Newenham, Sir Edward, 28, 49, 180
Newspapers, 72–73
Nicola, Col. Lewis, 19
Night patrol, 89
Non-intervention, 54–55
North Carolina, Governor and Council,
    122

O

Ocean navigation, 70, 111–113
Orphans, 74, 123–124, 160

P

Paine, Thomas, 196
Pardon, 125
Parliament of Great Britain, 8–10, 84

Publications of
The Mount Vernon Ladies' Association

———————————— ✺ ————————————

MOUNT VERNON HANDBOOK. One hundred and twenty-eight pages; one hundred thirty-nine color illustrations.

THE GARDENS & GROUNDS AT MOUNT VERNON: HOW GEORGE WASHINGTON PLANNED AND PLANTED THEM by Elizabeth Kellam de Forest. Photographs by Ted Vaughan. One hundred sixteen pages; seventy-eight color illustrations.

GEORGE WASHINGTON, A BRIEF BIOGRAPHY by William MacDonald. Forty-six pages; twelve illustrations.

MAXIMS OF GEORGE WASHINGTON, collected and arranged by John Frederick Schroeder. Introduction by Gerald R. Ford. Illustrated.

THE LAST WILL AND TESTAMENT OF GEORGE WASHINGTON, edited and annotated by Dr. John C. Fitzpatrick. Sixty-seven pages.

THE MOUNT VERNON COOKBOOK. Two hundred fifty-two pages; thirty-four line drawings, eight color illustrations.

NOTHING MORE AGREEABLE: MUSIC IN GEORGE WASHINGTON'S FAMILY by Judith S. Britt. One hundred twenty-four pages; ten color illustrations.

MOUNT VERNON: THE STORY OF A SHRINE by Gerald W. Johnson with extracts from the diaries and letters of George Washington selected and annotated by Charles Cecil Wall. Illustrated; one hundred and twenty-two pages.

PRESENCE OF A LADY: MOUNT VERNON 1861-1868 by Dorothy Troth Muir. Illustrated; ninety pages.

MOUNT VERNON COLORING BOOK. Twenty-two pages.

WASHINGTON'S MOUNT VERNON. Ninety-three color photographs by Taylor Biggs Lewis, Jr., text by Joanne Young.

THE CHILDREN OF MOUNT VERNON: A GUIDE TO GEORGE WASHINGTON'S HOME by Miriam Anne Bourne. Illustrated by Gloria Kamen. Fifty-nine pages.

GEORGE WASHINGTON: CITIZEN-SOLDIER by Charles Cecil Wall. Two hundred twenty-six pages, forty-four illustrations.

GEORGE WASHINGTON'S RULES OF CIVILITY. Introduction by Letitia Baldrige. Illustrated.

OTHER AVAILABLE PUBLICATIONS

GEORGE WASHINGTON'S CHINAWARE by Susan Gray Detweiler and Christine Meadows. Two hundred and forty-four pages; two hundred and sixteen illustrations (fifty-five in color). Abrams, for the Barra Foundation.

THE DIARIES OF GEORGE WASHINGTON. Vols. I-VI (1748-1799). Edited by Donald Jackson and Dorothy Twohig. University Press of Virginia.

THE PAPERS OF GEORGE WASHINGTON. Edited by W.W. Abbot and Dorothy Twohig. Colonial Series, Revolutionary War Series, Presidential Series. University Press of Virginia.

HURRAH FOR ARTHUR! A MOUNT VERNON BIRTHDAY by Anne Denton Blair. Illustrated by Carol Watson. Seven Locks Press.

Price List Available by Mail

Mount Vernon Ladies' Association
Mount Vernon, Virginia 22121